W. S. Gilbert:
A Century of Scholarship and Commentary

W. S. GILBERT:
A CENTURY
OF SCHOLARSHIP
AND COMMENTARY

Edited and with an Introduction by

JOHN BUSH JONES

Assistant Professor of English
University of Kansas

Foreword by

BRIDGET D'OYLY CARTE

New York University Press · New York
1970

In Memory of my Father

Is life a boon?
   If so, it must befall
   That Death, whene'er he call,
Must call too soon.
   —*The Yeoman of the Guard,* Act I.

Acknowledgments

Anonymous review of *The Bab Ballads*. Reprinted from *The Athenaeum*, No. 2163 (April 10, 1869).

Review of *The Bab Ballads* by "M. B." Reprinted from *The Contemporary Review*, Vol. XI (1869).

"Mr. Gilbert as a Dramatist," anonymous. Reprinted from *The Theatre*, June 26, 1877.

"Mr. W. S. Gilbert," by William Archer. Reprinted from *English Dramatists of Today* by William Archer (1882), by permission of Sampson Low, Marston, & Co., Ltd. The essay first appeared in *St. James Magazine*, Vol. XLIX (1881).

"An Autobiography," by William Schwenck Gilbert. Reprinted from *The Theatre*, n. s. Vol. I (1883).

"A Classic in Humour," by Max Beerbohm. Reprinted from *The Saturday Review* (London), Vol. XCIX (1905) by permission of William Heinemann, Ltd.

"The English Aristophanes," by Walter Sichel. Reprinted from *The Fortnightly Review*, Vol. XCVI (1911) by permission of *Contemporary Review*.

"W. S. Gilbert: A Mid-Victorian Aristophanes," by Edith Hamilton. Reprinted from *Theatre Arts Monthly*, Vol. XI (1927).

"W. S. Gilbert's Topsy-Turvydom," by Isaac Goldberg. Reprinted from *Bookman*, Vol. LXVII (1928).

"The Victorianism of W. S. Gilbert," by Henry Ten Eyck Perry. Reprinted from *The Sewanee Review*, Vol. XXXVI (1928), by permission of Henry Ten Eyck Perry and *The Sewanee Review*.

"W. S. Gilbert," by Arthur Quiller-Couch. Reprinted from *Studies in Literature, Third Series* by Sir Arthur Quiller-Couch (1929), by permission of the Cambridge University Press.

"Gilbert and Sullivan," by G. K. Chesterton. Reprinted from *The Eighteen-Eighties*, edited by Walter de la Mare (1930), by permission of the Cambridge University Press. The essay originally appeared in *Cornhill Magazine*, Vol. LXIX (1930).

"Taking Gilbert's Measure," by Charles E. Lauterbach. Reprinted from the *Huntington Library Quarterly*, Vol. XIX (1956) by permission of the *Huntington Library Quarterly*.

"The Satire of *The Yeomen of the Guard*," by Robert A. Hall, Jr. Reprinted from *Modern Language Notes*, Vol. LXXIII (1958) by permission of the John Hopkins Press.

"The Twisted Cue," by Herbert Weisinger. Reprinted from *The Agony and the Triumph* by Herbert Weisinger (1964), by permission of Herbert Weisinger and the Michigan State University Press.

"In Search of Archibald Grosvenor: A New Look at Gilbert's *Patience*," by John Bush Jones. Reprinted from *Victorian Poetry*, Vol. III (1965) by permission of John Bush Jones and *Victorian Poetry*.

"*The Gondoliers*," by David A. Randall. Reprinted from *Papers of the Bibliographical Society of America*, Vol. LIX (1965), by permission of David A. Randall and *Papers of the Bibliographical Society of America*.

"Gilbert and Sullivan's *Princess Ida*," by David A. Randall. Reprinted from *Papers of the Bibliographical Society of America*, Vol. LIX (1965), by permission of David A. Randall and *Papers of the Bibliographical Society of America*.

"The Printing of *The Grand Duke*: Notes Toward a Gilbert Bibliography," by John Bush Jones. Reprinted from *Papers of the Bibliographical Society of America*, Vol. LXI (1967), by permission of John Bush Jones and *Papers of the Bibliographical Society of America*.

"The Genesis of *Patience*," by Jane W. Stedman. Reprinted from *Modern Philology*, Vol. LXVI (1968) by permission of Jane W. Stedman and *Modern Philology*.

Contents

Foreword

This collection of articles and studies made by Mr. Jones, ranging in date from 1869 to the 1960's, should be of interest to all W. S. Gilbert students and enthusiasts, as it brings together in one volume a great deal of material that today would otherwise not be easily available to them. The collection is a fair representation of both English and American writers on Gilbert, professional scholars as well as popular critics of literature and the theatre. Many of the early essays in this collection appeared originally in books and magazines which are now out of print, and it is only now that pieces written during Gilbert's lifetime and in the first decades of this century are once again brought into print for the scholar and general reader alike. The more recent studies included here reveal that Gilbert continues to be the subject of considerable scholarly and critical attention. Perhaps the publication of this collection will encourage still more students of the theatre to turn their attention to W. S. Gilbert and the Gilbert and Sullivan operas.

I wish it every success.

BRIDGET D'OYLY CARTE

15th October, 1969

Introduction

I

Taking Gilbert Seriously

It is now more than a hundred years since W. S. Gilbert brought into print the first collection of his Bab Ballads in book form. These verses, and, more notably, his comic operas in collaboration with Sir Arthur Sullivan made Gilbert a popular and, for the most part, critical success in his own day; a part of the continuing theatrical tradition of England and America in this century; and, via the phrase "Gilbert-and-Sullivan," a veritable synonym for witty, melodic, occasionally biting, and always intelligent, if sometimes ludicrous, entertainment. "Nonsense," remarks Lady Saphir in *Patience*, "yes, perhaps—but oh, what precious nonsense!"

And yet, until quite recently, Gilbert has not fared

so well among serious students of literature and the theatre as he has with the play-going public at large. This is not to say that he is not liked; rather, he has not been and is not studied, except by a very few. Recently a friend who, like myself, *has* been engaged in research on W. S. Gilbert, admitted some embarrassment in having to own up to being a "Gilbert man." This did not seem to him quite as "respectable" or "legitimate" for an English professor as being, for instance, a "Shakespeare man," or a "Twain man," or a "Dickens man." And yet, if we but briefly touch upon some obvious aspects of his career, we may ask ourselves why a stigma should be attached to the study of Gilbert. Because he was a popular dramatist? So was Shakespeare. Because he was, primarily, a humorist? So was Mark Twain. Or because he was a commercial success? So was Dickens.

The answer to the question of Gilbert's failure to attract more scholarly investigation than he has lies not so much in the facts of his career, but, it would seem, in the fundamental nature of his most lasting works. The Bab Ballads and the Savoy Operas have nothing if not an air of frivolity, and what could be more natural than to treat frivolity frivolously? It is a great mistake, however, to dismiss that which appears ridiculous as merely irresponsible. Gilbert was, in his most notable pieces, a satirist, or, at the very least, an ironist. Despite the common accusation that he did not have a coherent philosophy or a program of reform for his society—an accusation very likely true—he saw quite steadily what he did not like, what was false, sham, and hypocritical, without going to the extreme of the malcontent in railing against the whole world indiscriminately. We cannot take the malcontent seriously for his raillery knows no limits; he spreads his venom broadcast. But the legitimate satirist is selective in his attacks;

his selectivity implies thought, and thought, seriousness. Hence, in whatever garb of the ludicrous and nonsensical Gilbert may have cloaked his satire, beneath that garb is the form of logic and common sense—the fundamental seriousness with which all responsible satire begins and ends. Says Jack Point, "For he who'd make his fellow-creatures wise/ Should always gild the philosophic pill!" Perhaps, then, if Gilbert's seriousness were better understood, his significance would be more widely recognized.

Another likely reason that Gilbert is still very much appreciated yet very little studied sounds rather like one of the dramatist's own paradoxes on which so many of his libretti turn. It will be allowed that Gilbert was possibly the most outstanding and certainly the most distinctive (in his collaborations with Sullivan) English dramatist between Sheridan and Wilde, and yet the period in which he wrote witnessed a sharp decline in the literary quality of drama, if not, perhaps, in its theatricality. What is it, then, to be the best in an age of apparent mediocrity? Posterity, something for which Gilbert claimed to have little regard, may have supplied the answer. Of all the English dramatists of the mid-nineteenth century, only Gilbert has remained constantly and continuously in the theatrical repertory of the English-speaking world. In fact, the Gilbert and Sullivan operas hold the record for the longest continual presentation by professional theatrical companies, second only to the plays of Shakespeare. Other English dramatists of earlier ages may be occasionally revived by university, repertory, or professional theatres, but someone, somewhere, is always presenting Gilbert and Sullivan. Surely this must count for something. If these plays are still so eminently stage-worthy, there should be something in Gilbert's texts (and, of course, in Sullivan's music)—the very substance from which the stage performance emanates—which justifies serious investigation and critical examination.

There have been, over the past few years, some definite signs of change in scholarly attitude from easy dismissal of nineteenth-century English drama to a careful and impartial investigation of it on its own terms. Several anthologies of nineteenth-century British plays have been published; courses in Victorian drama are being taught in major universities; historical and critical studies of melodrama and other forms of "popular entertainment" have appeared. With this awakening of academic interest in the Victorian theatre in general has come a renewal of scholarly interest in Gilbert in particular. We are perhaps approaching that time in which, as G. K. Chesterton prophesied in his introduction to Godwin's study of Gilbert, "it will be found . . . that this Victorian nonsense will prove more valuable than all that was considered the solid Victorian sense. . . . And it may be that in the remote future that laughter will still be heard, when all the voices of that age are silent."

II

"My object all sublime . . ."

The fact that few academicians have seen fit to deal with Gilbert until quite recently is not meant to imply that his works were wholly neglected by critics, commentators, and occasional researchers during his own lifetime and in the earlier decades of the twentieth century. If such were indeed the case, the present volume would be ridiculously slim, and one of its major aims would be almost entirely negated. For one of the primary purposes of this collection of essays is to demonstrate, through the chronological arrangement of the material, the changing and developing attitudes, approaches, and methodologies in dealing with Gilbert and his works. The articles run from the sketchy, personal, opinionated, and—interestingly enough—anonymous reviews of *The Bab Ballads* in 1869, through the analytical, objective, and generously footnoted researches of professional scholars in the 1960's. In between are examples of largely "appreciative criticism" (G. K. Chesterton, Walter Sichel), articles whose inspiration may be traced back to the "psychologizing" craze much in vogue in the 1920's (Isaac Goldberg, Arthur Quiller-Couch), studies in sources and parallels (Edith Hamilton), and other commentary and scholarship of a varied nature. A quick glance at the table of contents reveals that only in the last decade or so have scholars devoted entire articles to intensive studies of Gilbert's individual works, several of these falling into the category of that most "scientific" literary study, analytical and descriptive bibliography. In passing, however, it may be noted that Gilbert *was* taken seriously by some serious people in his own day, as evidenced in the essay by William Archer, the first great friend and translator of Ibsen's work in England.

In addition to providing an historical overview of Gilbert scholarship, this volume should furnish the reader —both professional student of nineteenth-century drama and casual "Savoyard"—with some valuable insights contained in essays not readily available before. Virtually all the selections appeared in periodicals—many of them now defunct or difficult to locate except in major libraries— and, save for a few pieces subsequently published in books not dealing exclusively with Gilbert, none of the present essays have been reprinted before. Needless to say, I do not agree with all the interpretations and critical evalua-

tions expressed in these articles, nor do I expect the reader
to do so. Rather, a number of the pieces are presented
chiefly for their historical interest in demonstrating toward
what flights of fancy interpretations of Gilbert's works can
soar.

Given the relatively small body of material written
on Gilbert, the principles of selecting items for this collection were fairly simple. I have tried to give space to all
major literary and dramatic critics who have written on
Gilbert (exclusive of reviews of particular productions),
and also to include many of the lesser known but serious
scholars recently or currently engaged in analytical studies
of the dramatist. It is unfortunate that the writers of some
of the best book-length works on Gilbert (Reginald Allen
and Audrey Williamson, to name only two) have not
produced the kinds of separate pieces which fall within
the scope of this collection. Also, it will be observed that
the name of George Bernard Shaw is absent from the contents, the reason being that his reviews were primarily on
Sullivan's music rather than Gilbert's libretti. Finally,
with the exception of Gilbert's own "Autobiography," all
articles of reminiscence and biography have been cate-
gorically excluded.

The texts of all the essays are complete and intact
in the form in which they first appeared. Only obvious
spelling and punctuation errors have been silently corrected. Some correction of factual error—primarily mis-
quotation of Gilbert's works—has been made in the text,
but in each case the original (erroneous) reading is supplied in a note. The numbering of footnotes has been
regularized, and all numbered notes are those of the re-
spective authors of the essays. Editorial notes are designated by symbols.

I would like publicly to thank the authors of copyrighted essays, and all the publishers and other holders of subsisting copyrights, for their permission to reprint such material included in this collection. I am especially grateful to Dean William P. Albrecht and the Graduate School of the University of Kansas for the research grant which has aided in the preparation of this volume.

John Bush Jones

Lawrence, Kansas
November 9, 1969

W. S. Gilbert:
A Century of Scholarship and Commentary

Anonymous *and* "M.B."

Two Reviews of The Bab Ballads

(1869)

The Bab Ballads,—Much Sound and Little Sense.
By W. S. Gilbert, With Illustrations by the author.
(Hotten.)—These "Bab Ballads" are the dreariest and
dullest fun we ever met with; they have no real humour
nor geniality, nor have they the broad farce of burlesque;
they are wooden, both in the verses and in the illustrations; the jokes are entirely destitute of flavour. To have
real fun you must have a real human heart, for fun requires sympathy quite as much as sentiment. Humour
quaint and whimsical, like Charles Lamb's or Hood's,
requires an insight into the most contradictory moods and
tenses of human nature, and a power of love for all human
things inspiring and underlying the sense of whimsicality.
The "Bab Ballads" do not contain a single thread of
interest, nor a spark of feeling. The illustrations are pain-

ful not because they are ugly, but because they are inhuman.

The Bab Ballads. By W. S. Gilbert, with Numerous Illustrations, Drawn by the Author. London: J. C. Hotten. These ballads—the key-note of which is struck by the vignette of the baby thumping the piano-keys at baby-random—appear to be entirely without pretension. It is a curious fact that they read better at a second or third glance than they do at first, and that, utterly trivial and mechanical as they appear, a certain truthfulness of work-manship does after a time disclose itself to those who look at them more than once. This, of course, no one will do who is impatient of sheer punchinello nonsense, with sheer commonplace for the raw material of the fun. But genuine fun there assuredly is in the "Bab Ballads," while some of the little wood-cuts, from the author's own hand, are almost better than the verses. The chief difficulty criticism finds in dealing with the latter is to find out the author's point of leverage for his admirably fluent non-sense. How does he manage to get a start? This we cannot make out. All we can say is, that the contrast between the mechanical and apparently causeless insanity of the con-ception, and the ordered, luminous, and musical sanity of Mr. Gilbert's manner, does in fact yield an odd sort of humour. It is something as if Praed, with Frankenstein in his mind, had tried to make a human humourist, and only succeeded in making a marionette humourist, with clockwork fun in his inside. And yet you enjoy it, though the fun is nearly always cockney fun; *i.e.,* you require a knowledge of London, and the temporary and superficial aspect of modern life, to enter into it. In "Peter the Wag" a policeman loses his way "near Poland Street, Soho;" but nobody would see the joke who did not know how easy

it is to lose yourself in that astonishing maze of a neighbourhood which lies between Leicester Square and Oxford
Street. In one or two cases, the drawings are simply
unpleasant, and the serious ballads are not successful; but
the only one we really object to is "Disillusioned." In the
ballad called "Bob Polter," there is a lesson which not
only teetotallers, but a great many other people who try to
instruct the poor and ignorant might advantageously lay
to heart. They do not know what a disgusting prig the
model workman, as they draw him, really is; but Mr.
Gilbert has caught and fixed him in his true colours, and
has shown that, instead of acting as a bait or incitement
to good conduct, he acts as a deterrent.

Anonymous

Mr. Gilbert as
a Dramatist

(1877)

It is now some time since Mr. W. S. Gilbert published in a collected form a selection from his "Original
Plays"; and, although viewed from the standpoint of today, the selection is not all that we could wish, it possesses
considerable interest and value. With the *Palace of Truth*,
the *Princess*, and *Pygmalion and Galatea*, we would rather
bind up *Broken Hearts* and *Dan'l Druce* than *Charity*,
which seems to us not only unworthy of its place in the
book, but to be characteristic of none of its author's
dramatic styles; but for chronological reasons this was impossible, and we must wait for a further edition of "Original Plays," before the collection can be deemed thoroughly satisfactory. In any case, however, *Charity* should
have been omitted; as an acting play it is far inferior to
the same author's comedy *On Guard*, which finds no place

here, and as a literary effort it is at once pretentious and poor.

It is just now the fashion to decry Mr. Gilbert and his work, in the same way that a few years back every one was gushing over him as the playwright of the day, and was holding up his fairy comedy as the chief dramatic achievement of the day. A turn of Fortune's wheel, a few indiscreet revivals, some foolish public squabbles, a little want of temper and a great want of tact—and fickle public opinion pronounces Mr. W. S. Gilbert to be one of the rockets that come down like sticks, sneers at his past success, and covertly predicts his future failure. Of course we shall be told that the playwright's relations with this coadjutor or with that have nothing to do with the question, and that the verdict pronounced by the public in the dispute of Hodson *v.* Gilbert does not affect the judgment passed upon the acting of the one or the writing of the other. That it ought not to do so we may readily admit; but we need not, therefore, shut our eyes to the fact that here, as elsewhere, we are only too apt to do that which we ought not to do; and we may take it for granted that the appreciation of the dramatist's merits is for the moment blunted in some quarters by considerations which should never have been placed before us at all.

In many ways the volume now before us deserves careful attention. In so far as it serves to confirm its author's high position amongst the dramatists of the day it does what few similar collections could do for contemporary playwrights; in so far as it shows the development of the author's powers it suggests advancement yet to come. The plays can, for the most part, be read as well as acted, and the reviewer could conscientiously mark passage after passage as thoroughly worthy of quotation. Could as much as this be said for most of the popular authors whose works are chiefly in demand upon the stage? Could we, if the poetic dramas of Mr. Wills were left out of the question, name many of the current productions of our stage which are worthy of a place in the library? Is it not a little that Mr. Gilbert's plays should, for the most part, stand this test; it is not a little that we should find in them the quality of finished workmanship, added to that knowledge of practical stage effect, which is so often made to supply the lack of all literary polish. Mr. Gilbert's muse, if she never explores the regions of very deep and genuine feeling, and if her flights are never very high, always preserves an even and rhythmical course, always chooses her verbal way with the utmost care, and always expresses herself with graceful precision. Mr. Gilbert never boggles his work by hurrying it, by careless reliance upon the intrinsic power of his subject to atone for clumsiness of expression, or by the confusion which results from the pretended inspiration of a third-rate poet. Speech after speech might be quoted from either *The Palace of Truth* or from *Pygmalion and Galatea*, or even from the far inferior *Wicked World*, in illustration of the author's simple strength of diction; and we may content ourselves with Ethais's fine description to Selene of that inconstancy of mortal love which she in her unworldliness, is so slow to comprehend.

> Ah, my Selene, picture to thyself
> A man—linked for his life to one he loves.
> She is his world—she is the breath he breathes;
> In his fond eyes the type of purity.
> Well, she is false—all women are—and then
> Come tidings of his shame, the damning words
> "I love another, I have cheated thee."
> At first it cannot be, it is a dream,

And when by slow procession, step by step,
He sees in it the waking from a dream.-
His heavy heart stands still—he dies a death,
A momentary death—to wake again
Into a furious life of hot revenge;
His hand against all men; his maddened tongue
Calling down curses on his cheated self;
On him who stole his love, on all but her
Who has called down this crowing curse on him!
To find *her* love a lie, *her* kiss a jest,
Her cherished bywords a cold mockery—
Oh, there are words
For other agonies, but none for this!

The description, too, given by Galatea of her first sleep
and dream and waking is exquisite in diction as in
thought; the difficulty, indeed, is to choose where the
language is throughout so admirably chosen for its
purpose.

Mr. Gilbert, in fact, has considerable command of
pure, strong, nervous English; and his blank verse, if it
does not appeal to the ear with any great charm of melody
or bold refreshing beauty, is consistently free from the
ignorant defects of metre which are so frequently found
in the poetry of our contemporary stage. It is always
studiously correct, and what is more the correctness is attained without any awkward inversion of the component
parts of the sentences. Hence it flows easily and naturally;
and the ear which hit upon the effective ring of the "Bab
Ballads" proves that it is not at fault in efforts more
ambitious and more sustained. By those, indeed, who have
composed music to the words of Mr. Gilbert it is said, that
his lines, where he wishes it, are thoroughly singable, a
fact which makes us look forward with all the more inter-

est to the comic opera of which he is to supply the libretto
to Mr. Arthur Sullivan. At the end of the volume now
before us the author has, with a boldness by no means
injudicious, printed his *Trial by Jury,* a trifle which, apart
altogether from its rich original humour, forms throughout an excellent example of the art of judicious expression. Every word in song, chorus, and recitative possesses
an effect which can be realised in vocal interpretation,
and not a thought or joke is wasted in that over-elabora-
tion, which is the fault of so many kindred efforts. What,
for example, could be happier, in their way, than the
following verses, many of whose lines have already taken
their place as familiar quotations?—

When I, good friends, was called to the bar
      I'd an appetite fresh and hearty,
And I was as many young barristers are
      An impecunious party.
I'd a swallow-tail coat of a beautiful blue,
      A brief which I bought of a booby,
A couple of shirts, and a collar or two,
      And a ring that looked like a ruby.

In Westminster Hall I danced a dance,
      Like a semi-despondent fury;
For I thought I should never hit on a chance
      Of addressing a British jury.
But I soon got tired of third-class journeys,
      And dinners of bread and water;
So I fell in love with a rich attorney's
      Elderly, ugly daughter.

The rich attorney he jumped with joy,
      And replied to my fond professions:

"You shall reap the reward of your pluck, my boy,
    At the Bailey and Middlesex Sessions;
"You'll soon get used to her looks," said he,
    "And a very nice girl you'll find her!
She may very well pass for forty-three
    In the dusk with a light behind her."

Every verse, every line, every word tells—and this without any apparent effort.

It seems strange that in these days of revivals some manager is not found to reproduce that most graceful of extravaganzas, *The Princess,* one of Mr. Gilbert's earlier dramatic works. A single extract from this daintiest of skits serves to remind us how immeasurably superior in calibre and aim it is to the popular burlesque of the period; and few who know it on the stage will pronounce it to be necessarily wanting in capabilities for effective stage representation, especially in these days of fast advancing woman's rights. Psyche, rallied upon her renunciation of mankind, exclaims, in defence of her resolution—

Senseless? No!
It's based upon the grand hypothesis
That as the Ape is undeveloped Man,
So man is undeveloped woman.

To which defence a handsome young man makes reply:—

Then,
This of all others is the place for us!
If man is only undeveloped woman,
We men, if we work hard indeed,

And do our utmost to improve ourselves,
May, in good time, be women!

When Mr. Gilbert wrote his *Dan'l Druce, Black-smith,* it was assumed, and not unnaturally, that he wished to vindicate himself and his work against the charge of coldness of temper, lack of sympathy, and want of heart; and on many sides the vindication was held to be sufficient and complete. Assuredly the motive of this first play, the single-hearted, and at the last, unselfish love of the misanthrope for his adopted child, is pure, and true, and elevated; but like the motive of *The Palace of Truth,* it is, though in a different sense, not Mr. Gilbert's own. The indebtedness to George Eliot and to Madame de Genlis is admitted, and there is nothing unworthy in the dramatist's use of his legitimately-chosen materials. But the fact remains that these two pieces do not form any fair trial of the bent of the author's genius. From our present point of view this matters little in the case of the French fairy tale, but it means a good deal in that of *Silas Marner.* The author takes refuge, as it were, from himself in the finest conception of our first novelist; and in doing so he seems to prove, in more ways than one, that he is actuated, of course unconsciously, by instinct. The great fault of his "Original plays" as we lay them down and strive to judge them, however impartially, as a whole, is their want of definite purpose and meaning. The moral, for the most part cynical, which is to be drawn from Mr. Gilbert's work, is one which never seems genuine and thorough. When we are most moved, as by Galatea's love for her human creator, we have an uncomfortable notion that the playwright is laughing in his sleeve at our emotion. When, in *Sweethearts,*—not included here, by the way,—the heroine is so deeply touched by her recollections of a love gone by, we cannot feel quite sure that we should not smile at her old-maidenly devotion; and we are never allowed to enjoy our full fling of contempt at the expense of Prince Philamir, or Pygmalion, or, to recur to *Broken Hearts,* the lover of poor Vavir. The work is very clever, very symmetrical, and very neat; but it is never very sincere, and in consequence it can rarely, if ever, bring home to us any sincere conviction.

Of one objection which has been raised against Mr. Gilbert's fairy comedies, that of artificial construction and puppet-like movement, it is by no means difficult to dispose. The very charge appears to indicate a hopeless lack of imaginative power on the part of the objector. If we cannot be content to breathe for an hour or two the magic atmosphere into which we are introduced; if we complain because a scarf is supposed to make a substantial man invisible, and because people's veracity varies from scene to scene in accordance with the varying ownership of a certain casket; if we hold it a mechanical trick for Galatea to be an exaggerated ingénue, for Chrysal to be a truth-telling liar, and for Selene to be, as she herself says, a jealous "devil," then must the mechanism of all plays more fanciful than the modern comedy or the realistic drama offend our reason and jar upon our matter-of-fact sense. Of course there is a good deal of mechanical movement in the action of the fairy-play, much that may be called tricky by those who will not give it its fair attribute of cunning ingenuity. But the mechanism—to describe thus roughly the minor motives of the action—is not only perfectly legitimate, it was inevitable from the first, if such a hint as that given by Queen Titania was ever to be carried out upon the stage. The most beautiful stage-poem that ever was written might be ruthlessly condemned by this rule-of-thumb measurement and criticism of avoirdupois.

Where we have to find fault is in the fact that the dramatist is too often led away after the fashion indicated in that prologue to the *Wicked World,* which appropriately introduces the present volume. He seems to have felt that his play was based upon a mis-reading of the word "love," a species of *double entendre* on a much magnified scale. We cannot quote the whole passage, but a few excerpts may serve to suggest the misunderstanding upon which the whole three acts are founded:—

> You have been taught, no doubt, by those
>   professing
> To understand the thing, that Love's a blessing:
> Well, *he* intends to teach you the reverse—
> That love is not a blessing, but a curse!
>
> To prove his case—a poor one I admit—
> He begs that with him you will kindly flit
> To a pure fairy-land that's all his own,
> Where mortal love is utterly unknown.
>
> As perfect silence undisturbed for years
> Will breed at length a humming in the ears,
> So, from their very purity within,
> Arise the promptings of their only sin.
> Forgive them? No! Perhaps you will relent
> When you appreciate their punishment.
> But prithee, be not led too far away
> By the hack author of a mere stage-play.
> It's easy to affect this cynic tone,
> But let me ask you, had the world ne'er known
> Such Love as you and I and he must mean,
> Pray where would you or I or he have been?

All this is very ingenious, and it forms a perfectly lucid exposition of the subject of the comedy. But it is not convincing, nor when we come to think it out, apart altogether from the effects produced from certain scenes by certain players, does it seem adequate to the task of sustaining our interest in the intricate fairy story unfolded before us. The conception of the play rather than its execution savours of trickiness,—it is a feat of mental gymnastics.

Mr. W. S. Gilbert is, however, an author of dauntless perseverance and courage; and if he has, as we believe, been working hitherto in a wrong groove, we may hopefully look to see him direct his future efforts towards a worthier goal. With all deductions made, and all faults found, it is impossible to lay down these "Original Plays" without being conscious that in their original and effective treatment, and their literary charm of expression, we have legitimate grounds, too, for congratulating ourselves on the possession of a living dramatist who has done so much to refine stage-humour, and to elevate the intellectual purpose of our lighter dramatic entertainments. It is probable that Mr. Gilbert's name will live in association with efforts not to be included in any collection of his plays which can yet be made; but in the meantime a hearty welcome is to be given to most of the work which he has chosen to transfer from the ephemeral existence of the stage to a more lasting life in the library.

William Archer

Mr. W. S. Gilbert

(1881)

By right of success, if for no other reason, Mr. W. S. Gilbert stands foremost among present-day dramatists. Few, if any, contemporary writers for the stage have made so much money from that source alone, none has acquired so wide a fame. The name of Gilbert, coupled generally with that of Sullivan, it is true, is known throughout Greater Britain. Mr. Gladstone is not, Lord Beaconsfield was not, more famous. They have only made the laws of a people—Mr. Gilbert has written the songs, and, better still, invented the popular catch-words not of one but of two great nations.

Far be it from me to deny that he has other claims besides that of success, to a leading place on the roll of our dramatists. On the contrary, I wish to emphasize at the outset my respect for him as the most striking individuality, the most original character our theatre of to-day can boast. He is not a mere spinner of verbal humour.

He is not a mere constructor or adapter of comic or pathetic situations. Other dramatists have qualities which he has not, or has only in a minor degree; but in all his work we feel that there is an "awakened" intellect, a thinking brain behind it. He impresses us as a man who has looked at life with his own eyes, and has looked below the surface. There is a certain irony in his treatment of it, and that not only, nor even mainly, when he is professedly ironical. His so-called cynicism is shallow enough, but even it is genuine in so far as it proceeds from a genuine temperament. In short, he is not merely *l'homme sensuel moyen,* to use Mr. Matthew Arnold's phrase, who has more or less turn for making jokes and more or less eye for superficial eccentricities of character, which he looks at through spectacles borrowed from Charles Dickens. This is the ordinary English dramatist, but this is not Mr. Gilbert, and therefore in my opinion he is the most interesting figure in our dramatic literature. The very fact that he is personally by no means popular in the theatrical world is not without its significance. This may arise partly from adventitious circumstances, such as his severity as a stage-manager—a severity which produces admirable results—and may be partly due to absolute faults of character. Of this I have no means of judging, nor does it affect my argument, which is, that in such a world as that of the London theatres no one can be thoroughly popular who is not either an accomplished Philistine or an accomplished hypocrite. That Mr. Gilbert is not thoroughly popular, and holds himself more or less aloof from theatrical society, is at least a negative indication of some depth of character. And, after all, even in that peculiar form of literature the modern English drama, a man's works should receive their main interest from his character. This is why so few contemporary English plays can claim to rank as literature—they give but slight indications of character, and what they do indicate is absolutely uninteresting. Mr. Gilbert's, on the other hand, manifest a strong and interesting individuality, and this, it seems to me, is their chief distinction.

The mention of the word literature suggests another of Mr. Gilbert's peculiar merits. He is almost alone in the attempt to give literary grace and finish to his work. His attempt is not always successful, so far at least as the grace is concerned, but any effort in that direction is a thing to be grateful for. I shall have some criticisms to make on his literary workmanship, in the course of this paper; but it would be ungracious not to admit at the outset that its faults seldom or never arise from mere slovenliness, which is in itself a rare distinction in these latter days, when three-act comedies are written in three nights and re-written at rehearsal.

Here let me admit that the word "Dramatists," in the title of this work requires qualification. A certain shade of contempt attaches to the word "playwright," otherwise I should have used it. Were "dramatist" to be taken in its strict sense, this series would be reduced to two, or at the most three, papers, none of which should deal with Mr. Gilbert. For he is not a dramatist. He is essentially a humorist whom circumstances have led to write for the stage. Long habit, and no doubt a certain natural bent, have given him a mastery of stage technique, but he has never created a character or written a drama. In two or three instances he has chanced upon a truly dramatic subject, and has treated it seriously, and in a measure successfully. But in none of his plays is there the growth and development, the action and reaction of character and incident, in short, the creative and inventive force which go to make a true drama.

In the category of serious plays,[1] I reckon "Dan'l Druce," "Sweethearts," "Charity," and, shall I say, "Gretchen"? As it is not fantastic and still less amusing, this seems to be the only head under which it can come.

"Dan'l Druce" is Mr. Gilbert's nearest approach to a drama. Its motive, taken from "Silas Marner," is exquisitely conceived, but it remains a play of lost opportunities. It consists of two dramatic incidents, the one occupying the first act, the other the second and third. The first act is a little play in itself, and should have been called a prologue, to use a word often abused, but precisely fitted for the present case. Its chief fault lies in the letter which Sir Jasper Combe leaves with the infant Dorothy.—"Be kind to the child, and it shall profit thee. Grieve not for thy gold, it hath taken this form." Sir Jasper had evidently been reading "Silas Marner" in the course of his flight from the Roundheads, or such an idea would never have occurred to him. The British public certainly requires to have an idea shoved down its throat, but this is ramming it home with a ramrod. The prologue over, there remains matter for a full and rounded drama, in three or even more acts, not merely for the incident in two acts which Mr. Gilbert gives us. The true drama surely lies in the struggle in Dan'l Druce's mind after he has discovered Sir Jasper Combe to be Dorothy's father— the struggle between love and duty, the doubt as to what course of action duty really claims, perhaps the adoption of a wrong course and its punishment. In Mr. Gilbert's play Dan'l is entirely passive. Time after time chance takes choice out of his hands. At the end of the second act the curtain falls upon a trumpery and utterly illogical misunderstanding with Geoffrey Wynyard, which has even not the excuse of theatrical effectiveness, since it breaks the sympathy with Dan'l. This is a badly arranged episode,

not an organic portion of the drama. The scene with
Reuben Haynes in the third act is a little better, for it is
at least rational. Indeed, the drama might be made to lie
in some such temptation as that to which Dan'l here
momentarily yields, better motived and more fully developed. On the other hand, the turn of affairs which
shows Dan'l to be Dorothy's father after all, and Sir
Jasper the betrayer of Dan'l's wife, is extremely bad. It is
a violent and improbable *coup de théâtre* which produces
no effect, and if anything spoils the motive. It is as hard
to swallow as a camel, and as unsatisfactory as a gnat. The
result is in the inverse ratio of the effort, which is precisely the wrong proportion.

The love-scene in "Dan'l Druce" is one of the pretti-
est bits of writing Mr. Gilbert has done, and Dorothy is
a theatrically effective character; yet it is perhaps she who
proves most plainly how far Mr. Gilbert's mechanical skill
falls short of the true dramatic gift. The fact that her
dialect is precisely that of the Bible may be passed over,
though I see no reason to suppose that a village girl in
the reign of Charles II would speak exactly as certain
divines wrote in the reign of his grandfather. But if one
were seeking an example of theatrical effectiveness as opposed to dramatic truth, it would be difficult to find a
better than the following soliloquy:

> *Dor.* Geoffrey returned! and Geoffrey a stalwart
> mariner, and grown to man's estate! I can scarce
> believe it. Of a truth I could weep for very joy! I was
> but a child when he left, and now—I am seventeen!
> Geoffrey loved children—it may be that he will be
> displeased with me now that I am a woman. I am
> rejoiced that I am decked in my new gown—it is
> more seemly than the russet, in which methinks I did

look pale. Geoffrey a man!—my old playmate a man! Pity that I have not my new shoes, for they are comely; but they compress my feet, and so pain me sorely. Nevertheless, I will put them on, for it behoveth a maiden to be neatly apparelled at all seasons.

No doubt Miss Marion Terry delivered this speech very charmingly, but it is none the less untrue to nature. Even worse is her appeal to Sir Jasper in the last scene, where she winds up a pathetic speech with the words "Oh, sir, if thou hast no care for him, yet *for the love of my mother* have pity upon me." This invocation is under the circumstances one of theatrical convention, not of dramatic truth. Worst of all is her intervention between her father and Sir Jasper, on the revelation of the latter's crime: "Father, spare him—be merciful—be just. He is an old man now—thou art an old man—is it in the winter of your lives, that the heartburnings of hot youth are to be avenged?" &c. &c. These words might come well from the "Colonial Bishop-elect" of "Charity"—Dorothy's intervention should have been silent or almost so. The fact that he does not appreciate the value of silence is one evidence of the undramatic quality of Mr. Gilbert's talent. He leaves nothing to divination or even to action. He never gets into those depths of human nature where words are useless, or if he ever gets there he does not know it.

I have dwelt on "Dan'l Druce," because it seems to me a typical play. It illustrates admirably the limitations of Mr. Gilbert's talent on its serious side. He might have given its action the beautiful, natural curve of a rocket— the resultant between the impetus of dramatic circumstance and gravitation in the shape of the universal forces of human nature. He has chosen instead to make it a cracker—its course an arbitrary zigzag, accentuated by irrelevant explosions.

"Sweethearts" is a pleasant little piece, rather mechanical in its humour now and then, but full of healthy, human feeling, and on the whole the most satisfactory of Mr. Gilbert's serious plays. There is, indeed, an almost French grace about its conception which gives it a place apart in the modern English drama.

As "Charity" was a failure, and is consequently less known than the majority of Mr. Gilbert's plays, I may give a short account of its plot. Frederick Smailey, son of Mr. Jonas Smailey, is engaged to Eve, the daughter of a certain Mrs. Van Brugh. This lady's property all comes from her godfather, to whom Smailey is next-of-kin. Mrs. Van Brugh, who is an extremely charitable lady, has rescued from the streets and taken into her service a tramp named Ruth Tredgett, thereby exciting the unqualified disapproval of Smailey, who holds that "Society had decided that a woman who has once forfeited her moral position shall never regain it." A detective employed by Smailey discovers that at the time of Mrs. Van Brugh's marriage her husband had another wife alive; and as her godfather's will describes her as "wife of Richard Van Brugh, Esq.," all the property reverts to Smailey as next-of-kin. He forces her to confess that she never even went through the ceremony of marriage with Captain Van Brugh, and then refuses to believe this, and tries to get up a case against her for bigamy. To this end he advertises for the burial certificate of the first Mrs. Van Brugh. Unfortunately for him, Ruth Tredgett proves to be a girl whom he himself seduced in Melbourne many years previously, and who has in her possession a burial certificate of a certain Martha Vane, which was forged by Smailey about that time in order to defraud a burial society. This Martha Vane was the wife of Captain Van Brugh, separated from him and going by her maiden name. Smailey is thus caught in his own trap, and is arrested at the end of the piece. His son has, of course, meanly broken off his engagement with Eve as soon as the troubles of the family commenced, and the Van Brughs, as the curtain falls, determine to sail to a new land with their friend, Dr. Athelney, a "Colonial Bishop-elect."

One cause of the failure of this play is clear enough even from the above sketch. The plot is unpleasant and extremely involved, while the unravelling of it is effected by means of a series of coincidences which quite transcend the bounds of probability. But the main cause of failure lay in the character of Smailey. Intended as a satirical portrait of the modern Pharisee and hypocrite, he is in reality a repulsive and self-contradictory caricature. Mr. Gilbert has failed to repress his bias towards burlesque. "The Smaileys are a very old and very famous family," says Mr. Smailey; "Caius Smaileius came over with Julius Caesar." And again, in a serious scene with his son, "If Caius Smaileius heard that one of his race was about to marry into a tainted family, I believe the doughty old Roman would turn in his tumulus." The extravagance of these speeches might be amusing in the mouth of Sir Joseph Porter or of Major-General Stanley: in that of Mr. Smailey it merely destroys all illusion. Worse, if possible, is his speech to Ruth Tredgett, "In my case allowance should, in common charity, be made for follies that arise from extreme youth and—and inexperience. I was barely forty then." The relation, too, between the father and son is absolutely impossible. That two such "anointed scoundrels" should live together for twenty-five years, each believing the other to be an honest man, is a simple absurdity. But Mr. Gilbert does

not make it clear whether or not Smailey is conscious of
his own villainy. He occasionally keeps up his hypocrisy
even in his soliloquies, especially if an amusing effect is to
be got by so doing. It is a truism, of course, that many
great rogues believe themelves highly respectable people;
but Smailey is not consistently conceived as one of this
type. One moment he seems a conscious scoundrel, and the
next unconscious, his speeches being dictated, not by the
necessity of his character, but by the exigencies of momentary effect. If Mr. Gilbert had any distinct conception
of the character he wished to draw, it was probably something after the fashion of Bulstrode in "Middlemarch,"—

> But frequently he rather fatally misses
> Who ventures to shoot with the bow of Ulysses.

This remark applies with double force to "Gretchen."
Mr. Gilbert is of the opinion that Goethe's "Faust" is not
a stage play, but a philosophical treatise upon human nature written in dramatic form. "It is scarcely going too far
to say," he adds, "that in those versions of 'Faust,' which
are current on the English, French, and Italian stages, the
great master would hardly recognize his own handiwork.
Whether it is allowable so to trim, patch, lop, mutilate,
and disfigure an immortal work in order to adapt it to an
arena for which its creator never designed it, is a point
upon which the reader will form his own opinion. I trust,
however, that in preferring to re-model for purely dramatic purposes the entire story of Gretchen's downfall, I
shall at least be absolved from a charge of intentional irreverence towards the grandest philosophical work of the
century." The result is that he has transmuted the marvellous legend into a commonplace and painful seduction-

story. His plea for total reconstruction might have been relevant had he been under any compulsion to place "Faust" upon the English stage at all. He was not; and even if he had been, the necessity for total reconstruction in general would not have justified the particular form which his reconstruction has taken.

His Faustus is not the weary student who has "durchaus studirt" all the world's wisdom, and after all knows only that he can know nothing. He is a blasé young man whose mistress has played him false, and who has consequently turned monk. A more utterly shallow character was never conceived, unless perhaps it be that of Mephisto —for this is the name of Mr. Gilbert's fiend, shorn of his tail in more senses than one. He is a sort of long-winded Dick Deadeye, only that his cynicism is good-humoured instead of snarling. He reminds one of Macaulay's recommendation to Robert Montgomery, that he should alter a few lines in his poem of "Satan," and rechristen it "Gabriel." His influence on the character of Faustus is nil. Indeed, the whole effect he produces in the play is to show Faustus a vision of Gretchen, to make love to Martha, and to cause Faustus' hair to grow with preternatural rapidity. The whole tragedy lies in Faustus' tonsure. In the first act he has a shaven crown concealed by a skull-cap: in the second, the next day, he has a full crop of ambrosial curls. Hence Gretchen never suspects that he is a priest, and it is his unguarded revelation of this fact that suddenly drives her to despair and death. Her sorrow at the sacrilege she has committed—a perfectly conventional and factitious emotion—is the cause of the catastrophe. Indeed, it is his character of Gretchen that one can least forgive Mr. Gilbert. He may say that we have no right to compare her with Goethe's Margarete, but, right or no right, we cannot help it. If she were even the faintest reflex of that exquisite incarnation of "das Ewig-Weibliche," she would be tolerable. But her ingenuousness is modern throughout, and perfectly self-conscious. Mr. Gilbert is responsible for the paradox, not I. She is a moral—I mean a moralizing, Gretchen. She is tolerant, not ignorant, of evil. When the penitent Lisa returns to the village, she cries,—

> Oh, sisters, is it fit
> That we should judge our sister, or withhold
> The mercy that we pray for, day by day?

She is eminently religious; sometimes high-church, sometimes evangelical. In short, there is not a breath of freshness, not a throb of life about her. No drop of warm blood runs in her veins, no thought of nature's teaching grows, flower-like, in her mind. To make up for this she can put all her thoughts into words, very precise and well-chosen words, and plenty of them. Here is a specimen— one speech addressed to Faustus—

> Ah, Heaven is kind to me, for all my sin!
> For when my heart is more than common sad,
> I need but close my eyes—and all at once,
> I wander at my will amid the days
> When thou and I may face the world again.
> And yet I am no fitting mate for thee,
> Thou, a great lord—rich, honour'd, and
>   beloved—
> I a poor simple, untaught, peasant girl!
> Yet bear with me—my love shall plague thee little,
> Though ever and anon I come to thee
> With faltering step and tearful downcast eyes,
> A timid suppliant for such alms of love
> As thou in thy good will mayst grant to me.

So, when thou seest, kneeling at thy feet,
Thy poor, mad, love-sick, trusting, trembling wife,
Throw her in charity one little flower
Out of the boundless garden of thy heart,
That she may go rejoicing on her way.

Now listen to six lines of Margarete's:—

Du lieber Gott! was so ein Mann
Nicht alles alles denken kann!
Beschämt nur steh 'ich vor ihm da,
Und sag' zu allen Sachen ja.
Bin doch ein arm unwissend Kind,
Begreife nicht, was er an mir find't.

I seem to find more humanity in these lines than in all "Gretchen" put together—and yet "Gretchen" is a drama and "Faust" is a "philosophical treatise!" The death-scene is as verbose and conventional as the rest of the play—epithets which are too often applicable to Mr. Gilbert's pathos. It leaves us unmoved and cold. St. Patrick is said to have lighted a fire with icicles, but the age of miracles is past.

"Gretchen" is written throughout in blank-verse, and so are the five fantastic plays of which I shall next have to speak. Supposing each play to contain on an average 1500 lines—a modest computation—we find that Mr. Gilbert has written at least 9000 lines of blank-verse. Of these 9000 I venture to assert that there is not one which has the smallest metrical beauty. As a rule they are correctly enough measured off into ten syllables, but there is not one whose cadence lingers in the memory. Occasionally, they are positively bad. Such lines as the following are inexcusable:—

Who could look on that face and stifle love?

and

Tell me more of her!
                Well—
                            What did she say?

Here every emphasis falls in the wrong place with unerring precision. Could a more dragging line be imagined than

Even though Heaven's armaments be ranged;

or

While he sat all day fuddling at the ale-house.

Sometimes a very slight alteration in the order of words would make an extremely wooden line tolerably graceful.

My heavy debt is multiplied tenfold

would surely have a better fall in this form,—

My heavy debt is tenfold multiplied

and the line

Sang once more in the great green waving trees,

might be transposed thus—

Sang in the great green waving trees once more.

But it is the negative and not the positive defects of his verse which seem to me fatal—its absence of merits and not its faults. I said that not one line lingered in my memory, but that was not literally correct. After a pretty close study of the blank-verse plays on the stage and in book form, I remember one line, that in which he has called in apt alliteration's artful aid to produce this lingual masterpiece—

Lapped in a lazy luxury of love.

A perusal of his six poetical plays recalls Lowell's remark about the moral Gower,—"As you slip to and fro on the frozen levels of his verse, which give no foothold to the mind . . . you learn to dread, almost to respect, the powers of this indefatigable man." I omit the unkind quotation from Wordsworth, which the reader who has suffered from Gower or Gilbert may look up for himself in Lowell's essay on Chaucer. But Gower had more excuse than Mr. Gilbert for manufacturing wooden verse, since his had only to be read while Mr. Gilbert's was written to be spoken by a generation of actors, who, as a rule, are notoriously incapable of delivering any verse whatever. True, the old Haymarket company, for which several of the plays were written, was not so bad in this respect as the company which played "Gretchen." But, at best, why choose this hampering medium of expression? Even in the hands of a poet and a master of its mysteries, it is of questionable effect in dramatic work. Shakespeare himself seldom or never wrote a whole play in blank-verse. Mr. Gilbert is neither a poet nor a master of its mysteries, and in binding himself to cut his thoughts into lengths of five feet, he has merely made their expression needlessly verbose. He has seldom been betrayed into positive errors of style, though even in this respect he is not immaculate. Galatea, for instance, remarks, looking at a mirror—

> How beautiful! I'm very glad to know
> That both our tastes agree so perfectly.

This solecism has evidently slipped in through the exigencies of the metre, but such cases are rare. The sole use of the verse, however, is to cloak poverty of dialogue, meagreness of thought and imagery—richness of thought and imagery, too great, if that be possible, for expression in prose, would have been its sole excuse.

In two instances also, the verse is useful in giving a certain consistency to plays whose slightness of motive would, without it, be too apparent. "The Wicked World" and "Broken Hearts" are pretty fantasies which, developed in very much narrower compass, and by a true poet, might have taken an abiding place in literature. Mr. Gilbert's cold and mechanical fancy was quite inadequate to their treatment, and he marred them, the former especially, by touches of vulgarity, of which I shall have more to say when I come to deal with "Pygmalion and Galatea."

But first a few words as to "The Palace of Truth." In this play, the keynote of Mr. Gilbert's peculiar talent is struck, his style of satire is epitomized. His most successful works have all for their scene an imaginary Palace of Truth, where people naively reveal their inmost thoughts, unconscious of their egotism, vanity, baseness, or cruelty. Touches of this peculiar mannerism are apparent in earlier works, such as the two fantastic farces, "Creatures of Impulse" and "The Gentleman in Black"; but it was first consistently adopted in "The Palace of Truth." The comedy is constructed and written with a good deal of ingenuity. It is so thoroughly fantastic, both in motive and treatment, that its cynicism does not become repulsive. The spotless Lady Mirza is a well-conceived figure, and her downfall an extremely effective touch. Altogether, the play is in itself one of Mr. Gilbert's best pieces of work; but it acquires double importance from the fact that since he discovered "The Palace of Truth," he has hardly ever succeeded in freeing himself from its enchantment. He conceives the whole world as subject to the spell. He seldom cares to use the talisman which frees him from its influence, and when he wants to use it, he sometimes seems to have mislaid it. It was the magic of "The Palace of Truth," for instance, that spoiled the semblance of nature in "Charity," and contributed largely to its failure.

That he has touched nothing which he has not adorned cannot, unfortunately, be said of Mr. Gilbert. As he vulgarized the legend of Faust, so he vulgarized in an even greater degree the legend of Pygmalion and Galatea. His initial mistake lay in giving the sculptor a wife, and introducing the element of jealousy in a very modern and commonplace form. But even if we accept this as a necessary device for giving the story interest and consistency on the stage, it is impossible to accept his development of the theme in detail. It is remarkable that Mr. Gilbert, whose peculiar form of humour is based upon a strong logical faculty, should work out the problem of psychology presented by a vivified statue in a peculiarly illogical form; and it is also remarkable that he, who as a librettist has so successfully steered clear of vulgarity, should have treated this theme in a peculiarly vulgar fashion.

As we have no scientific record of a statue coming to life, the probable moral and intellectual condition of a being so created is left to the widest conjecture. The playwright may assume for it any stage of development he pleases, and his audience will readily grant his assumption. But if his work is to have any claim to artistic value he must not assume all sorts of different stages of development at every second word his creation utters. He must not make her a child in one speech, a woman of the world in the next, and an idiot in the next again. Of course it would be an extremely difficult task clearly to define in all its bearings and details the particular intellectual condition assumed at the outset, and then gradually to indicate the natural growth of a fuller consciousness. Difficult it would be, but by no means impossible; nay, it would be this very problem which would tempt the true dramatist to adopt such a theme. Mr. Gilbert has not even essayed the task. He regulates Galatea's state of consciousness by the fluctuating exigencies of dialogue whose comedy is levelled straight at the heads of the old Haymarket pit—never in the least over them. Shortly after she comes to life occurs the following passage:—

Pyg:	O woman—perfect in thy loveliness?
Gal:	What is that word? Am I a woman?
Pyg:	Yes.
Gal:	Art thou a woman?
Pyg:	No, I am a man.

Gal: What is a man?
Pyg: A being strongly framed,
              To wait on woman and protect her from
              All ills that strength and courage can avert;
              To work and toil for her that she may rest;
              To weep and mourn for her that she may
                  laugh;
              To fight and die for her that she may live!
Gal: (*after a pause*): I'm glad I am a woman.
Pyg: So am I.

Then, a little further on, the conversation takes this turn:—

Gal: I wish that I could look upon myself,
              But that's impossible.
Pyg: Not so indeed.
              This mirror will reflect thy face. Behold!
              (*Hands her a mirror.*)
Gal: How beautiful; I'm very glad to know
              That both our tastes agree so perfectly;
              Why, my Pygmalion, I did not think
              That aught could be more beautiful than
                  thou,
              Till I beheld myself. Believe me, love,
              I could look in this mirror all day long.
              So I'm a woman!
Pyg: There's no doubt of that!
Gal: Oh happy maid to be so passing fair!
              And happier still Pygmalion, who can gaze,
              At will upon so beautiful a face!
Pyg: Hush! Galatea—in thine innocence
              Thou sayest things that others would
                  reprove.

Gal:	Indeed, Pygmalion; then it is wrong
	To think that one is exquisitely fair?
Pyg:	Well, Galatea, it's a sentiment
	That every other woman shares with thee;
	They *think* it—but they keep it to
	themselves.
Gal:	And is thy wife as beautiful as I?
Pyg:	No, Galatea, for in forming thee
	I took her features—lovely in themselves—
	And in the marble made them lovelier still.
Gal:	(*disappointed*): Oh! then I'm not original?

Thus Galatea does not know that she is a woman, but knows the possibility of disagreement in taste, though Pygmalion is the only living creature she has seen; does not see the futility of self-praise any more than an inhabitant of the Palace of Truth, yet sees the distinction between an original and a copy. Next day occurs the following dialogue:—

Pyg:	Leucippe comes,
	And he shall comfort thee till I return;
	I'll not be long!
Gal:	Leucippe! Who is he?
Pyg:	A valiant soldier.
Gal:	What is that?
Pyg:	A man
	Who's hired to kill his country's enemies.
Gal:	(*horrified*): A paid assassin!
Pyg:	(*annoyed*): Well, that's rather strong.

Here we find that Galatea has got the length of knowing the enormity of taking life, and appreciating the fine

distinction between taking it of one's own motive and
taking it for money. Yet it appears the next moment, when
Leucippe enters with a fawn he has killed, that she does
not know the difference between man and the brute creation. To point out even the more glaring inconsistencies
of this sort would be an interminable task, as there is not
the smallest attempt at consistency. Nor, I need scarcely add,
is there any attempt at local colour, or the reproduction of
Greek habits and modes of thought. As the play is purely
fantastic, this was scarcely to be demanded. Only, with
modern forms of thought and expression, was it necessary
to import into the action a strong flavouring of modern
vulgarity? Even the extracts I have given above show tend-
encies in that direction, which come out still more
strongly in certain other passages with Pygmalion. But it is
in the following scene, and some others of a like nature,
that the taint is strongest. The personages are Galatea and
Chrysal, an old and ugly art patron:—

Gal: (*who has been examining him in great
wonder*):

Tell me, what are you?

Chry: What *am* I?

Gal: Yes; I mean, are you a man?

Chry: Well, yes; I'm told so.

Gal: Then believe them not,
They've been deceiving you.

Chry: The deuce they have!

Gal: A man is very tall, and straight, and strong,
With big brave eyes, fair face, and tender
voice.
I've seen one.

Chry: *Have* you?

Gal: Yes; you are no man.

Chry: Does the young person take me for a
   woman?

Gal: A woman? No; a woman's soft and weak,
  And fair, and exquisitely beautiful.
  I am a woman; you are not like me.

Chry: The gods forbid that I should be like you,
  And farm my features at so much an hour!

Gal: And yet I like you, for you make me laugh;
  You are round and red, your eyes so small,
  Your mouth so large, your face so seared
   with lines,
  And then you are so little and so fat!

Chry: (*aside*): This is a most extraordinary girl.

Gal: Oh, stay—I understand—Pgymalion's skill
  Is the result of long experience.
  The individual who modelled you
  Was a beginner very probably?

Chry: (*puzzled*): No. I have seven elder brothers.
   Strange
  That one so young should be so very bold.

Gal: This is not boldness, it is innocence;
  Pygmalion says so, and he ought to know.

Chry: No doubt, but I was not born yesterday.
  (*Sits.*)

Gal: Indeed! I was. (*He beckons her to sit beside
  him.*)
      How awkwardly you sit.

Chry: I'm not aware that there is anything
  Extraordinary in my sitting down.
  The nature of the seated attitude
  Does not leave scope for much variety.

Gal: I never saw Pygmalion sit like that.

Chry: Don't he sit down like other men?

Gal: Of course!
  He always puts his arm around my waist.

Chry: The deuce he does! Artistic reprobate!

Gal: But you do not. Perhaps you don't know
          how?

Chry: Oh, yes; I *do* know how!

Gal: Well, do it then!

Chry: It's a strange whim, but I will humour her.
          You're sure it's innocence? (*Does so.*)

Gal: Of course it is.
          I tell you I was born but yesterday.

Chry: Who is your mother?

Gal: Mother!—what is that?
          I never had one. I'm Pygmalion's child;
          Have people usually mothers?

Chry: Well,
          That is the rule.

Gal: But then Pygmalion
          Is cleverer than most men.

Chry: Yes, I've heard
          That he has powers denied to other men,
          And I'm beginning to believe it!

It must be remembered, in excuse for Mr. Gilbert, that he was writing not only for the Haymarket audience, but for the Haymarket management, and that such parts as Chrysal, and, in the "Palace of Truth," King Phanor, were demanded by Mr. Buckstone. Nevertheless, it is painful to see such elements imported into the treatment of a theme like that of "Pygmalion and Galatea."

"The Princess," the only blank-verse play I have not yet mentioned, is a neat burlesque, good-humoured beyond Mr. Gilbert's wont. It is not free from a tinge of vulgarity, but is witty, lively, and on the whole a favourable specimen of the lighter order of his work.

Written in prose, and placed in modern England, "Engaged" and "Tom Cobb" are yet as purely fantastic as any of the blank-verse plays. They are among Mr. Gilbert's most original works, but are of very different merit. "Engaged" was a success, "Tom Cobb," if I remember rightly, a comparative failure—need I say that the latter is by far the better play? The scene of both is laid in Mr. Gilbert's patent Palace of Truth. The characters are presented, as it were, with their moral skins off, for the satire very seldom gets more than skin deep. They are divested of the wrappings and integuments which generally shield our vanities and meannesses from the common gaze. I say our vanities and meannesses, for it is to be noted that in no single instance, unless it be that of Zeolide in "The Palace of Truth" itself, does Mr. Gilbert's flaying process reveal any unexpected nobleness or generosity. It is this which, in a sense, takes the sting from his cynicism. It is so unrelieved, that we recognize it as a mere trick or mannerism, and not the result of genuine insight. The jester who railed at every one from king to scullion, offended no one. Had he made exceptions, and shown reverence to Lancelot, or even to Arthur himself, the rest of the court might have resented his jibes as being personal, and not merely professional.

"Engaged" is a repulsive, vulgar, and—extremely amusing play. It shows us eight personages all actuated by the most unblushingly mercenary motives, who confess these motives in the most unblushing way, and with the air of uttering the noblest sentiments. The intrigue is really ingenious in its absurdity. Turning upon a Scotch marriage, it involves the *dramatis personae* in an amatory imbroglio of unparalleled complexity. Cheviot Hill—inimitably played by the late Mr. George Honey—is an extremely parsimonious and extremely erotic young man. The train in which he is travelling is thrown off the line by a virtuous Scotch peasant, Angus Macalister, who makes his living by wrecking trains. Emerging from the wreck "a moral pulp, a mash, a poultice," as he himself describes his condition, Cheviot meets Maggie Macfarlane, the sweetheart of the virtuous Angus. He forgets that he is engaged to Minnie Symperson, and at once proposes to her, when the following scene ensues:—

Mag: Ah, kind sir, I'm sairly grieved to wound sae true and tender a love as yours, but ye're ower late; my love is nae my ain to give ye. It's given ower to the best and bravest lad in a' the bonnie Borderland!

Ch: Give me his address that I may go and curse him!

Mag: (*kneels to Cheviot*): Ah, ye must not curse him. Oh, spare him, spare him, for he is good and brave, and he loves me, oh, sae dearly! and I love him, oh, sae dearly, too! Oh, sir, kind sir, have mercy on him, and do not—do not curse him, or I shall die! (*Throwing herself at his feet.*)

Ch: Will you, or will you not, oblige me by telling me where he is, that I may at once go and curse him?

Ang: (*coming forward*): He is here sir; but dinna waste your curses on me. Maggie, my bairn (*raising her*), I heard the answer ye gave to this man, my true and gentle lassie! Ye spoke well and bravely, Meg—well and bravely! Dinna heed the water in my 'ee—it's a tear of joy and gratitude, Meg—a tear of joy and gratitude!

Ch: (*touched*): Poor fellow! I will *not* curse him! (*Aloud.*) Young man, I respect your honest emotion. I don't want to distress you, but I cannot help loving this most charming girl. Come, is it reasonable to quarrel with a man because he's of the same way of thinking as yourself?

Ang: Nay, sir, I'm nae fasht, but it just seems to drive a' the bluid back into my hairt when I think that my Meg is loved by anither! Oh, sir, she's a fair and winsome lassie, and I micht as justly be angry wi' ye for loving the blue heavens! She's just as far above us as they are! (*Wiping his eyes and kissing her.*)

Ch: (*with decision*): Pardon me, I cannot allow that.

Ang: Eh?

Ch: I love that girl madly—passionately—and I cannot possibly allow you to do that—not before my eyes, I beg. You simply torture me.

Mag: (*to Angus*): Leave off, dear, till the poor gentleman's gone, and then you can begin again.

Ch: Angus, listen to me. You love this girl?

Ang: I love her, sir, a'most as weel as I love mysel'!

Ch: Then reflect how you are standing in the way of her prosperity. I am a rich man. I have money, position, and education. I am a much more intellectual and generally agreeable companion for her than you can ever hope to be. I am full of anecdote, and all my anecdotes are in the best possible taste. I will tell you some of them, some of these days, and you can judge for yourself. Maggie, if she married me, would live in a nice house in a good square. She would have wine—occasionally. She would be kept beautifully clean. Now, if you really love this girl almost as well as you love yourself, are you doing wisely or kindly in standing in the way of her getting all these good things? As to compensation—why, I've had heavy expenses of late—but if—yes, if thirty shillings—

Of course the bargain is struck, but comes to nothing, as Cheviot forthwith falls in love with another young lady. The second act takes place on the day appointed for the marriage of Cheviot and Minnie Symperson, and here is part of a love-scene between the bride and bridegroom:

Ch: Dear me! To think that in half an hour this magnificent dress will be *my* property.

Min: Yes. Dear papa said that as you had offered to give the breakfast at your house, he would give me the best dress that money could procure.

Ch: Yes, I *did* offer to provide the breakfast in a reckless moment; that's so like me. It was a rash offer, but I've made it, and I've stuck to it. Oh, then there's the cake.

Min: Oh, tell me all about the cake.
          (*Cheviot and Minnie sit on sofa.*)

Ch: It's a very pretty cake. Very little cake is eaten at a wedding breakfast, so I've ordered what's known in the trade as the three-quarter article.

Min: I see; three-quarters cake, and the rest wood.

Ch: No; three-quarters wood, the rest cake. Be sure, my dear, you don't cut into the wood, for it has to be returned to the pastry-cook to be filled up with cake for another occasion. I thought at first of ordering a seven-eighths article; but one isn't married every day, it's only once a year—I mean it's only now and then. So I said, "Hang the expense; let's do the thing well." And so it's a three-quarters.

Min: How good you are to me! We shall be very happy, shall we not?

Min: Then how shall we spend our evenings?

Ch: We'll have pleasant little fireside games. Are you fond of fireside games?

Min: Oh, they're great fun.

Ch: Then we'll play at tailoring.

Min: Tailoring? I don't think I know that game.

Ch: It's a very good game. You shall be the clever little jobbing tailor, and I'll be the particular customer who brings his own materials to be made up. You shall take my measure, cut out the cloth (real cloth, you know), stitch it together, and try it on; and then I'll find fault like a real customer, and you shall alter it until it fits, and when it fits beautifully that counts one to you.

Min: Delightful!

Ch: Then there's another little fireside game which is great fun. We each take a bit of paper and a pencil and try who can jot down the nicest dinner for ninepence, and the next day we have it.

Min: Oh, Cheviot, what a paradise you hold open to me.

I need go no further. These quotations sufficiently indicate the tone of the play, and the style of its humour. That it is extremely funny cannot be denied, especially when it is played with the business-like earnestness which Mr. Gilbert manages to impart to his interpreters. But it leaves a bitter taste in the mouth. It is as unpleasant and degrading as "Gulliver's Travels," without their deep human truth. Its cynicism is as irrelevant as it is exaggerated.

A much pleasanter, if not much cleverer work, is "Tom Cobb." It is a delicious piece of absurdity, very neat in its conception, and without a dull scene in its short, crisp action. The satire now and then takes a deeper grasp than is usual with Mr. Gilbert, especially in the scene at the beginning of the third act, where the Effingham family, mistaking Tom Cobb for the poet-warrior Major-General Fielding, gush over his most commonplace remarks, and come to the conclusion that "Shakespeare never said anything like them." Perhaps my preference is exaggerated, but this play, trifling as it is, seems to me the happiest of all Mr. Gilbert's works,—that in which the maximum of effect is attained with the minimum of (apparent) effort. It will surely be revived before long.

"Foggerty's Fairy," on the other hand, though it contained much clever work, failed by reason of a lack of the very quality of logic which is generally Mr. Gilbert's strong point. The idea is that of a man, who, by supernatural aid, overcomes the irrevocableness of the past. To avoid unpleasant consequences he "obliterates" a part of his past life. But in the process another set of events is substituted for those which actually occurred. He finds himself hampered as much as ever by the consequences of this new past, and from these difficulties the action is evolved. Now it is clear that the new chain of events which is substituted is an entirely arbitrary invention of the dramatist, not growing out of any logical necessity in the idea. The natural, or rather the logical, effect of "obliterating" a certain portion of one's life would be to carry one back to the point at which the obliteration commenced. The device did not result in a paradox, but in a wild absurdity. This might have been tolerated had it been carried out with particular tact and skill; but, as a matter of fact, though many of the scenes were very funny, it was felt that others were vulgar, strained, and unpleasant, and that in one or two instances Mr. Gilbert was quite unwarrantably repeating himself. Hence the play met with scant approval.

Mr. Frederic Harrison is of opinion that the age which can tolerate "H.M.S. Pinafore" cannot read Homer. The obvious reply is that the age must be very one-sided. Such a remark coming from a man like Mr. Harrison, suggests an inquiry as to whether he has ever seen "Pinafore." Perhaps he has; but in that case he cannot have seen the opera-bouffes which "Pinafore" and its family have in a measure—a small measure, alas!—succeeded in supplanting. Had he seen "Les Cloches de Corneville," to take one of the least objectionable examples, and compared its inane and vulgar buffoonery with the crisp neatness and literary and musical finish of "Pinafore," he would have been too thankful for small mercies to breathe a word against the reputation of that most famous craft which ever hoisted the British flag. Truly the step from the Odyssey to "Pinafore" is scarcely a greater descent than from "Pinafore" to an average opera-bouffe in its English dress. The wall which divides the stage of the Opera Comique from that of the Globe for years divided humour from inanity, art from horse-play, refinement from vulgarity, literature from the lowest form of literary hack-work.

"Princess Toto" was Mr. Gilbert's first operatic effort of any importance. It was not successful, but both in idea and writing it was very clever. Its music was composed by Mr. Frederick Clay—Mr. Gilbert had not yet found the musical collaborator whose talent has shown itself so congenial with his own.

"Trial by Jury" was the first effort in a new field, and

was so successful that the "pardners," as Bret Harte would call them, have since unremittingly "worked the claim," which has proved a very Tom Tiddler's ground, giving a larger yield at each stroke of the shovel. "The Sorcerer," "H.M.S. Pinafore," "The Pirates of Penzance," and "Patience," have followed in unbroken though not in quick succession. They have been treated with contumely by other critics besides Mr. Frederic Harrison, but they have taken the popular ear, and, what is more, they have become part of the national life. In the healthiest if not the loftiest way, they have enhanced the gaiety of nations. In so far as they have prevented Mr. Gilbert from doing serious work, we may perhaps regret their success; but I, for one, do not refuse to be comforted even on this score. Only Mr. Gilbert could have written "The Pirates of Penzance," whereas we have several playwrights who could have written "Dan'l Druce," and one or two who might even have perpetrated "Gretchen." As for the farces we might have had in their stead, it seems to me that the operas are fully equal in point of quaint humour to anything Mr. Gilbert has done, while Mr. Sullivan's music appears to have the power of soothing his savage breast, and sweetening the gall and bitterness which flavour such a play as "Engaged."

The humour of the operas is a thing by itself—so much so, that I have known people with an otherwise well-developed sense of the ridiculous, whom it seemed completely to elude. There is a good deal of the Palace of Truth mannerism in it, but this is not the whole secret. Indeed the operas are more closely akin to the "Bab Ballads" than to "The Palace of Truth," Mr. Gilbert having actually, with the frugality of true genius, worked up several ideas from those early productions. A strong logical faculty is the basis of this humour. *Reductio ad absurdum* is its favourite method of procedure. Maxims of morality car-

ried to their logical extreme and developed into paradoxes
are its chosen playthings. In "Pinafore," for instance, much
of the fun is extracted from the logical development of the
modern idea of consideration for inferiors, or rather the
broader principle of essential equality modified by acci-
dental distinctions of rank and office. In "The Pirates,"
material is found in pushing to its logical extreme the idea
of duty. In "Patience," much of the action turns upon the
absurdities which may be deduced from a literal acceptance of common maxims on love and unselfishness.

> How quaint the ways of paradox!
> At common sense she * gaily mocks,

might be the motto of the whole series. The "contrast yet
kinship," to use Mr. Carlyle's phrase, between the every-
day comomn-sense application of these principles and Mr.
Gilbert's apparently logical deductions from them, forms
the basis of our enjoyment. There is a general inclination
to attribute to these operas, or at any rate to the last three,
a serious satiric purpose. Nothing could be more mistaken.
Not even "Patience" is to be taken as a satire. It is an
extravaganza, pure and simple, and so are its predecessors.
Genuinely satiric touches are no doubt interspersed, but
we are no more meant to conclude from "Patience" that
Mr. Gilbert believes "aestheticism" as a whole to be a sham
and a craze, than we are to conclude from "The Pirates"
that he believes our police as a body to be arrant cowards.
That they are not satires in the true sense of the term is
proved by the fact that they leave every one's "withers un-
wrung." Satire which meets with universal acquiescence is
unworthy of the name. The only person I ever heard of

* Archer writes "it" for "she."—Ed.

who felt himself aggrieved by Mr. Gilbert's "satire" was a sailor at Portsmouth, who loudly resented the disparaging terms applied by Captain Corcoran to Ralph Rackstraw in "Pinafore."

I have no hesitation in calling these operas the most characteristic productions of our contemporary English stage. Their humour, as I have tried to show, is original if not profound, their literary workmanship is thorough, and they are, like Mr. Cheviot Hill's anecdotes, all in excellent taste. I do not mean to say that occasional speeches do not occur, which the most rigid fastidiousness might wish eliminated. A few of the sayings, for instance, placed in the mouth of the Lady Jane in "Patience," are in questionable taste. But such cases are very rare, and quite unimportant. They do not affect the broad fact that Mr. Gilbert, as author and stage manager, has succeeded in producing a style of entertainment fitted *virginibus pueris-que,* yet capable of affording to intelligent men amusement not altogether despicable in its intellectual quality. Mr. Sullivan's share in this result cannot be overrated. It is quite evident that composer and librettist have learned to work together in the most literal sense of the term, and this is one of the great advantages they possess over all competitors. It is impossible to appraise the precise amount of credit due to each, but Mr. Gilbert's humour is evidently the fecundating principle. His share, too, is the more important in so far as it is the greater advance upon previous and contemporary examples of work of the same class. Light French music may or may not be equal or superior to Mr. Sullivan's; the difference between Mr. Gilbert's librettos and those of the ordinary opera-bouffe adapters, is the difference between positively good and positively bad. Let us hope that Fortune and his Muse will continue to favour him in this sphere, though not to the exclusion of more ambitious work.

Notes

1. I do not mention "Randall's Thumb," as it is an early work of crude construction, which Mr. Gilbert has not included in the collected edition of his plays. It possesses, however, especially in the humorous part, which is almost wholly unconnected with the serious action, some distinct touches of the peculiar manner which its author has since developed. "The Ne'er-do-Weel," too, has been in a measure disowned by its author, who has probably recognized that the merits of its opening are insufficient to redeem the absurdities of its development and close.

William Schwenck Gilbert

An Autobiography

(1883)

I have been asked by the editor of this Magazine* to
give an account of myself. I was born on the 18th of November, 1836, at 17, Southampton Street, Strand. I was
educated privately at Great Ealing and at King's College,
intending to finish up at Oxford. But in 1855, when I was
nineteen years old, the Crimean war was at its height, and
commissions in the Royal Artillery were thrown open to
competitive examination. So I gave up all idea of Oxford,
took my B.A. degree at the University of London, and read
for the examination for direct commissions, which was to
be held at Christmas, 1856. The limit of age was twenty,
and as at the date of examination I should have been six
weeks over that age I applied for and obtained from Lord
Panmure, the then Secretary of State for War, a dispensa-
tion for this excess, and worked away with a will. But the
war came to a rather abrupt and unexpected end, and no

* *The Theatre.*—Ed.

more officers being required, the examination was indefinitely postponed. Among the blessings of peace may be reckoned certain comedies, operas, farces, and extravaganzas which, if the war had lasted another six weeks, would in all probability never have been written. I had no taste for a line regiment, so I obtained, by competitive examination, an assistant clerkship in the Education Department of the Privy Council Office, in which ill-organized and ill-governed office I spent four uncomfortable years. Coming unexpectedly into possession of a capital sum of £300, I resolved to emancipate myself from the detestable thraldom of this baleful office; and on the happiest day of my life I sent in my resignation. With £100 I paid my call to the Bar (I had previously entered myself as a student at the Inner Temple), with another £100 I obtained access to a conveyancer's chambers; and with a third £100 I furnished a set of chambers of my own, and began life afresh as a barrister-at-law. In the meantime I had made my appearance in print. My very first plunge took place in 1858, I think, in connection with the late Alfred Mellon's Promenade Concerts. Madame Parepa-Rosa (at that time Mdlle. Parepa), whom I had known from babyhood, had made a singular success at those concerts with the laughing-song from "Manon Lescaut," and she asked me to do a translation of the song for Alfred Mellon's play-bill. I did it: it was duly printed in the bill. I remember that I went night after night to those concerts to enjoy the intense gratification of standing at the elbow of any promenader who might be reading my translation, and wondering to myself what that promenader would say if he knew that the gifted creature who had written the very words he was reading was at that moment standing within a yard of him? The secret satisfaction of knowing that I possessed the power to thrill him with this information was enough, and I preserved my incognito.

In 1861 *Fun* was started, under the editorship of Mr. H. J. Byron. With much labour I turned out an article three-quarters of a column long, and sent it to the editor, together with a half-page drawing on wood. A day or two later the printer of the paper called upon me, with Mr. Byron's compliments, and staggered me with a request to contribute a column of "copy" and a half-page drawing every week for the term of my natural life. I hardly knew how to treat the offer, for it seemed to me that into that short article I had poured all I knew. I was empty. I had exhausted myself: I didn't know any more. However, the printer encouraged me (with Mr. Byron's compliments), and I said I would try. I did try, and I found to my surprise that there *was* a little left, and enough indeed to enable me to contribute some hundreds of columns to the periodical throughout his editorship, and that of his successor, poor Tom Hood! And here I may mention, for the information and encouragement of disheartened beginners, that I never remembered having completed any drama, comedy, or operatic libretto, without feeling that into that drama, comedy, or operatic libretto, I had poured all that I had, and that there was nothing left. This is a bogey which invariably haunts me, and probably others of my kind, on the completion of every work involving a sustained effort. At first it used to scare me; but I have long learnt to recognize it as a mere bogey, and to treat it with the contempt it deserves.

From time to time I contributed to other magazines, including the *Cornhill, London Society, Tinsley's, Temple Bar,* and *Punch.* I furnished London correspondence to the *Invalide Russe,* and I became the dramatic critic to the now defunct *Illustrated Times.* I also joined the Northern

Circuit, and duly attended the London and Westminster Courts, the Old Bailey, the Manchester and Liverpool Assizes, and Liverpool Sessions and Passage Court. But by this time I was making a very decent income by my contributions to current literature, whereas at the Bar I had only earned £75 in two years. So I stuck to literature, and the Bar went by the board. I was always a clumsy and inefficient speaker, and, moreover, an unconquerable nervousness prevented me from doing justice to myself or my half-dozen unfortunate clients.

Of the many good and staunch friends I made on my introduction into journalism, one of the best and staunchest was poor Tom Robertson, and it is entirely to him that I owe my introduction to stage work. He had been asked by Miss Herbert, the then lessee of St. James's Theatre, if he knew any one who could write a Christmas piece in a fortnight. Robertson, who had often expressed to me his belief that I should succeed as a writer for the stage, advised Miss Herbert to entrust me with the work, and the introduction resulted in my first piece, a burlesque on "L'Elisir d'Amore," called "Dulcamara; or, the Little Duck and the Great Quack." The piece, written in ten days and rehearsed in a week, met with more success than it deserved, owing mainly, to the late Mr. Frank Matthews' excellent impersonation of the title-role. In the hurry of production there had been no time to discuss terms, but after it had been successfully launched, Mr. Emden (Miss Herbert's acting manager) asked me how much I wanted for the piece. I modestly hoped that, as the piece was a success, £30 would not be considered an excessive price for the London right. Mr. Emden looked rather surprised, and, as I thought, disappointed. However, he wrote the cheque, asked for a receipt, and when he had got it, said: "Now take a bit of advice from an old stager who knows what he is talking about: never sell so good a piece as this for £30 again." And I never have.

My first piece gave me no sort of anxiety. I had nothing in the matter of dramatic reputation to lose, and I entered my box on the first night of "Dulcamara" with a *coeur leger*. It never entered my mind that the piece would fail, and I even had the audacity to pre-invite a dozen friends to supper after the performance. The piece succeeded (as it happened), and the supper party finished the evening appropriately enough, but I have since learnt something about the risks inseparable from every "first night," and I would as soon invite friends to supper after a forth-coming amputation at the hip-joint.

Once fairly afloat on the dramatic stream, I managed to keep my head above water. "Dulcamara" was followed by a burlesque on "La Figlia del Reggimento," called "La Vivandière," which was produced at what was then the Queen's Theatre, in Long Acre, and excellently played by Mr. J. L. Toole, Mr. Lionel Brough, Miss Hodson, Miss M. Simpson, Miss Everard (the original Little Buttercup of "H.M.S. Pinafore"), and Miss Fanny Addison. The "Vivandière" ran for 120 nights, and was followed at the Royalty Theatre by the "Merry Zingara," a burlesque on the "Bohemian Girl," in which Miss M. Oliver, Miss Charlotte Saunders, and Mr. F. Dewar appeared. This also ran 120 nights, but it suffered from comparison with Mr. F. C. Burnand's "Black-Eyed Susan," which it immediately followed, and which had achieved the most remarkable success recorded in the annals of burlesque.

Then came the opening of the Gaiety Theatre, for which occasion I wrote "Robert the Devil," a burlesque on the opera of that name, and in which Miss Farren appeared. This was followed by my first comedy, "An Old Score," which, however, made no great mark. But there

was a circumstance connected with its production which
may serve as a hint to unacted authors. As soon as I had
written the piece I had it set up in type—a proceeding
that cost me exactly five guineas. I sent a copy of it to Mr.
Hollingshead, and within one hour of receiving it he had
read and accepted it. He subsequently informed me that
he read it at once *because it was printed. Verb. sap.*

I wrote several "entertainments" for Mr. German
Reed, including "No Cards," "Ages Ago" (in collaboration
with Mr. F. Clay), "Our Island Home," * "Happy Ar-
cadia," "A Sensation Novel," and "Eyes and No Eyes"—
pieces which have at least this claim upon the gratitude of
playgoers, that they served to introduce to the stage Mr.
Arthur Cecil, Mr. Corney Grain, Miss Leonora Braham,
and Miss Fanny Holland—all of whom made their début
in one or other of these little pieces.

I had for some time determined to try the experiment
of a blank verse burlesque in which a picturesque story
should be told in a strain of mock-heroic seriousness; and
through the enterprise of the late Mrs. Liston (then man-
ageress of the Olympic) I was afforded an opportunity of
doing so. The story of Mr. Tennyson's "Princess" supplied
the subject-matter of the parody, and I endeavoured so to
treat it as to absolve myself from a charge of wilful irreverence. The piece was produced with signal success, owing in
no small degree to the admirable earnestness with which
Miss M. Reinhardt invested the character of the heroine.
Her address to the "girl graduates" remains in my mind as
a rare example of faultless declamation. It was unfortunately necessary to cast three ladies for the parts of the

* Due either to Gilbert's occasionally faulty memory or to a rather
remarkable printer's error, "Island" appears as "Highland" in the
original.—Ed.

three principal youths, and the fact that three ladies were dressed as gentlemen disguised as ladies, imparted an epicene character to their proceedings which rather interfered with the interest of the story. The success of the piece, however, was unquestionable, and it led to a somewhat more ambitious flight in the same direction.

Immediately after the production of the "Princess" I was commissioned by the late Mr. Buckstone to write a blank verse fairy comedy on the story of "Le Palais de la Verité," a subject which had been suggested to me by Mr. Palgrave Simpson. The piece was produced at the Haymarket Theatre with an admirable cast, which included Mr. Buckstone, Mr. Everill, Mrs. Kendal, Miss Caroline Hill, and Miss Fanny Gwynne, and it ran about 150 nights. A day or two before the production of the piece I was surprised to receive a packet containing twenty-four dress circle seats, twenty-four upper-box seats, twenty-four pit seats, and twenty-four gallery seats, for the first night. On inquiry I discovered that by immemorial Haymarket custom these ninety-six seats were the author's nightly perquisites during the entire run of a three-act play. I assured Mr. Buckstone that I had no desire to press my right to this privilege, which seems to be a survival of the old days when authors were paid in part by tickets of admission. I believe that the Haymarket was the only theatre in which the custom existed. Under Mr. Buckstone's conservative management very old fashions lingered on long after they had been abolished at other theatres. I can remember the time (about thirty-eight years since, I think) when it was still lighted by wax candles. The manager of the Haymarket, in Court dress, and carrying two wax candles, ushered Royalty into its box long after other managers had left this function to their deputy, and the old practice of announcing that a new play "would be repeated every night until further notice" survived until the very close of Mr. Buckstone's management.

"Pygmalion and Galatea" followed the "Palace of Truth," and achieved a remarkable success, owing mainly to Mrs. Kendal's admirable impersonation of Galatea. Mr. Buckstone, Mr. Howe, Miss Caroline Hill, and Mrs. Chippendale were the other noteworthy members of the cast. This was followed by "The Wicked World," a fairy comedy in three acts, and "Charity," a modern comedy in four acts, which achieved but an indifferent success in London, although it was played with much credit in the country, under Mr. Wilson Barrett's management.

In the meantime the Court Theatre had been built and opened by Miss Marie Litton. I was commissioned to write the opening comedy, "Randall's Thumb," and its successor, "On Guard." This was followed by a parody on "The Wicked World," called "The Happy Land," with which I had some concern, although it was mainly written by Mr. Gilbert à Beckett. The origin of this piece, which attracted extraordinary attention owing to certain impersonations of three leading statesmen—impersonations which were subsequently forbidden by the Lord Chamberlain—was as follows:—Mrs. Bancroft (at that time lessee of the Prince of Wales's Theatre) had arranged to give a private performance to her personal friends, and she asked me to write a wild burlesque for the occasion. I constructed a political parody on my own piece, "The Wicked World," and incidentally I told the plot to Miss Litton, who expressed a great desire to produce the piece at the Court Theatre, but that was out of the question, as the burlesque was intended for Mrs. Bancroft's private performance. That performance, however, was postponed indefinitely, owing to a domestic affliction, and I then told

Miss Litton that the subject of the piece was at her service. Miss Litton gave the plot to Mr. Gilbert à Beckett, who completed it, with some slight assistance from me.

This was followed by an adaptation of "Great Expectations," which achieved no success worth mentioning. It afforded, however, a curious example of the manner in which the Censorship of those days dealt with plays submitted to it for license. It seems that it was the custom of the then Licenser of Plays to look through the MS. of a new piece, and strike out all irreverent words, substituting for them words of an inoffensive character. In "Great Expectations," Magwitch, the returned convict, had to say to Pip, "Here you are, in chambers fit for a Lord." The MS. was returned to the theatre with the word "Lord" struck out, and "Heaven" substituted, in pencil!

Soon after the production of "Pygmalion and Galatea" I wrote the first of many libretti, in collaboration with Mr. Arthur Sullivan. This was called "Thespis; or, the Gods Grown Old." It was put together in less than three weeks, and was produced at the Gaiety Theatre after a week's rehearsal. It ran eighty nights, but it was a crude and ineffective work, as might be expected, taking into consideration the circumstances of its rapid composition. Our next operetta was "Trial by Jury," which was produced at the Royalty Theatre, under Miss Dolaro's management, with surprising success, due in no slight degree to poor Fred Sullivan's admirable performance of "the Learned Judge." The success of this piece induced Mr. D'Oyly Carte (at that time the managing director of a newly formed "Comedy Opera Company") to commission us to write a two-act opera for the Opéra Comique. "The Sorcerer" was the result of this commission, and it deserves to live in the memory of theatre-goers on account of its having introduced Mr. George Grossmith and Mr. Rutland Barrington to the professional stage. "The Sorcerer" ran for six months, and was followed by "H.M.S. Pinafore," which ran for two years. To this succeeded the "Pirates of Penzance," which ran for a year, and this in turn was followed by "Patience." The success of these pieces induced Mr. D'Oyly Carte to build the Savoy Theatre expressly for them. "Patience" was transferred to the Savoy after having run for six months at the Opéra Comique. It derived new life from its new home, and ran, in all, nineteen months. It is, perhaps, unnecessary to add that its successor, "Iolanthe," is still drawing excellent houses. A new opera is on the stocks, and will probably be produced in October.

I have omitted to record, in their proper places, "Dan'l Druce," and "Engaged," produced at the Haymarket, under Mr. J. S. Clarke's management, and in which Miss Marion Terry made a signal success; "Sweethearts," a two-act comedy produced at the Prince of Wales's under Mrs. Bancroft's management; "Broken Hearts," a three-act play in blank verse, in which Miss Bessie Hollingshead particularly distinguished herself, produced at the Court Theatre, under the management of Mr. Hare; "Tom Cobb," a three-act farcical comedy, produced at the St. James's Theatre, under Miss Litton's management; "Gretchen," a four-act blank verse play, produced at the Olympic by Mr. Neville; "The Ne'er do Weel," an absolute failure at the Olympic; "Foggerty's Fairy," another failure at the Criterion. I have translated three farces or farcical comedies from the French, and I have adapted two English works, namely, "Great Expectations," and "Ought We to Visit Her?" With these exceptions all the plays I have written are original.

Max Beerbohm

A Classic in Humour

(1905)

I have been ranging to and fro through a new edition
of the "Bab Ballads." It is some years since I possessed any
edition but Mr. Gilbert's own meagre and miserable selection of fifty. So I have joy in the recapture of many half-
remembered masterpieces.

This joy is chastened in several ways. Messrs. Macmillan and Co. seem to have conspired with their printers and
binders to test, once and for all, the strength of the reading
public. To have packed so much leaden weight into a
mere octavo is a really marvellous achievement. It is an
achievement that I regret. I regret, too, that Mr. Gilbert
has interspersed his Savoy lyrics throughout the volume.
These have, certainly, points of kinship with the "Bab
Ballads." They have a spiritual affinity, but in manner and
method they are very different. They do not blend here:
they interrupt. "Songs of a Savoyard" was, like the "Fifty
Bab Ballads," an inadequate selection, and I am glad to

find here many lyrics that were not there. But they ought to be published in a separate volume. They well deserve it. Of course one misses the tunes; but one is more than consoled by perception of those exquisite little qualities which the tunes obscured. It makes so very little difference whether a song that is sung be sense or twaddle, and good sense or bad. It is so very hard to distinguish through music the quality of the words. If you knew Shakespeare's songs only through the settings sung on the stage, you would guess but dimly at the beauty of them. To appreciate them, you must read them. Mr. Gilbert is not a poet, as we understand the term; but there never was a more delicious versifier; and to verses music is as fatal as to poems. So let the lyrics of Mr. Gilbert be read as widely as may be. But let them not be wedged into the "Bab Ballads." And let the next edition of the "Bab Ballads" be purged also of its author's new and revised illustrations. These are amusing drawings. But they are not the old drawings. That fact alone suffices to condemn them. Our vision of all the strange persons who figure in the "Bab Ballads" has been formed, once and for all, by their author's own first vision of them. It is too late to change our vision. Any attempt at change we regard as a foolish violence—almost as an act of sacrilege. We should resent these new illustrations even if they were better than the old. And this they are not. In comparison with the old, they are tame and indefinite. They lack that splendid precision and concision which the old ones had in virtue of being cut directly on the block. Freedom to draw in pen and ink for process-reproduction has taken half the strength and fun out of Mr. Gilbert's technique. And, being conceptions made after long lapse of years, these drawings are not nearly so close in spirit as were the old ones to their subjects. "I have always felt," says Mr. Gilbert in his pref-

ace, "that many of the original illustrations to the 'Bab
Ballads' erred gravely in the direction of unnecessary
extravagance." So did the "Bab Ballads." That is why the
first drawings were so exactly right for them. To make
these new drawings equally right, Mr. Gilbert ought to
have rewritten the poems. I am glad that his innate love
for logic did not drive him to this double vandalism.

With all its faults, this new edition is for me a
treasure. The instinct of every human being is to share his
joys; and I should like everyone to delight as I do in the
"Bab Ballads." I dare say my wish is granted in so far as
my elders and my coevals are concerned. But I have my
doubts about my juniors. The fashion in humour changes
so subtly and so quickly. Of course, there are many acknowledged classics in humour. But they do not have on
us just that effect which it is the prime aim of humour.
They do not make us laugh outright. We revel respect-
fully in "The Sentimental Journey," for example, or in the
Essays of Elia, or in the adventures of Don Quixote or
Pantagruel. We are wreathed by them in fond smiles. But
I do not think we can conscientiously say that we ever
laugh outright at any passage in them. I do not think anyone has ever overheard us laughing thus. It would seem
that to appreciate thoroughly a work of humour, however
fine, we must be born in the very era in which it was written, or very soon after. The "Bab Ballads" were written, I
fancy, in the 'sixties. But when I was a child they were still
in their heyday. I heard many of them recited (recitations
were in vogue then) by the late Mr. Arthur Cecil, Mr.
Brandon Thomas, Mr. Tree, and other actors. It was a
matter of course, in those days, that everyone possessed a
copy of the "Bab Ballads" and often quoted from them.
My elders and my coevals still have this piety. But in that
growing class of vast and hirsute personages who, on closer

acquaintance, prove to me irrefutably that they were in their bassinettes when I was in the full stress of existence at school, I encounter many to whom the "Bab Ballads" are but a name. Shocked by their loss, I urge them to buy a copy forthwith. In deference to my advancing years, they do so. And subsequently they thank me. But their tone has not the ring of rapture that I had hoped to hear, and I am conscious of a gulf between us. They share fully with me my delight in such later humourists as Mr. Wilde, or Mr. Shaw, or Mr. Chesterton. They profess, considerately, to have as keen a joy as I in Mr. Gilbert. But they quote, with seeming relish, the pointless passages, and force me to undertake the quite futile task of exposition.

To expound the magic of the "Bab Ballads" is very like breaking a butterfly on a wheel, and has the disadvantage of being a far less easy operation—of being, indeed, an impossible operation. Magic would not be magic if it did not defy analysis. Those readers who do not of their own accord revel in the "Bab Ballads" will not acquire through a demonstration, however painful, the power to revel. The only real use of the demonstration is to exercise the brain of the demonstrator. What then, I ask myself—you need not listen—is the especial quality that distinguishes the "Bab Ballads" as a whole? That quality is, I think, the sheer silliness of them. I had almost said the sheer madness of them. But madness precludes deliberation. A clever man cannot, by taking thought, become mad. But he may become silly. "Madness" was a tempting word, because it implies a kind of largeness and wildness, whereas "silliness" implies something rather little and tame; and the silliness of the "Bab Ballads" is on a truly large and a wild scale. So soon as he had determined to be silly, Mr. Gilbert let himself go—took the bit between his teeth, and charged wildly forward. That is the main difference between the

"Bab Ballads" and the Savoy operas. In those operas one feels always a cold and calculating method throughout the silliness—a keen logical faculty presenting a more or less serious criticism of life. The "Bab Ballads" are in the manner of a riot. In some of them, of course—the famous "Etiquette" for example—one finds the industrious satirist at work. But the great majority of them, and those that I love best, are mere high-spirited inventions or distortions, with no critical significance whatsoever. Consider such masterpieces as "Annie Protheroe," or "Gregory Parable LL.D.," or "The Bishop and the 'Busman." There is no satire on capital punishment in the first of these: simply a fantasia on the private life of "a gentle executioner, whose name was Gilbert Clay."

> And, if it rained, the little maid would stop at
>   home and look
> At his favourable notices, all pasted in a book,
> And then her cheek would flush—her swimming
>   eyes would dance with joy
> In a glow of admiration at the prowess of her boy.

The story of the little maid's rescue of her former lover from the headsman's block is a joy for ever. But it cannot be twisted into any semblance of satire. It is a triumph of sheer silliness. The same criticism applies to "Gregory Parable LL.D."—"no man alive could him nonplus with vocative of filius"—and to all the best of the other ballads. I admire the ingenuity of the stories; but it is always a rollicking ingenuity, without one taint of reason in it.

If I took these ballads and made their plots mere précis, in ordinary prose, the result would be (for me) extremely good to read. But a good third of their fun depends on Mr. Gilbert's casual embroideries (as in the verse quoted from "Annie Protheroe"), and on the eccentricities of his vocabulary. I enjoy the story of Babette's love for a very stout English sailor who leant gracefully against posts on the quay of Boulogne. But how impoverished that story would be if we had not Mr. Gilbert's own description of the captain's view of the situation!—

> He wept to think a tar of his
>   Should lean so gracefully on posts,
> He sighed and sobbed to think of this,
>   On foreign, French, and friendly coasts.
> "It's human natur', p'raps—if so,
> Oh isn't human natur' low?"
>
> He called his Bill, who pulled his curl,
>   He said, "My Bill, I understand
> You've captivated some young gurl
>   On this here French and foreign land.
> Her tender heart your beauties jog—
> They do, you know they do, you dog.
>
> "You have a graceful way, I learn,
>   Of leaning airily on posts,
> By which you've been and caused to burn
>   A tender flame on these here coasts.
> A fisher gurl, I much regret,—
> Her age, sixteen—her name Babette."

When I analyse the delightfulness of this passage, I find that it consists mainly in the sudden changes of tone in the Captain's manner—his ranging between extreme vulgarity and gentility, and between sternness and jocularity. Note, too, the cunning repetition of "French and friendly." All the "Bab Ballads" abound in such tricks, and much of the fun depends on them. But, artist though Mr. Gilbert is, his art is always natural and spontaneous. He is never academic. Had he been a don at one of the Universities, he would have polished and polished his verses till half the fun had been polished out of them. He would have been a mere Calverley. Humour must be spontaneous; else it is deadly. And the artistic expression of humour must, likewise, be spontaneous, to a certain degree. It is well for Mr. Gilbert, and for me, that when he wrought the Ballads he was in the thick of the rough-and-tumble Bohemian journalism of the 'sixties. Art was too strongly innate in him to be killed by that atmosphere. Elsewhere it would have become over-refined for the purpose of these Ballads.

Walter Sichel

The English Aristophanes

(1911)

When a new voice makes a new world dance to a new
tune we acknowledge a genius. Sometimes he does so in
a way that may be pursued: he founds a school which ex-
pands. So, after many colloquial experiments, Montaigne's
essay in essays blossomed into the present cosmopolitan
novel which barely permits its forefather to recognise himself. But sometimes his enchantment is limited to his own
originality, which no copyist can develop. He has achieved
all that was possible in his peculiar sphere: he is a phenomenon. Such was Aristophanes; such, in his measure, Sir
William Gilbert—both, in whatever respects incomparable with each other, wholly incomparable with anyone
else; both, poet-ironists and creators of fresh provinces;
both, inverters of what is termed the real, and realisers of
the world's inversions.

Gilbert has left us, but his works will not easily pass away so long as poetic humour and prose-fairyland hold their own, so long as "superior persons" are kept at a respectful distance. His dramatic humoresques have already become literature, and in both aspects they are signal. Our English Aristophanes was eminently a stylist and constructor. He was a master of the comic and lyric stage in nearly all their departments. His rhymes and his rhythms harmonise even the most extravagant of his capers and caprices, and, while they dance hand and foot with them, they restrain their antics almost severely. He is the most critical of creators, the most creative of critics in an atmosphere which he may be said to have rediscovered. For that atmosphere, despite the centuries, *is,* after all, the atmosphere of Aristophanes. Their world is one not of nonsense but of sense upside down. It laughs thought into us. And though it is in both cases a sphere as light as down, it is not ethereal, but a borderland between empyrean and the too solid earth. Its welkin rings with every-day laughter, and the mirage of a masquerade contrasts the countenances with the vizors. Truth smiles from the bottom of a most sparkling fountain, the spray of which is hued with rainbow ironies. With all the magic of its background, the victory of whim is short-lived. It is the triumph of hypothesis, resembling one of those systems that proceed logically from paradox: inconsequence turns consequent, while fantasy lends wings to the logic of the illogical:—

> How quaint the ways of paradox,
> At common sense she gaily mocks.[1]

Both Aristophanes and Gilbert were pure ironists. Direct

satire maps out the country which it invades, but irony is always on the confines of ambiguous territory. As we survey its inhabitants they seem to be in perpetual somersaults—and yet they are always standing on their feet. Here, however, Gilbert parts company with the great Greek who mocked at loftier foibles with an irony often gigantic. It is true that his English counterpart has depth, and even a "philosophy"—a very English outlook on life and love rendered in very English lyrics, the philosophy of cultivated common sense. But in Aristophanes, the poetical side overpowers the practical, and in him there is a fine, fierce frenzy of the ludicrous which Gilbert lacks. Gilbert joined a mathematical precision to a very strong dash of the muse; there was *par excellence* Euclid in his Aristophanes. The featness and neatness of craftsmanship possessed him. Aristophanes probably thought of himself as before all things a shrewd man of the world, and, in like manner, Gilbert may have regarded himself as mainly a poet. A poet he was by instinct, with a charming lyrical gift, and, throughout, a topsy-turvy pathos which transforms tears to laughter. But his very restrictions accentuate the originality of his works. Combined in their varied fulness they find no parallel in our language. Compared with kindred whimsies they stand out supreme, while in metrical grace and fantastic flexibility Aristophanes himself does not surpass him.

He was more of a poet than many solemn pretenders to the name. But he was not mainly a poet, even allowing for the restrictions of his scope. The critic in him predominated, and checked or ridiculed the flight. Yet he could abandon himself, and in his modern fantasies there was room for the pathos which Aristophanes wholly missed. Gilbert's irony has its own soft leaven, and sometimes displays it. Lines like

> Proud as a war-horse—fair as the dawn of day—
> Staunch as a woman—tender as a man! [2]

and (of sleep)—

> . . . 'Twas but a dream!
> Once every day this death occurs to us,
> Till thou and I and all who dwell on earth
> Shall sleep to wake no more.[3]

and the noble retort of the sculptor to the insolent art-patron's lackey:—

> I am an artist and a gentleman.
> He should not reckon Art among his slaves:
> She rules the world—so let him wait on her.[4]

are not readily forgotten.

Out of airy and fairy nothings he raised a local habitation and a name which are distinctively his own. But as distinctively they are local. He is an English Aristophanes, just as Fielding would have loved to have been in his *Tom Thumb*—an English Aristophanes with all the limits involved in the remoteness and the insularity.

> For he himself has said it,
> And it's greatly to his credit
>   That he is an Englishman.

and

In spite of all temptations
To belong to other nations,
　　He remains an Englishman.

Gilbert, like Aristophanes, was an artist to the core. His feeling for symmetry and proportion was native and needed no emphasis. In one faculty, indeed, he may be said to have excelled Aristophanes himself—in concentration. Not only is Gilbert's phrasing terse and trenchant, but his lyrical comedies are of the kind that leave an impression of length without ever being long—intaglios reduced from statues, or, to vary the metaphor, miniatures with the quality of pictures. They are his own *Bab Ballads* dramatised, acted epigrams. Rarely do they exceed some forty pages of print; indeed, *Pinafore* falls short of thirty pages, while the *Sorcerer* and the *Pirates of Penzance* occupy little over that amount. Yet how spacious these are in the hearing, how their plot distends, how excellently they read! Their facets gleam in the setting of the study as effectively as they do under the limelights. He is lambent. This art of condensation concerns the very gestures of the persons that emphasise the fantastic world which surrounds them. Their topsy-turvydom is written in italics, yet it is never mis-shapen. It is, in fact, *character*—the character of inversion. The inversion is often a toy inversion, but their character is no toy and it breeds familiarity. The persons are humanised elfs or elfinised mortals with momentary motives and glimpses of actions that, none the less, lend us the feeling of protracted acquaintance. They pass from mouth to mouth, and memory to memory, till they become types and proverbs. That is surely a mark of creative genius. They are normal in their abnormality. Their very child's play is grown-up, and though the artist only draws fleeting profiles, the beholder takes away with him the genuine expressiveness of life at full length. They are never perversions; they are versions, and lively versions. Fantasies in shadowland, they are not phantoms; and so it happens that inside all their gossamer vagaries their solid substance begets human intimacy attracting general welcome, and workaday acceptance. That is why they in no sense resemble some of those bizarre and bloodless ephemerals who serve a newer satire as pegs for passing paradox, and are debarred from stature and the vitality of quotation. Gilbert's characters, it must be insisted, breathe. They are no marionettes to be danced on the wires of a dramatic essayist. Nor are they ever morbid. Their madness is sane, and their follies are sympathetic. Still less are they merely intellectual figments. They feel as well as think. And so Gilbert's works form a sort of *scherzo serioso* relating him, however gaily, to the tragicomedy of existence. Two characteristics in this connection he shares with Sheridan and with Thackeray. He is a sentimentalist tilting at sentiment, and he has what is hardly found outside English literature—the true schoolboy's love of fun. Three specimens may suffice. The first comes from the "doesn't matter" patter in *Ruddigore,* and it is paralleled by the

> In a river, in a meadder
> Took a header, and a deader
>   Was Ophelia.

From the *Mountebanks*—

> If I had been so lucky as to have a steady brother
> Who could talk to me as we are talking now to one
>   another—

Who could give me good advice when he
    discovered I was erring
(Which is just the very favour which on you I am
    conferring),
My story would have made a rather interesting
    idyll,
And I might have lived and died a very decent
    indiwiddle.

The second occurs in the poetical *Princess Ida*—

For adder-like his sting lay in his tongue;
His "sting" is present, though his "stung" is past.

The third is a prose-quip on the lips of Foggerty:—

Miss Spiff, you will not insist on your bond. You
will be merciful! You will not dash the cup—the—
dash it, the *jug* of happiness from my lips.

And this, too, is paralleled in *Tom Cobb* by Matilda's
retort to her lover's boast of "I'm a qualified practitioner
. . . ! I've passed the College of Surgeons."—*"So have I,
dear, often."* Such verbal horseplays are not of Gilbert's
higher or subtler satire, with its lights and shadows, but
romping fun is always its rough foundation—the quarry of
his statues. These practical jokes impart elasticity and freedom; wit and his humour spring out of them, and they,
like his common sense and humanity, find expression even
in his most sardonic touches and pervade what I cannot
help regarding as his ironic masterpiece, the unlyrical *Engaged.* This quality is the more remarkable when we consider to what grace it is allied. It would be difficult to beat

Pygmalion's compliment to his wife Cynisca—a compliment truly poetical—

> Why, here's ingratitude, to slander Time,
> Who in his hurried course has passed thee by!
> Or is it that Cynisca won't allow
> That time *could* pass her by, and never pause
> *To print a kiss upon so fair a face?*

Gilbert is best known by his operettas, but some of his chief creations are the satires without songs given before his genius won a wider popularity through the marriage of his muse to Sullivan's entrancing music. Who now reads or sees *Charity?* Yet it is well worth reading, and might be revived with advantage on the stage. It handles what would now be termed a problem with insight, exposing the subterfuges of false philanthropy and transfiguring the loving kindness of an erring heroine. The tramp, "Ruth Tredgett"—the simple objective of both—reveals herself seriously, and in one of her sentences she strikes the very keynote of all Gilbert's future work. "We meet in a strange way after so many years," exclaims the hypocrite "Smailey," encountering his former victim. "Yes," she answers, "we do meet in a strange way. But it's a topsy-turvy world, ain't it?" There we get Gilbert's whole gay-grave faculty— the inverting power which deals breezily with the cant of coincidence. That note had, of course, been struck in his *Bab Ballads,* but Gilbert came to see that there was more than farce in it, and that the quaint pathos which he had singled out in his ballad of the poor ballet-girl was universal. That is his irony. Everywhere it seizes on the *impasses* of existence and the strange contrasts of the commonplace. He saw them in all the conventions around him, and still more in the sham defiance of those conventions. A straight line *was* a straight line, and his ingenuity revelled in devising comical retributions for such as persisted in calling it crooked. Solemn shams and pompous incapacity were his butts, but everywhere he put these old laughing-stocks into new positions, till their futility became piteous, and everywhere he descried a sort of romance, and weird glamour, in the familiar. Give him a garret and a broken-down *beau,* and he would at once evolve trains of circumstance outvying Aladdin's palace. Or give him a stingy philanderer and the Scotch marriage laws—the Nemesis of Greek tragedy is in sight. Give him a stray "bobby," and at once, in a ruined chapel by moonlight, which does *not* contain the tombs of the "modern major-gineral's ancestors"—a whole chorus of heroic constables will assure us that—

> When the coster's finished jumping on his mother
> He loves to lie a-basking in the sun.
> Ah, take one consideration with another,
> The policeman's lot * is not a happy one.

Give him a buccaneer, and a sea-faring syndicate that disdains to plunder an "orphan" and has transformed a nursemaid into "a piratical maid of all work," will be as picturesque or prosaic as you please. Give him a stalwart sentry, and he turns into a stammering philosopher, perpending under the moon why—

> . . . Every child that's born alive
> Is either a little Liberal or else a little
> Conservative.

* Sichel writes "life" for "lot."—Ed.

Or let him deal with a modern squire, or a modern faddist, or a modern altruist, or the would-be "wicked" baronet—and with all the worn machinery of shepherds and shepherdesses joined to intensified types of melodrama, he would upset the modern scene and outdo the *Castle of Otranto.* The romance or poetry might be derided, but they were there, and there in the neighbourhood of chignons and frock-coats. Dairymaids and countesses, knights of industry and knights of empire, faddists and financiers, all jostle on each other, while pirates and gondoliers are reduced to proportions which fit alike the clerk and the diplomatist. The medley tingles with colour and suggestion, yet all is real, though all is fancy. Imagination runs riot among the commonest crockery of the obvious; out of a cheap squib shoots a gorgeous variety of display. And the converse process is quite as prominent. An Arabian Nights Entertainment soon sinks to the level of a modern newspaper. The spells even of Fortunatus's cap only bore and bewilder their wearers. The magician turns out to be nothing more than "the resident Djinn, number seventy, Simmery Axe," who dances incantations over a tea-pot; and could anyone else but Gilbert have set a stiff Lord Chancellor leaping a refined cancan in his robes, or, on the other hand, have romanticised him into the lover of a fairy who is also his ward? * Here the two processes meet. But everywhere plain commercial principles, with punctuality and dispatch, animate all the winged ministers of air. And nowhere does anyone seem what he is, or is anybody what he seems. Fact *is* stranger than fiction if only we look round and into as well as at it. Jack Point in

---

* This is not precisely accurate. At present the Lord Chancellor loves Phyllis, a shepherdess and his ward, but not a fairy; earlier he had indeed married a fairy, Iolanthe, presumed dead till the end of the play.—Ed.

the *Yeomen of the Guard* is surely Gilbert himself: "Oh sir, a pretty wit, I warrant you—a pretty, pretty wit!":—

> I've jest and joke
>   And quip and crank,
> For lowly folk
>   And men of rank.
> I ply my craft
>   And know no fear,
> I aim my shaft
>   At prince or peer.
> At peer or prince—at prince or peer,
>   I aim my shaft and know no fear.
>
> I've wisdom from the East and from the West
>   That's subject to no academic rule;
> You may find it in the jeering of a jest,
>   Or distil it from the folly of a fool.
> I can teach you with a quip, if I've a mind;
>   I can trick you into learning with a laugh.
> Oh, winnow all my folly and you'll find
>   A grain or two of truth among the chaff.*
>
> *   *   *
>
> When they're offered to the world in merry guise
> Unpleasant truths are swallowed with a will;
> For he who'd make his fellow-creatures wise
> Should always gild the philosophic pill.

In *Foggerty's Fairy* Gilbert started his peculiar prose-fairyland with its romance and realism alike upside down. The fairy "Rebecca," who causes the complications beset-ting the path of the perplexed little hero, is a practical and entirely English fay. The routine of the supernatural

* Sichel writes "philosophic" for "truth among the."—Ed.

is represented as a business, and she is ever eager for return to the coryphean tasks in her far from gossamer world. She is, indeed, less a fairy than a glorified *figurante*. By recklessly invoking her aid to wipe out an embarrassing incident in his past, Foggerty has also accepted the condition of obliterating all the possible consequences of that incident, and so he only finds himself plunged from one hopeless dilemma into others more hopeless. Stripped of its magic, his plight really amounts to what is called a loss of memory, through which in the second act he becomes absolutely puzzled as to where or how or who he is. And the whim is worked out with an algebraical exactness, and with strict adherence to character, since the motives are always true, however feigned may be the positions and actions. Nowhere is a better example of his union of the practical and the poetical, and he was practical enough to repeat long afterwards several of his *Foggerty* lines in his *Yeomen of the Guard.* This logic of fantasy stamps his pathos also. *Sweethearts* is the most pathetic of his pieces, yet with what a cruel consequence he depicts the jilting heroine of the first act and the forgetful hero of the second. And how closely the irony treads on the heels of the pathos! "Am I an old man, or you an old woman, because the earth contrives to hurry round the sun in three hundred and sixty-five days? Why, Saturn can't do it in thirty years. If I had been born on Saturn I should be two years old, ma'am, a public nuisance in petticoats." So, too, in *Broken Hearts,* the next most moving of his more serious achievements. The hunchback "Mousta" is a sort of Caliban in the enchanted island where the sad and fair insurgents against love have transferred their affections to the trees and fountains. Yet he is invested with a sort of remorseless pathos that only makes him the more horrible as he becomes more pitiable. The sole pathos unmixed with irony centres round the self-effacement of the loved and lovely "Vavir." Here Gilbert feels finely, and her dying moments deserve to live. Hilda, the friend of her soul, the "sister" for whom she has sacrificed herself, stands by her side—

Vavir
(*very
faintly*):
It is too late—too late! I feel the hand
Of Death upon my heart. So let it be.
My day is spent—my tale is nearly told!

Hilda:
Vavir—Vavir!
Have pity on us! Gentle little soul,
Fly not to thine appointed Heaven—
not yet—
Not yet—not yet! Eternity is thine;
Spare but a few brief years to us on Earth
And still Eternity remains to thee!
He loves thee—Florian loves thee well!
Oh, Death,
Are there no hoary men and aged women
Weeping for thee to come and comfort
them?
Oh, Death—oh, Death—leave me this
little flower!
Take then the fruit, but pass the
blossom by!

Vavir
(*very
feebly*):
Weep not: the bitterness of death is past,
Kiss me, my sister. Florian, think of me—
I loved thee very much! Be good to her.
Dear sister, place my hand upon my dial.
Weep not for me; I have no pain indeed.
Kiss me again; my sun has set. Good
night!
Good night!

Once more, take the tragic irony in *Comedy and Tragedy* where a woman's heart comes to its climax in a few pages. The courtiers think that Clarice is only performing one of her parts while she betrays her agony at the deadly duel which is being fought outside:—

Clarice: You look at me, but you do not move.
                Gentlemen, I am not acting; I am in
                fearful earnest. Oh! my love! my love!
                and I have done this! As I speak my
                husband is being killed.

It is not so much the words said, but the situation and the feelings flashed on us by a few bold strokes after an elaborate prelude of artificial gaiety. And throughout his *Dan'l Druce* runs an undercurrent of the pathos that befits a transferred paraphrase of *Silas Marner*. Here, however, the pathos is less effective, as, after the first act, it is unhelped by strong dramatic moments, and its rendering is all along unpointed by the Gilbertian irony. It tends occasionally to touch on the genre which Gilbert so often satirised, just as Sheridan in his *Pizarro* lapsed into the conventions which his *Critic* destroyed and immortalised.

These examples of Gilbert's pathos are not often remembered, nor is the ironical pathos of his absurdities borne in mind. Instances meet us on every page; the whimsical catastrophes and derided ecstasies, the false sentiments, have usually a real appeal of their own. Recall one of his least-known and jauntiest farces—*Tom Cobb*. "What's the use of socks to a man who's going to blow his brains out," exclaims that unfortunate medical student to the Irish "colonel"-landlord's prosaic daughter, Matilda. "I never saw his face," says her friend Caroline of her newspaper lover, "but I have seen his soul!" "What's his soul like?" rejoins Matilda:—

Caroline:	Like? Like the frenzied passion of the antelope, like the wild fire of the tiger-lily. Like the pale earnestness of some love-sick thundercloud that longs to grasp the fleeting lightning in his outstretched arms.
Matilda:	Was he often like that?
Caroline:	Always.
Matilda:	A pleasant man in furnished lodgings! And where did ye see his soul?
Caroline (*sits*):	He poured it in the columns of the *Weybridge Watchman*, the local paper of the town that gave him birth. Dainty little poems, the dew of his sweet soul, the tender frothings of his soldier brain . . . the huckstering men of law appraise my heart-wreck at five thousand pounds.

Here we strike the keynote of *Engaged*—a grotesque with a very tangible background where affected simplicity and maudlin avarice are worked up and out to their extremes, yet where, somehow, we feel with, while we laugh, at their tormenting *imbroglios*. How the impostures of Belvawney and his fatal eyes are brought home and made quite natural! How tragic is the falsetto of Belinda at the

wedding feast! And how irresistible are the designing art-
lessness of Minnie, the canny tears of Maggie, and the
gushing shifts of that parsimonious Lothario, Cheviot Hill!
Or, to return to *Tom Cobb,* how the high-faluting of
the out-at-elbows "Effinghams" (foreshadowing *Patience*)
hardly excludes a kind of compassion for them and for the
son whose "life is one protracted misfit." "My boy," says
the father with distorted dignity, "sneer not at these
clothes. They have been worn for many years by a very old,
but very upright man. Be proud of them. No sordid
thought has ever lurked behind that waistcoat. That hat
has never yet been doffed to vicious wealth. Those shoes
have never yet walked into the parlours of the sinful." "A
blessing on him," sighs Caroline. "Is he not benevolent?"
To which replies Tom, "Yes, he looks so. Why do benevolent people have such long hair? Do they say to themselves,
'I am a benevolent person, so I will let my hair grow,' or
do they let it grow because they are too benevolent to cut
it off?

Irony always makes the great and the little, the masks
of Comedy and of Tragedy, exchange places. But Gilbert
makes them exchange and re-exchange places again and
again, and with an infinite network of involution defying
disentanglement. So much so that at length we can scarcely
escape from the Chinese puzzle, and give credence to illusion within illusion—all mutually destructive—just as if
each were an isolated matter of fact. This is why a farcical
pathos is always possible to him—at the close of *Ruddigore,* for example, where he introduces "Hannah's" touching and teaching little ballad:—

> There grew a little flower
>   'Neath a great oak tree.

When the tempest 'gan to lower
    Little heeded she;
No need had she to cower,
For she dreaded not its power—
She was happy in the bower
    Of her great oak tree!
        Sing hey,
        Lackaday!
    Let the tears fall free,
    For the pretty little flower and the great oak
      tree.

When she found that he was fickle,
    Was that great oak tree,
She was in a pretty pickle,
    As she well might be—
But his gallantries were mickle,
For Death followed with his sickle,
And her tears began to trickle
    For her great oak tree.

Said she, "He loved me never,
    Did that great oak tree,
But I'm neither rich nor clever,
    And so why should he?
But though Fate our fortunes sever
To be constant I'll endeavour,
Ay, for ever and for ever,
    To my great oak tree."

Gilbert's irony is changeable as an April morning, and it is on his lights and shadows that we all love to dwell, yet one or two more of his less volatile turns may still engage us till we pass to his more familiar vein. Take his power of analysis. There is an excellent sample in *Pygmalion and Galatea*. The statue has just come to life.

Galatea: Is this the world?
Pygmalion: It is.
Galatea: This room?
Pygmalion: This room is portion of a house;
             The house stands in a grove; the grove
                 itself
             Is one of many, many hundred groves
             In Athens.
Galatea: And is Athens then the world?
Pygmalion: To an Athenian—yes.
Galatea: And am I one?
Pygmalion: By birth and parentage, not by descent.
Galatea: But how came I to be?
Pygmalion: Well—let me see;
             Oh—you were quarried in Pentelicus;
             I modelled you in clay—my artisans
             Then roughed you out in marble—I in
                 turn
             Brought my artistic skill to bear on you,
             And made you what you are—in all but
                 life—
             The gods completed what I had begun,
             And gave the only gift I could not give.
Galatea: Then this is life?
Pygmalion: It is.
Galatea: And not long since
             I was a cold, dull stone! I recollect
             That by some means I knew that I was
                 stone;
             That was the first dull gleam of
                 consciousness:
             I became conscious of a chilly self,
             A cold, immovable identity,

I knew that I was stone, and knew no
    more!
Then by an imperceptible advance,
Came the dim evidence of outer things,
Seen—darkly and imperfectly—yet
    seen—
The walls surrounding me, and I alone.
That pedestal—that curtain—then a
    voice
That called on Galatea! At that word,
Which seemed to shake my marble to the
    core,
That which was dim before, came
    evident.
Sounds that had hummed around me
    indistinct,
Vague, meaningless—seemed to resolve
    themselves
Into a language I could understand;

    *   *   *

My limbs grew supple, and I moved—
    I lived!
Lived in the ecstasy of newborn life,

    *   *   *

Lived in a thousand tangled thoughts of
    hope,
Love, gratitude—thoughts that resolved
    themselves
Into one word, that word, Pygmalion.
    (*Kneels to him.*)

Pygmalion: I have no words to tell thee of my joy,
O woman—perfect in thy loveliness!

Galatea: What is that word? Am I a woman?

Pygmalion: Yes.

Galatea: Art thou a woman?

Pygmalion:	No, I am a man.
Galatea:	What is a man?
Pygmalion:	A being strongly framed
	To wait on woman, and protect her from
	All ills that strength and courage can avert;
	To work and toil for her that she may rest;
	To weep and mourn for her, that she may laugh:
Galatea (*after a pause*):	To fight and die for her, that she may live!
	I'm glad I am a woman.
Pygmalion:	So am I.
	(*They sit.*)

This is earnest enough irony, and the conclusion is very characteristic. It brings us to close quarters with Gilbert's attitude towards the sexes. I have said that he was a sentimentalist tilting against sentiment, and the statement is borne out by nearly all his stage-heroes and heroines. No one had a deeper reverence for manly manhood and womanly womanhood; none a more piercing scorn for their affections or the reversal of their types. The whole of *Engaged* forms a satirical homily on this theme. But Gilbert also seems to have held that the theory of affinities verged perilously on nonsense. He thought that under normal conditions any normal man would suit any normal woman, and he delights in the whimsical application of this cynical common sense. "Cynical" is perhaps hardly the epithet, yet what is the cynic but the denuder of the super-imposed—the microscope of motives? Woman was made, not for competition, but marriage. We get this starting-point in *Pygmalion* again, where the wife, Cyn-

isca, was vowed in girlhood to virginity as "a holy nymph
of Artemis." "How terrible!" exclaims Myrine:—

Cynisca: It seemed not so to me;
                 For weeks and weeks I pondered
                    steadfastly
                 Upon the nature of that serious step
                 Before I took it—lay awake at night,
                 Looking upon it from this point and
                    that,
                 And I at length determined that the vow
                 Which to Myrine seems so terrible,
                 Was one that I, at all events, could keep.
Myrine: How old wast thou, Cynisca?
Cynisca: I was ten!
                 Well—in due course I reached eleven,
                    still
                 I saw no reason to regret the step;
                 Twelve—thirteen—fourteen saw me still
                    unchanged;
                 At fifteen it occurred to me one day
                 That marriage was a necessary ill
                 Inflicted by the gods to punish us,
                 And to evade it were impiety;
                 At sixteen the idea became more fixed;
                 At seventeen I was convinced of it.
Pygmalion: In the meantime she's seen Pygmalion.

The conclusion here too is equally characteristic both
in form and meaning. In the *Wicked World* again the
fairy-queen Selene protests to Ethais her "strange, irrational belief" in him. "Is that so strange?" answers her
knight, and this is his adorer's explanation:—

> Nay, my love, reflect,
> I am a woman, and thou art a man;
> Well, thou art comely, so in truth am I;
> We meet and love each other . . .
>
>   * * *
>
> And why?
> Because I see in thee, or thou in me,
> Astounding virtue, brilliant intellect,
> Great self-denial, venerable years,
> Rare scholarship, or godly talent? No!
> Because, forsooth, we're comely specimens
> Not of our own, but Nature's industry!

He is convinced that vanity plays a large part in love. We get Maggie in *Engaged* flattering her face in the brook; and Yum-Yum is an *ingenue* self-complacent to a marvel:—

> The sun, whose rays
> Are all ablaze
> With ever-living glory,
> Does not deny
> His Majesty—
> He scorns to tell a story.
>
> He don't exclaim,
> "I blush for shame,
> So kindly be indulgent."
> But, fierce and bold,
> In fiery gold,
> He glories all effulgent!
>
> I mean to rule the earth,
> As he the sky—
> We really know our worth,
> The sun and I!

A little "dross" is naturally an added relish. "Belinda has £500 a year; it is not much, but it would at least save me from starvation," sighs Belvawney. And at the very outset in Gilbert's buoyant *Trial by Jury* we find the unblushing avowal of the defendant accused of deceiving

> . . . a girl confiding,
> Vows *et cetera* deriding.

—The confession that

> I soon got tired of third-class journeys
>   And dinners of bread and water;
> So I fell in love with a rich attorney's
>   Elderly, ugly daughter;*

and, in his previous romance, when he

> . . . used to mope, and sigh, and pant
> Just like a love-sick boy,

that

> . . . joy incessant palls the sense
>   And love unchanged will cloy,
> And she became a bore intense,
>   Unto her love-sick boy.

> With fitful glimmer burnt my flame,
>   And I grew cold and coy;

* These lines are a part of the Judge's confession, *not* the Defendant's.—Ed.

At last one morning I became
Another's love-sick boy.

In *Ruddigore* (which Gilbert offered to call "Kensington Gore" to such as misliked the title) we get "perhaps the only village in the world that possesses an endowed corps of professional bridesmaids who are bound to be on duty every day from ten to four," and in *The Mountebanks* we find a masquerade of jealousy (with an excellent song on it) and of exchanged lovers worthy of the *Midsummer Night's Dream*. In *The Mikado* love stands quite on the Japanese (or British) level, while in *Pinafore* and *The Sorcerer* the same points of view are evident. Nonchalance and surprise attend all their developments; in *Patience* there are the dragoons with—

We've been thrown over, we're aware;
But we don't care—but we don't care.
There's fish in the sea, no doubt of it,
As good as ever came out of it.
And some day we shall get our share,
So we don't care—so we don't care.

And there is always a fixed boundary to romance:—

Young man, despair,
    Likewise go to,
Yum-Yum the fair
    You must not woo,
    It will not do;
    I'm sorry for you,
You very imperfect ablutioner.

While the selfishness of the "little fireside games" in
Engaged—tailoring with "real cloth, you know; and if it
fits it counts one to you"—almost fires the mind of Cheviot
Hill. But on the whole a sturdy and wholesome affection—
the sort of tender loyalty that runs right through Trollope's novels—holds Gilbert's heart even while his pleas-
antries play with it. Elsie's song at the end of *The Yeomen
of the Guard,* which

> . . . is sung with the ring
> Of the song maids sing
> Who love with a love life-long O!

Patience's two love-songs, the last the most poetical, of

> Love that will aye endure
> Though the rewards be few;

the first, that warns with sadness,

> If love is a nettle that makes you smart,
> Why do you wear it next your heart?

Teresa's dirge in *The Mountebanks*—

> My heart it is sad and a-weary my head,
> For I weep and I die for the love that is dead

—all these, with many more, attest his wholesome love of
love's wholesomeness. And, above all, that frank apotheo-

sis of the "English Girl" in *Utopia,* which gains double point from its place on the company-promoter's lips and remains as a protest against the decadence and anaemia trounced in *Patience* by

> Then a sentimental passion of a vegetable fashion
>   Must excite your languid spleen,
> An attachment à la Plato for a bashful young
>   potato,
>   Or a not-too-French French bean.

The last stanza of this "English Girl" may well be re-called—

> Her soul is sweet as the ocean-air,
> For prudery knows no haven there;
> To find mock modesty, please apply
> To the conscious blush and the down-cast eye.
> Rich in the things contentment brings,
>   In every pure enjoyment wealthy,
> Blithe as a beautiful bird she sings,
>   For body and mind are hale and healthy.
> Her eyes they thrill with a right good will—
>   Her heart is light as a floating feather—
> As pure and bright as the mountain rill
>   That leaps and laughs in the Highland heather!
>
> Go search the world and search the sea,
> Then come you home and sing with me,
> There's no such gold and no such pearl
> As a bright and beautiful English girl.

Gilbert certainly never dethroned womankind; he inclines to "the side of the angels," after all. His worst blows were reserved for man. As his Lady Psyche sings in *Princess Ida*:

> For the Maiden fair whom the monkey craved.
>   Was a radiant Being
>   With brain far-seeing—
> While a Man, however well-behaved,
> At best is only a monkey shaved.

Gilbert's outlook on the social and political horizon was the same. He exalted order and freedom and discipline. He abominated the greed of monopoly whether it styled itself Socialism, or Finance, or the Cabinet. He dragged down the pretenders from their thrones, and unmasked them with a quip or a moral. On every blatant bore and finicking faddist he "drew" his "snickersee." He

> . . . has got them on his list;
> They really won't be missed.

And he probes the evergreen fallacies of shallow optimism:

> Society has quite forsaken all her wicked courses,
> Which empties our police courts and abolishes
>   divorces—
>   Divorce is nearly obsolete in England.

> No tolerance we show to undeserving rank or
>   splendour,
> For the higher his position is, the greater the
>   offender,
>   That's a maxim that is prevalent in England.

We have solved the labour question with
  discrimination polished,
So poverty is obsolete and hunger is abolished—
  We are going to abolish it in England.

Our peerage we've remodelled on an intellectual
  basis,
Which certainly is rough on our hereditary races—
  We are going to remodel it in England.

The Brewers and the Cotton Lords no longer seek
  admission,
And Literary Merit meets with proper recognition—
  As Literary Merit does in England.

  It really is surprising
  What a thorough Anglicising
We have brought about—Utopia's quite another
  land;
  In her enterprising movements
  She is England—with improvements,
Which we dutifully offer to our motherland!

As for the present posture in England of bumptious
yet sensitive Socialism, listen to the true words of *Pinafore*:—

Boatswain:	Ah! Sir Joseph's a true gentleman: courteous and considerate to the humblest.
Ralph:	True, Boatswain; but we are not the very humblest. Sir Joseph has explained our true position to us. As he says, a British seaman is any man's equal excepting his; and if

	Sir Joseph says that, is it not our duty to believe him?
All:	Well spoke! Well spoke!
Dick:	You're on a wrong tack, and so is he. He means well, but he don't know. When people have to obey other people's orders, equality's out of the question.
All (*recoiling*):	Horrible! Horrible!

Or hear *The Sorcerer*:—

Alexis:	. . . I have addressed navvies on the advantages that would accrue to them if they married wealthy ladies of rank, and not a navvy dissented.
Aline:	Noble fellows! And yet there are those who hold that the uneducated classes are not open to argument! And what do the Countesses say?
Alexis:	Why, at present, it can't be denied, the aristocracy hold aloof.
Aline:	The working man is the true Intelligence, after all!
Alexis:	He is a noble creature when he is quite sober.

And then there are the promises of "Marco" and of "Giuseppe" in *The Gondoliers*: they might have been proffered by the parliamentary Jacobins of to-day:—

For everyone who feels inclined,
Some post we undertake to find
Congenial to his frame of mind—
    And all shall equal be.

The Chancellor in his peruke—
The Earl, the Marquis, and the Dook,
The Groom, the Butler, and the Cook—
    They all shall equal be.

The Aristocrat who banks with Coutts,
The Aristocrat who hunts and shoots,
The Aristocrat who cleans our boots—
    They all shall equal be.

*   *   *

Sing high, sing low,
Wherever they go,
They all shall equal be.

"Don Alhambra's" famous song (one of Gilbert's very best) in *The Gondoliers* about the king who "promoted everybody" sums up the moral:—

Lord Chancellors were cheap as sprats
And Bishops in their shovel hats
Were plentiful as tabby-cats—
    In point of fact too many.

Ambassadors cropped up like hay,
Prime Ministers and such as they
Grew like asparagus in May,
    And Dukes were three a penny.

*   *   *

The King, although no one denies
His heart was of abnormal size,
Yet he'd have acted otherwise
    If he had been acuter.

The end is easily foretold,
When every blessed thing you hold
Is made of silver or of gold,
    You long for simple pewter.

When you have nothing else to wear
But cloth of gold and satins rare,
For cloth of gold you cease to care—
    Up goes the price of shoddy.

In short, whoever you may be
To this conclusion you'll agree,
When everyone is somebodee,
Then no one's anybody.

But "equality" spells monotony as well as tyranny, and the politicians who thrive on or abet it meet with a chastisement not inappropriate to the present junctures, though it was inflicted nearly a quarter of a century ago:—

Ye supple M.P.'s who go down on your knees,
    Your precious identity sinking,
And vote black and white as your leaders indite
    (Which saves you the trouble of thinking).
For your country's good fame, her repute, or her
        shame,
    You don't care the snuff of a candle—
But you're paid for your game when you're told
        that your name
    Will be graced by a Baronet's handle.
Oh! allow me to give *you* a word of advice—
The title's uncommonly dear at the price!

Nor does aggressive philanthropy escape the lash. Mr. Chesterton (who I doubt little would compare Gilbert with Dr. Johnson) has somewhere said that in the next revolution the gutters will run red with the blood of philanthropists. I am disposed to agree with him. In *Princess Ida* "King Gama" thus describes his amiable calling:—

> If you'll give me your attention, I will tell you
>   what I am!
> I'm a genuine philanthropist—all other kinds are
>   sham.
> Each little fault of temper and each social defect
> In my erring fellow-creatures I endeavor to
>   correct.
> To all their little weaknesses I open people's eyes
> And little plans to snub the self-sufficient I devise;
> I love my fellow-creatures—I do all the good I
>   can—
> Yet everybody says I'm such a disagreeable man!
>   And I can't think why!

Gilbert's "philosophy" is to make the best of what comes—plain and direct like all thoughts, however fanciful the arabesques that decorate them. As he puts it in *Ruddigore,* which, taken all for all, is perhaps the most brilliant of his extravaganzas, not excepting *Iolanthe* or *The Mikado,*

> Every season has its cheer,
> Life is lovely all the year.

Or, as he varies the theme in *The Gondoliers:*—

> Try we lifelong, we can never
>   Straighten out life's tangled skein:
> Why should we in vain endeavour,

Guess and guess and guess again?
　　Life's a pudding full of plums,
　　Care's a canker that benumbs,
Wherefore waste our elocution
On impossible solution?
Life's a pleasant institution:
　　Let us take it as it comes.

Set aside the dull enigma,
　　We shall guess it all too soon;
Failure brings no kind of stigma—
　　Dance we to another tune!
　　　String the lyre and fill the cup,
　　　Lest on sorrow we should sup.
Hop and skip to Fancy's fiddle,
Hands across and down the middle—
Life's perhaps the only riddle
　　That we shrink from giving up!

"I take things as I find them, and I make the best
of them . . . that's true philosophy," says "Clarice" in sus-
pense to "Pauline" at the opening of *Comedy and Tragedy*. But there are deeper notes than these, and one of
them—struck by "Fairfax" in the *Yeomen*—sounds with
solemnity now that Gilbert has himself made his exit. It
renders his own voice:—

Why, sir, it is no light boon to die swiftly and surely
at a given hour and in a given fashion! Truth to tell,
I would gladly have my life; but if that may not be,
I have the next best thing to it, which is death.
Believe me, sir, my lot is not so much amiss.

This is serious; but Gilbert's gaiety is irrepressible
and irresistible, breaking through every suggestion of

gloom or despair. Some of his lyrics have an irresponsible flow of rarefied nonsense, quite unique, and quite apart from their extreme ingenuity of structure. They elude classification, yet a few instances will show that there is a real relationship between these poems of wandering paradox.

> Oh, happy the blossom
>   That blooms on the lea,
> Likewise the opossum
>   That sits on a tree.
> But when you come across 'em,
>   They cannot compare
> With those who are treading
> The dance at a wedding,
> While people are spreading
>   The best of good fare.
>
> Oh, wretched the debtor
>   Who's signing the deed!
> And wretched the letter
>   That no one can read!
> But very much better
>   Their lot it must be
> Than that of the person
> I'm making this verse on,
> Whose head there's a curse on—
>   Alluding to me!

The next shows the same unconnected connectedness of word-picture:—

> Cheerily carols the lark
>   Over the cot,
> Merrily whistles the clerk
>   Scratching a blot.

But the lark
And the clerk,
I remark
    Comfort me not.

Over the ripening peach
    Buzzes the bee,
Splash on the billowy beach
    Tumbles the sea.
But the peach
And the beach,
They are each
    Nothing to me.

These are both from *Ruddigore,* but a third belongs to *The Mikado,* and is sung by "Ko-Ko," together with the mature "Katisha," on the motif of beauty even in blood-thirstiness:—

There is beauty in the bellow of the blast,
    There is grandeur in the growling of the gale,
        There is eloquent outpouring
        When the lion is a-roaring,
And the tiger is a-lashing of his tail;
        Yes, I like to see a tiger,
        From the Congo or the Niger,
And especially when lashing of his tail.[5]

*   *   *

There is beauty in extreme old age—
    Do you fancy you are elderly enough?
        Information I'm requesting
        On a subject interesting
    Is a maiden all the better when she's tough?

*   *   *

Are you old enough to marry, do you think?
    Won't you wait till you are "eighty in the shade"?

There's a fascination frantic
In a ruin that's romantic:—
Do you think you are sufficiently decayed?

And Gilbert's really wonderful patter-songs, rivalling the "parabaseis" of Aristophanes, are among the most enjoyable of his fancies. That of the Lord Chancellor in *Iolanthe* beginning

When you're lying awake
With a dismal headache

is perhaps the most exhilarating, rising with a *crescendo* of imaginary horrors and sinking into the *diminuendo* of nightmare. Many such will occur to the recollection, notably the Mikado's paean of punishments. But there is one which has never, I believe, been published about the affable and generous railway director who "tipped all the outside porters" and

Gave his friends some shooting
In his little place at Tooting.

Eventually, through a series of amusing misfortunes, he falls on evil days, and now

The shareholders are all in the Work'us,
And *he* sells lights in the Regent Circus.

How good, too, is his irony even on irony; and how unexpected! To illustrate its idioms would be to re-quote his plays, but one song has been half forgotten and must be recalled. It comes from *Princess Ida,* and it is sung by the redoubtable "Arac":—

> This helmet, I suppose,
> Was meant to ward off blows;
>   It's very hot,
>   And weighs a lot,
> As many a guardsman knows,
> So off that helmet goes.

> This tight-fitting cuirass
> Is but a useless mass;
>   It's made of steel,
>   And weighs a deal,
> A man is but an ass,
> Who fights in a cuirass,
> So off goes that cuirass.

> *   *   *

> These things I treat the same *(indicating the leg pieces)*
> (I quite forget their name),
>   They turn one's legs
>   To cribbage-pegs.
> Their aid I thus disclaim,
> Though I forget their name.

Nowhere, too, is his irony more marked than in *Rosencrantz and Guildenstern,* where the soliloquising Hamlet figures as the worst bore in England. Nor should the *Pirates'* disclaimer of poetry be omitted: it brings us back again to our starting point of Gilbert's own faculty of deromanticising what he also romanticises:—

> Although our dark career
>   Sometimes involves the crime of stealing,

> We rather think that we're
>   Not altogether void of feeling.
> Although we live by strife,
>   We're always sorry to begin it,
> And what, we ask, is life
>   Without a touch of Poetry * in it.

To which replies the chorus,

> Hail, Poetry, thou heaven-born maid,
> Thou gildest e'en the pirate's trade!
> Hail, flowing fount of sentiment!
> All hail, Divine Emollient!

This review would have no claim to the very ghost of completeness without some mention of the most poetical of his songs; songs that, as Sullivan once pointed out to the present writer, were always singable, and lend themselves far more naturally to music than the words, for example, even of Tennyson. The many from *Patience,* including the "Silver Churn," need no fresh mention, nor the "Sighing softly to the river" from *The Pirates;* nor, of course, "Titwillow" from *The Mikado,* and several ditties in *Iolanthe;* nor many another familiar strain and canzonet that rank Gilbert and Sullivan in the rounded cycle of English ballad music. But three perhaps less well-remembered songs may here be allowed citation. The first is again from *Princess Ida,* one of his two versions of the *Princess,* just as in *Gretchen* he took an old subject into his versatile hands. It has the true Restoration ring:—

* Sichel writes "poetic" for "of Poetry."—Ed.

Whom thou hast chained must wear his chain,
　　Thou canst not set him free;
He wrestles with his bonds in vain,
　　Who lives by loving thee.
If heart of stone for heart of fire
　　Be all thou hast to give,
If dead to me my heart's desire,
　　Why should I wish to live?

No word of thine—no stern command—
　　Can teach my heart to rove;
Then rather perish by thy hand
　　Than live without thy love!
A loveless life apart from thee
　　Were hopeless slavery.
If kindly death will set me free,
　　Why should I fear to die?

Thus, Hilarion's song, and the same wistfulness, this time
a wavering one, attaches to the following from *Ruddigore*. Metrically and inherently it is more delicate and
Herrick-like:—

To a garden full of posies,*
　　Cometh one to gather flowers,
　　And he wanders through its bowers,
Toying with the wanton roses,
　　Who, uprising from their beds,
　　Hold on high their shameless heads,
With their pretty lips a-pouting,
Never doubting, never doubting,
　　That for Cytherean posies
　　He would gather aught but roses.

* Sichel writes "In" for "To."—Ed.

In a nest of weeds and nettles,
   Lay a violet half-hidden,
   Hoping that his glance unbidden
Yet might fall upon her petals,
   Though she lived alone, apart,
   Hope lay nestling at her heart,
But, alas, the cruel waking
Set her little heart a-breaking,
   For he gathered for his posies
   Only roses—only roses!

The last, and saddest, is "Fairfax's" farewell, which has almost an Elizabethan or Jacobean savour. It may aptly close this imperfect tribute to the great satirist-singer:—

Is life a boon?
   If so it must befall
   That Death, whene'er he call,
Must call too soon.
   Though four-score years he give,
   Yet one would pray to live
Another moon!
   What kind of plaint have I,
   Who perish in July?
   I might have had to die
Perchance in June.

Is life a thorn?
   Then count it not a whit!
   Man is well done with it;
Soon as he's born,
   He should all means essay
   To put the plague away;

And I, war-worn,
  Poor, captured fugitive,
  My life most gladly give—
  I might have had to live
Another morn!

After these let none with any sense of song dare to deny that Gilbert was a minstrel born. I have sought to dwell on the strong fibre—the web and woof which the shuttle of his nimble ironies compounded. The tissue is firm beneath its glitter; there is purpose in his paradox. Gilbert has left England more than a legacy of pure and lasting laughter, though this is much indeed. He has bequeathed an inheritance of melody as well as of mirth, of thought, and criticism, as well as of whim and fantasy. These are not evanescent, and "another morn" will dawn on them, though it is always hard to prophesy the permanence of words wedded to music. But as literature the librettos will endure. The great Englishman, like the greater Greek, will long outlive the surroundings that his irony brought into such sharp yet such joyous relief. Posterity is a careless fellow, but his debt of gratitude is assured.

Notes

1. *The Pirates of Penzance*
2. *Broken Hearts*
3. *Pygmalion and Galatea*
4. *Ibid.*
5. With this Gilbertian stroke *cf.* "Especially Ellen MacJones Aberdeen," in his *Bab Ballads*.

Edith Hamilton

W. S. Gilbert:
A Mid-Victorian
Aristophanes

(1927)

"True Comedy," said Voltaire, "is the speaking picture of the Follies and Foibles of a Nation." He was thinking of Aristophanes, and no better description could be given of the Old Athenian Comedy. His words are, however, not all-inclusive; indeed they serve to point the difference between the comedy of Athens and the comedy of sixteenth-century England. The *Zeitgeist* of those periods of splendor and magnificent vigour was in many points, the most important points, alike. Athenian and Elizabethan comedy, too, have much in common; the resemblance between Aristophanes and certain of the comedy parts of Shakespeare jumps to the eye. The spirit of their times is in them. There is the same tremendous energy and verve and vitality; the same swinging, swashbuckling spirit; the same exuberant, effervescing flow of language; the same rollicking, uproarious fun. Falstaff is a character out of Aristophanes raised to the *nth* power; Poins, Ancient Pistol, Mistress Quickly, might have come straight out of any of his plays.

But this likeness, vivid though it is, is on the surface only. If one goes deeper it disappears. In so far as each man was a product of his time he resembled the other, but in their essential genius they were unlike. To read Aristophanes is in some sort like reading an Athenian comic paper. All the life of Athens is there: the politics of the day and the politicians; the war party and the anti-war party; pacifism, votes for women, free trade, fiscal reform, complaining tax payers, educational theories, the current philosophical and literary talk,—everything in short that interested the average citizen of that day was food for his mockery. To all such matters Shakespeare was completely indifferent. The mode of the moment, the purely passing show, was of no concern whatever to him. Aristophanes was the "speaking picture of the Follies and Foibles of his Nation." Shakespeare lived in an undated world.

The great age of Greek drama was nearing its close when Aristophanes began to write. Of the Old Comedy, as it is called, we have little; none of the plays of Aristophanes' often successful rivals, and only eleven of the many he himself wrote, but the genre is clearly to be seen in those eleven. There were but three actors. A chorus divided the action by song and dance (there was no curtain) and often took part in the dialogue. About half way through, the plot, a very loose matter at best, came practically to an end, and the chorus made a long address to the audience, which aired the author's opinions and often had nothing to do with the play. After that would follow scenes more or less connected. A dull picture this, of a brilliantly entertaining reality. Nobody and nothing escaped the ridicule of the Old Comedy. The gods came in for their share; so did the institutions dearest to the Athenians; so did the most popular and powerful individuals, often by name. The freedom of speech is staggering to our ideas. Athens was fighting a bitter war which was ultimately to crush her and to end the glory that was Greece, but Aristophanes was free to say exactly what he pleased. If an American had produced a play, after we entered the war, which represented General Pershing and Admiral Sims as wanting to desert; which denounced the war, praised the Germans, glorified the peace party, ridiculed Uncle Sam, that play would have had a short life, but that is just what Aristophanes did in play after play, and the Athenians, pro and anti-war alike, thronged to the theatre. The fundamental thing to the Athenian was a man's right to say what he chose.

The best known of Aristophanes' plays are the *Birds,* where Athens is shown up in contrast to the Utopian city the birds build in the clouds; the *Frogs,* a parody of popular writers; the *Clouds,* which makes fun of Socrates and the intelligentsia who "walk on air and contemplate the sun"; and three plays about women, the *Thesmophoriazusae,* the *Lysistrata,* and the *Ecclesiazusae,* in which the women take hold of literature, the war and the state, to the great betterment of all.

To find the writer most like Aristophanes one must go to an age as unlike his as Shakespeare's was like. The turbulent democracy that gave birth to the Old Comedy and the England over whose manners and customs Queen Victoria ruled supreme had nothing in common, and yet the mid-Victorian Gilbert of *Pinafore* fame saw eye to eye with Aristophanes as no other writer has done. The case with Shakespeare is reversed. The differences between Aristophanes and Gilbert are superficial; they are due to the differences of their time. In their essential genius they are alike.

The unknown is always magnificent. Aristophanes wears the halo of Greece, and is at the same time softly dimmed by the dust of centuries of scholarly elucidation. A comparison therefore with an author familiar and beloved and never really thought about wears a look of irreverence,—also of ignorance. Dear nonsensical Gilbert, and the magnificent Aristophanes, poet, political reformer, social uplifter, philosophical thinker, and a dozen other titles to immortality,—how is it possible to compare them? The only basis for true comparison, Plato says, is the excellency that is peculiar to each thing. Was Aristophanes really a great lyric poet? Was he really bent on reforming politics or ending democracy? Such considerations are beside the point. Shakespeare's glory would not be enhanced if Hamlet's soliloquy was understood as a warning against suicide, or if it could be proved that he was attacking the social evil in *Pericles*. The peculiar excellency of comedy is its excellent fooling, and Aristophanes' claim to immortality is based upon one title only, he was a master maker of comedy, he could fool excellently. Here Gilbert stands side by side with him. He, too, could write the most admirable nonsense. There has never been better fooling than his, and a comparison with him carries nothing derogatory to the great Athenian.

Striking resemblances, both general and particular, emerge from such a comparison. The two men fooled in the same way; they looked at life with the same eyes. In Gilbert's pages Victorian England lives in miniature just as Athens in Aristophanes'. Those sweet pretty girls, those smart young dragoons, those match-making mammas; those genial exponents of the value of a title, a safe income, a political pull; that curious union of sentimental thinking and stoutly practical acting; that intimate savor of England in the eighteen-eighties;—who has ever given it so perfectly as he? He was one of the cleverest of caricaturists, but the freedom Aristophanes enjoyed was not his, and his deft, clear-cut pictures of dishonesty and sham and ignorance in high places are very discreet and always nameless. Essentially, however, he strikes with the same weapon as his Greek predecessor. He, too, ridicules the things dearest to his countrymen: the aristocracy in *Iolanthe;* army training in the *Pirates;* the navy in *Pinafore;* English society in *Utopia Limited;* the law courts in *Trial by Jury;* the smart young intelligentsia with Oscar Wilde at their head in *Patience;* the new woman in *Princess Ida,* and so on through all his thirteen plays. It is never cruel, this ridicule, as Aristophanes' sometimes is, but this difference is the inevitable result of the enormous difference between the two men's environment. The Athenian was watching cold and hunger and bitter defeat draw ever nearer to Athens. The Englishman wrote in the safest and most comfortable world mankind has ever known. But underneath that difference their fundamental point of view was the same. They were topical writers, both of them, given over to the matters of the moment, and yet Aristophanes has been laughed with for two thousand years, and Gilbert has survived a half century of such shattering change, his England seems almost as far away from us. They saw beneath the surface of the passing show. They wrote of the purely ephemeral and in their hands it became a picture not of the "Follies and Foibles" of a day and a nation, but of those that exist in all nations and all ages and belong to the permanent stuff of human nature.

Of the two, Aristophanes has the bigger canvas, leagues

to Gilbert's inches, but the yard-stick is not a measure of art, and the quality of their comedy is the same. Grace, gaiety, lightness, charm, quintessential qualities of the Comic Spirit, mark them both. It is noteworthy that they resemble each other even in matters of technique which is wont to vary so greatly from age to age. In both men the fooling is the point, not the plot. In that subtle, individual thing, the use of metre, they are strikingly alike. The metre of a comic song is as important as its matter. No one understood that more clearly than Gilbert:

> All children who are up in dates and floor you
> with 'em flat,
> All persons who in shaking hands, shake hands
> with you like *that.*

Aristophanes understood it too as none better:

> [1]I'm swelling within like a cake full of yeast. I
> must talk or I'll blow into pieces.
> Get out of my way. Don't stop me, I say. Boy,
> bring me my togs and a topper.

This jolly line is a favorite with him, but he uses an endless variety. Examples will be found in the passages translated, in all of which, except the one passage indicated, I have reproduced the original metres. The effect of them is essentially that of Gilbert's.

A device of pure nonsense in Gilbert, which seems peculiarly his own, and which he uses, for example, in the second act of *Patience,* is the appeal to something utterly irrelevant that proves irresistible:

Grosvenor (*wildly*):	But you would not do it—I am sure you would not. (*Throwing himself at Bunthorne's knees, and clinging to him.*) Oh, reflect, reflect! You had a mother once.
Bunthorne:	Never!
Grosvenor:	Then you had an aunt! (*Bunthorne deeply affected.*) Ah! I see you had! By the memory of that aunt, I implore you.

He uses exactly the same device in the second act of *The Pirates*.

(*A struggle ensues between the Pirates and Police. The Police are overcome, the Pirates standing over them with drawn swords.*)

Sergeant:	To gain a brief advantage you've contrived, But your proud triumph will not be long-lived. On your allegiance we've a stronger claim— We charge you yield, in Queen Victoria's name!
King (*baffled*):	You do!
Police:	We do! We charge you yield, in Queen Victoria's name! (*Pirates kneel, Police stand over them triumphantly.*)

King: We yield at once, with humbled
                           mien,
                        Because, with all our faults, we
                           love our Queen.
                        (*Police, holding Pirates by the
                           collar, take out handkerchiefs
                           and weep.*)

Precisely the same nonsensical device is used by
Aristophanes. In the *Acharnians*[2] the magic appeal before
which all opposition melts is, not to an aunt or the Queen,
God bless her, but to a scuttle of coal, as it might have
been last year in England. Fuel was scarce in Athens just
then: war was raging.

The scene is a street in Athens. A man, Dikaeopolis
by name, has said something in favor of Sparta, Athens'
enemy. The crowd is furious:

Dikaeopolis: This I know, the men of Sparta, whom
                  we're cursing all day long,
               Aren't the only ones to blame for
                  everything that's going wrong.
Crowd: Spartans not to blame, you traitor?
               Do you dare tell such a lie?
               At him! At him, all good people. Stone
                  him, burn him. He shall die.
Dikaeopolis: Won't you hear me, my dear fellows?
Crowd: Never, never. Not a word.
Dikaeopolis: Then I'll turn on you, you villains.
               Would you kill a man unheard?
               I've a hostage for my safety, one that's
                  very dear to you.
               I will slaughter him before you. (*Goes
                  into house at back of stage.*)

Crowd: What is it he's gone to do?
                    How he threatens. You don't think he's
                        got a child of ours in there?
Dikaeopolis: (*from behind stage*): I've got something.
                    Now, you scoundrels, tremble, for I
                        will not spare.
                    Look well at my hostage. This will test
                        your mettle, every soul. (*He comes
                        out, lugging something behind
                        him.*)
                    Which among you has true feeling for
                        —a scuttle full of coal.
Crowd: Heaven save us! Oh, don't touch it!
                    We'll give in. Say what you please.

In the *Lysistrata* [3] occurs the following:

First Speaker: For through man's heart there
                        runs in flood
                    A natural and a noble taste for
                        blood.
Second Speaker: To form a ring and fight—
Third Speaker: To cut off heads at sight—
All: It is our right.

Matter and manner are perfectly Gilbert's. Anyone not
knowing the author would inevitably assign it to him, to
the *Princess Ida,* perhaps, along with:

    We are warriors three,
        Sons of Gama Rex,
    Like most sons are we
        Masculine in sex.

Bold and fierce and strong, ha! ha!
  For a war we burn.
With its right or wrong, ha! ha!
  We have no concern.

Aristophanes was amused by grand talk that covered empty content. The first scene in the *Thesmophoriazusae*[4] is a street in Athens. Two elderly men enter, one with the lofty air that befits a Poet and Philosopher, the other an ordinary, cheerful old fellow. He speaks first.

Mnesilochus: Might I, before I've lost my wind
      entirely,
  Be told where you are taking me,
      Euripides?

Euripides You may not hear the things which
  (*solemnly*):   presently
  You are to see.

Mnesilochus: What's that? Say it again. I'm not to
      hear—?

Euripides: What you shall surely see.

Mnesilochus: And not to see—?

Euripides: The things you must needs hear.

Mnesilochus: Oh how you talk. Of course you're
      very clever.
  You mean I must not either hear or
      see?

Euripides: They two are twain and by their
      nature diverse,
  Each one from other.

Mnesilochus: Hearing from seeing, eh?

Euripides: Even so. By nature diverse.

Mnesilochus: What's that—diverse?

Euripides: Their elemental parts are separate.

Mnesilochus: Oh, what it is to talk to learned
                people.

Gilbert was amused by the same thing. In the second
act of the *Princess Ida* the first scene is in the hall of the
Women's University. The principal has been addressing
the faculty and students, and as she finishes asks:

                    Who lectures in the Hall of Arts
                        today?
Lady Blanche: I, madam, on Abstract Philosophy.
                    There I propose considering, at
                        length,
                    Three points—the Is, the Might Be,
                        and the Must.
                    Whether the Is, from being actual
                        fact,
                    Is more important than the vague
                        Might Be,
                    Or, the Might Be, from taking
                        wider scope,
                    Is for that reason greater than the Is:
                    And lastly, how the Is and Might
                        Be stand
                    Compared with the inevitable Must!
Princess: The subject's deep.

Every kind of sham is dear to Aristophanes but espe-
cially the literary sham. He is forever making fun of him.
In the *Birds* Péisthetaerus, an Athenian, is helping the
birds found their new city in the clouds, which is called
Cloud-cuckoo-town. To it flock the quacks and the cranks.
A priest has just been chased off the stage when enter a
Poet, singing: [5]

> O Cloud-cuckoo-town!
> Muse, do thou crown
> With song her fair name,
> Hymning her fame.

Peisthetaerus:	What sort of thing is this? I say, Who in the world are you, now, pray?
Poet:	A warbler of a song, Very sweet and very strong, Slave of the Muse am I, Eager and nimble and spry, —As Homer says.
Peisthetaerus:	Does the Muse let her servants wear That sort of long, untidy hair?
Poet:	Oh, we who teach the art Of the drama, whole or part, Servants of the Muse, must try To be eager and nimble and spry, —As Homer says.
Peisthetaerus:	That nimbleness, no doubt is why You're all in rags. You are too spry.

Poet:	Oh, I've been making lovely, lovely
	    lays,
	Old and new-fashioned too, in
	    sweetest praise
	Of your Cloud-cuckoo-town.
	. . . And won't you see
	If you have something you can give
	    to *me?*

In the *Thesmophoriazusae*[6] Euripides and Mnesilochus are walking along the street:

Euripides:	That house is where great Agathon is living, The tragic poet.
Mnesilochus:	Agathon? Don't know him.
Euripides:	Why, he's the Agathon—
Mnesilochus (*interrupting*):	A big dark fellow, eh?

Euripides:	Oh, no, by no means. Haven't
	    you ever seen him?
	But let us step aside. His
	    servant's coming.
	He's got some myrtles and a pan
	    of coals.
	He's going to pray for help in
	    composition.

Servant:	Let sacred silence rule us here,
	Ye people all, lock up your lips,
	For the Muses are revelling
	    there within,
	The Queens of poetry-making.
	Let the air be still and forget
	    to blow,
	And the gray sea wave make
	    never a sound—

Mnesilochus:	Stuff and *non*sense.
Euripides:	*Will* you be quiet.
Servant (*scandalized*):	What's this I hear?
Mnesilochus:	Oh, just as you said. It's the air that's forgetting to blow.
Servant:	He's making a play. First the keel he will lay With neatly joined words all new,

Then the bottom he'll round,
And chisel the sound,
And fasten the verses with glue.
A maxim he'll take
And an epithet make,
And call by new names what is
old,
He'll form it like wax
And fill in the cracks,
And cast it at last in a mold.[7]
(*Enter Agathon. He has on a
silk dress and his hair is in
a net.*)

Mnesilochus: Who are you? Were you born a
man?
No, you're a woman surely.

Agathon: Know, sir, I choose my dress to
suit my writing.
A poet molds himself upon his
poems,
And when he writes of women
he assumes
A woman's dress and takes on
woman's habits.
But when he sings of men a
manly bearing
Is his therewith. What we are
not by nature
We take unto ourselves through
imitation.

Gilbert enjoyed the sham artist quite as much. In
Patience Act I, Scene I, the officers of the Dragoons are on
the stage:

Colonel:	Yes, and here are the ladies.
Duke:	But who is the gentleman with the long hair?
	(Bunthorne enters, followed by the Ladies, two by two.)
Bunthorne *(aside)*:	Though my book I seem to scan
	In a rapt ecstatic way,
	Like a literary man
	Who despises female clay,
	I hear plainly all they say.
	Twenty love-sick maidens they!
Bunthorne *(alone)*:	Am I alone
	And unobserved? I am!
	Then let me own
	I'm an aesthetic sham!
	This air severe
	Is but a mere
	Veneer!
	This costume chaste
	Is but good taste
	Misplaced!

Both writers make the same kind of jokes about military matters and the like. In the *Knights*[8] the two generals introduced were among the most famous of their time:

Demosthenes:	How goes it, poor old chap?
Nicias:	Badly. Like you.
Demosthenes:	Let's sing a doleful ditty and then weep.
	(Both sing, break down, and sob.)
Demosthenes:	No use in whimpering. We'd do better far

To dry our tears and find some good
    way out.

Nicias: What way? You tell me.

Demosthenes: No. Do you tell me.

If you won't speak I'll fight you.

Nicias: No not I.

You say it first and then I'll say it
    after.

Demosthenes: Oh, speak for me and say what's in
    my heart.

Nicias: My courage fails, If only I could say
    it

Neatly and sweetly, like Euripides.

Well then, say *sert,* like that, and say
    it smartly.

Demosthenes: All right. Here goes: *sert.*

Nicias: Good. Have courage now.

Say first *sert* and then *de,* repeating
    fast

The two words, very fast.

Demosthenes: Ah, yes. I get you.

Sert de, sert de sert, desert.

Nicias: You have it.

Well, doesn't it sound nice?

Demosthenes: It's *heavenly.*

But—but—

Nicias: What's that?

Demosthenes: They *flog* deserters.

Gilbert's jokes, of course, were in a lighter vein. There
is the Duke of Plaza-Toro:

In enterprise of martial kind,
  When there was any fighting,
He led his regiment from behind—
  He found it less exciting.

> But when away his regiment ran,
>   His place was at the fore, O—
>   That celebrated,
>   Cultivated,
>   Underrated
>   Nobleman,
>   The Duke of Plaza-Toro!

But the passage most like the one quoted from Aristophanes is the marching song of the Police in the *Pirates,* Act II.

> Mabel: Go, ye heroes, go to glory,
>   Though ye die in combat gory,
>   Ye shall live in song and story,
>   Go to immortality!
> Police: Though to us it's evident,
>   Tarantara! tarantara!
>   These intentions are well meant,
>   Tarantara!
>   Such expressions don't appear,
>   Tarantara! tarantara!
>   Calculated men to cheer,
>   Tarantara!
>   Who are going to meet their fate
>   In a highly nervous state,
>   Tarantara!

Politicians in Athens and in London seem very much the same. In the *Plutus*[9] a slave, Carion, meets one. He asks:

> You're a good man, a patriot?
> Politician: Oh, yes.

                                If ever there was one.
Carion: And, as I guess,
                                A farmer?
Politician: I? Lord save us. I'm not mad.
Carion: A merchant then?
Politician: Ah, sometimes I have had
                                To take that trade up—as an alibi.
Carion: You've some profession surely.
Politician: No, not I.
Carion: How do you make a living?
Politician: Well, there're several
                                Answers to that. I'm Supervisor
                                    General
                                Of all things here, public and
                                    private too.
Carion: A great profession that. What did
                                    you do
                                To qualify for it?
Politician: I *wanted* it.

So Gilbert in the song of the duke and duchess in the
Gondoliers:

        To help unhappy commoners, and add to their
            enjoyment,
        Affords a man of noble rank congenial
            employment;
        Of our attempts we offer you examples illustrative:
        The work is light, and, I may add, it's most
            remunerative.
        Small titles and orders
        For Mayors and Recorders
            I get—and they're highly delighted.
        M.P.'s baronetted,
        Sham Colonels gazetted,
            And second-rate Aldermen knighted.

In the *Knights*[10] an oracle has just foretold that Athens will be ruled some day by a sausage seller. At that moment one enters and is greeted with enthusiasm:

Demosthenes:	Dear Sausage-seller rise, our Saviour and the State's.
Sausage-seller:	What's that you say?
Demosthenes:	O happy man and rich. Nothing today, tomorrow everything. O Lord of Athens, blest through you.
Sausage-seller:	I see, sir, That you must have your joke. But as for me, I've got to wash the guts and sell my sausage.
Demosthenes:	But you are going to be our greatest man.
Sausage-seller:	Oh, I'm not fit for that.
Demosthenes:	What's that? Not fit? Is some good action weighing on your conscience? Don't tell me that you come of honest folk?
Sausage-seller:	Oh, dear me, no sir. Bad 'uns, out and out.
Demosthenes:	You lucky man. Oh, what a start you've got For public life.
Sausage-seller:	But I don't know a thing Except my letters.
Demosthenes:	Ah, the pity is That you know anything.

A parallel passage is Sir Joseph's song in *Pinafore:*

I grew so rich that I was sent
By a pocket borough into Parliament.
I always voted at my party's call,
And I never thought of thinking for myself at all.
I thought so little they rewarded me
By making me the Ruler of the Queen's Navee!

The woman joke, of course, is well to the fore with both men. It is ever with us. *Plus ça change, plus c'est la même chose.* Any number of passages might be selected. In the *Princess Ida* the new woman is described:

As for fashion, they forswear it,
    So they say—so they say;
And the circle—they will square it
    Some fine day—some fine day;

Each newly-joined aspirant
    To the clan—to the clan—
Must repudiate the tyrant
    Known as Man—known as Man.

They mock at him and flout him,
    For they do not care about him,
And they're "going to do without him"
    If they can—if they can!

The song of the duchess in the *Gondoliers* is even more in Aristophanes' vein:

On the day when I was wedded
    To your admirable sire,
I acknowledge that I dreaded
    An explosion of his ire.

I was always very wary,
  For his fury was ecstatic—
His refined vocabulary
  Most unpleasantly emphatic.

Giving him the very best, and getting back the very
    worst—
That is how I tried to tame your great progenitor
    —at first!

But I found that a reliance
  On my threatening appearance,
And a resolute defiance
  Of marital interference
Was the only thing required
  For to make his temper supple,
And you couldn't have desired
  A more reciprocating couple.

So with double-shotted guns and colours nailed
    unto the mast,
I tamed your insignificant progenitor—at last!

Aristophanes' ladies are of quite the same kind. They
form the chorus of the *Thesmophoriazusae*[11] and they
begin their address to the audience as follows:

We now come forward and appeal to you to hear
    how the men all flout us,
And the foolish abuse and the scandals let loose
    the silly things tell about us.
They say all evil proceeds from us, war, battles,
    and murder even,
We're a tiresome, troublesome, quarrelsome lot,
    disturbers of earth and heaven.

Now, we ask you to put your minds on this: if
    we're really the plague of your lives,
Then tell us, please, why you're all so keen to get
    us to be your wives?
Pray, why do you like us to be at home, all ready
    to smile and greet you,
And storm and sulk if your poor little wife isn't
    always there to meet you?
If we're such a nuisance and pest, then why—we
    venture to put the question—
Don't you rather rejoice when we're out of the way
    —a reasonable suggestion.
If we stay the night at the house of a friend,—I
    mean, the house of a lady,
You hunt for us everywhere like mad and hint at
    something shady.
Do you like to look at a plague and a pest? It seems
    you do, for you stare
And ogle and give us killing looks if you see us
    anywhere.
And if we think proper to blush and withdraw, as
    a lady, no doubt should be doing,
You will try to follow us all the more, and never
    give over pursuing.
But we can show you up as well,
The ways of a man we all can tell,
Your heart's in your stomach, every one,
And you'll *do* anyone if you're not first *done*.
We know what the jokes are you love to make,
And how you each fancy yourself a rake.

Parallels such as these could be given indefinitely.
The world moves slowly. Aristophanes in Athens, fifth
century, B. C., Gilbert in nineteenth century England,
saw the same things and saw the same humour in them.
Some things, however, were seen by the Athenian which

the Englishman was constrained not to see. And this fact constitutes the chief point of difference between them. What a gulf between the Old Comedy, so riotous and so Rabelaisian, and the decorous operettas that would never raise a blush on the cheek of Anthony Trollope's most ladylike heroine. A gulf indeed, but it is the gulf between the two periods. England's awful arbiter of morals, the formidable Queen in her prime, was the audience that counted in Gilbert's day, and it may be stated with certainty that Aristophanes himself would have abjured indecency and obscenity in that presence. Equally certainly if he had lived in the age, for example, of gentility, he would have tempered his vigour, checked his swiftness, moderated his exuberance. Gilbert is an Aristophanes plentifully watered down, a steady and stolid-y, jolly Bank-holiday, every day Aristophanes, a mid-Victorian Aristophanes.

The question is irresistibly suggested, if Gilbert had lived in those free-thinking, free-acting, free-speaking days of Athens, "so different from the home life of our own dear Queen," would he too have needed a Lord High Chamberlain

> to purge his native stage beyond a question
> of "risky" situation and indelicate suggestion.

There are indications that this is a possibility, even a probability, had there not always been before him the fear of that terrible pronunciamento: WE ARE NOT AMUSED.

Notes

1. *The Birds* 462-464. Aristophanes, of course, uses the Athenian equivalent for dinner clothes.
2. *Acharnians* 310-333 (with omissions).
3. Translated by Lawrence Housman 3-7.
4. *Thesmophoriazusae* 3-21.
5. *Birds,* 904 ff—except first four lines, not in original metre, which varies from line to line as English metre does not.
6. *Thesmophoriazusae.* 29-156 (with omissions).
7. In the original every line of this speech rhymes with all the others, one of the extremely few examples of the use of rhyme in Greek.
8. *Knights* 3-29 (with omissions).
9. *Plutus* 901 ff.
10. *Knights* 149-190 (with omissions).
11. *Thesmophoriazusae* 785 ff.

Isaac Goldberg

W. S. Gilbert's Topsy-Turvydom

(1928)

Almost seventeen years have passed since Sir William S. Gilbert sank to his death in the private lake of his own designing, on his famous estate, Grim's Dyke. True to the pantomimic traditions of his beginnings, he died like a Harlequin in a gallant attempt to rescue Columbine from drowning. His young guest was saved; himself, already an aged man, who had been cautioned by his physician to avoid swimming in cold water, succumbed not to drowning but to syncope. As the inquest showed, no water was found in his lungs; he was strong for a man of seventy-four, but his heart was unequal to the sudden task imposed upon it. It was a romantic end for one of the most realistic, yet most fanciful, of the late Victorians. It crowned the paradox that was his life.

There is more than one reason why Gilbert, at this

late date, should be of fresh interest to an age that has managed to invert the dictum of Peacock about his fellow Englishmen. They took their pleasures sadly; today, on the surface at any rate, we take even our sorrows with a certain not-too-innocent merriment. Gilbert, who may have been much of a puzzle to himself, was not easily classified. Most of what he wrote, and even more of what he thought, has disappeared forever into the limbo of outmoded things. Although he was occasionally sharper in self-criticism than was Sullivan, he could be notoriously wrong about his aims and his achievements to the point of stubborn humorlessness. There is something in Gilbert, in fact—and this holds true of him far more than it does of his gentle and charming collaborator—that carries him as a temperament, as a personality, straight into the complex life of our own twentieth century. On the one hand he looks back toward a simpler day,—toward the candles and gaslight and gigs and crinoline of the period in which he was born; on the other, there is a distinct, an unresolved conflict in his living that allies him to the hectic Freudianism and Watsonism of this tense, hypersophisticated era. It is an old question, recently revived, whether that entity which we know as Gilbert-and-Sullivan owes more to its first component or its second. It provides an excellent arena for academic discussion; on the whole, it is like debating the superiority of hydrogen to oxygen, when what one wants for one's thirst is—strangely—water.

Gilbert the Tory resented, surely, the double subserviency to which, as a British subject, he fell heir: the political ascendancy of the bourgeois, the fashionable rulership of womankind. Perhaps it would be too much to call him a rebel; he was an Englishman, after all. He attacked individual foibles rather than sociological error. This is so true, indeed, that even in his political burlesques and satires it is usually the person, not the institution, at which he aims. Had Gilbert and Sullivan centered their wit and humor upon social rather than personal targets, it is hardly probable that we should be listening to them today with an enthusiasm that recalls the frenzies of their first successes. The institution passes; the individual foible remains, making us the eternally fit laughter of the gods.

Homer had seven birthplaces; Gilbert was born in only two. Almost fifty years ago, the irrepressible Kate Field, hunter—and occasionally tamer—of literary lions, writing of Gilbert at the height of the craze for "Pinafore" in this country, spoke rather cryptically of his birth in Somersetshire. Thence, according to her account, he was "speedily brought to London, and then taken by his parents to Germany and Italy." According to his official biographers, however, Gilbert was born in the Strand, London, "in the house of his mother's doctor." Again a cryptic circumlocution. Why? The house of his mother's doctor was the house of his mother's father, who was a doctor. William Gilbert, father of the future librettist, had married Anne, second daughter of Dr. Thomas Morris, on February 14th of the same year—1836—in which their first and only son was born, on November 18th.

It is impossible to appreciate fully the son without at least a descriptive knowledge of the father. For the original map of Topsy-turvydom was outlined in the brain of the crotchety Gilbert père. Literary precursors are easy to discover; the Gilbertian librettos have more than one. There is, among the ancients, Aristophanes; fifteen years ago Mr. Sichel, writing in the *Fortnightly Review*, drew upon himself rather too much ridicule for having ventured to institute a comparison between Sir William and the Greek. And only this October, Miss Hamilton, in the *Theatre Arts Monthly*, returns unabashed to the theme. Shakespeare's Gonzalo, in "The Tempest," has a speech that seems to have been the model of an oft-quoted song from "The Gondoliers." "I the commonwealth," promises Gonzalo, "I would by contraries execute all things." But Gilbert is full of Shakespearian suggestions, and I should not be surprised to learn that his theory of comic acting, so well interpolated into his parody of "Hamlet" ("Rosencrantz and Guildenstern") derived in appreciable measure from the example of "A Midsummer Night's Dream." Again, and less probably, there is the suggestion of the theatrical writings of Richard Brome; Brome, active in the first half of the seventeenth century, is not important enough to figure in all the histories of English letters, but he has his place in the history of the Ballad Opera, and the curious will examine his "Antipodes" and "Jovial Crew" with something more than pedantic interest. "The Beggar's Opera," of course, is an acknowledged ancestor, ragged, uncouth, vulgar, of The Savoy Theatre; a close examination of its text—which, after two hundred years, holds its own against Gilbert's excessive refinements—reveals more than one line, more than one situation, that the Victorian must have remembered.

It would be easy, then, to show that much of what has passed for pure Gilbertianism, whether in the theory of comic acting, the practise of production, or the creative attitude, has plentiful precedent in England and on the continent. Yet, just as the Gilbertian theory of comic acting, despite all the sources that may be adduced from without, was founded essentially upon analogous traits in his own nature, so his Topsy-turvydom derives chiefly from himself and that part of himself which he owed to his father.

The elder Gilbert was, in his own way, a polygraph. After having retired from service as a navy doctor to live, at an early age, in literary leisure, he wrote a steady succession of plays, translations, novels, essays in political administration and tracts upon religious activities. He had the patriarchal temper, a phenomenon that antedates by many centuries the Victorian choler of the dominant, yet dominated, male. He wrote, with suspiciously uncanny discernment, of those who wavered on the tenuous line between sanity and lunacy. The accepted notion, fostered by Gilbert junior and too readily accepted by his commentators, has been that the father was encouraged to write by the success of his son. Perhaps he may have been encouraged to continue at writing; certainly he had published a number of things before his son became the talk of London for his clever take-offs on current plays in the weekly, *Fun,* and for the imperishable nonsense of the ballads that were first to be published as a book in 1869.

"Bab" was the signature of young Gilbert's drawings long before it became identified with his metrical merriment. And "Bab," among his Pooh-Bah activities as contributor to *Fun,* purveyor of burlesque to the London theaters, and town wit, found time to illustrate some books that his father had written for children. Certainly when he came to write "Pinafore" he did not forget his father's nightmare of adventures, "The King's Middy." The influence is much greater, however. For the elder Gilbert went about with a head populated by fairies and elixirs of love, by necromancers, wicked barons, orphans and morals. His "Memoirs of a Cynic" in time finds translation, by his son, into a series of satiric comic operettas; the pious ladies of "Facta Non Verba," by a lawless law of Topsy-turvydom are with a wave of the wand converted into a fairy chorus; "Contrasts," a political tract, by a magnificent whimsey may spring to exotic life in "The Mikado." These are not set down as literary sources; they represent the tricksy variations of themes as filtered through temperaments at once so similar and so unlike. To read through the masto- donic, three-story novels of the elder Gilbert, with their magic and madness; to labor through his tracts and theses; to plow through the childish didacticism of "The Magic Mirror" (1866) and "The King's Middy" (1869), is to understand the influences in which Gilbert as a child was reared. His father was, on this plentiful evidence, an anti- nomian spirit, an irascible stepchild of the moon; and Gilbert was the son of his father.

There were four sisters; as the only son of a masculine ruler, as the masculine elder of four females of the species, young Gilbert may easily have grown into the domineering type that he soon became at school, and, later, in life. A year after his birth a woman was on the throne. To the rule of the bourgeois was added the rule of the petticoat. King George was dead, and with him the prerogatives of the male in society; long live Queen Victoria.

No doubt it is to feed fat an ancient grudge; in any case, often, as I have sat before one of the Savoy operettas, with their recurrent types of the all-too fleshy, all-too un- married, predacious female, I have thought that I could see a malicious reference to the Queen. It is more certain that Gilbert everywhere populates his scene; not only as a Jack Point, in "The Yeomen of the Guard," with his auto- biographical whimsey; or a King Gama, in "Princess Ida," with his eyewinking confession of surliness, but under the wig of a Lord Chancellor, behind the uniform of a Private, before the hump of a Dick Deadeye. Gilbert's works, in- deed, are like a hall of mirrors—trick mirrors that work every distortion—along which he passes with an antic gait, delighted not least with the mirrors on the ceiling. Topsy- turvy? Yes and No. As when one inverts the figure eight; or turns upside down an hour-glass.

It is in his attiude toward the sweet young thing and her Gorgon elder sister that Gilbert is most self-revealingly interesting. He had a Yum-Yum complex and a Katisha-phobia. The man who hated Katisha bowed nevertheless to the rules that she, as chaperone, laid down for Yum-Yum. Not that he loved old age the less, but that he loved youth the more. At his own parties it was fairly an established convention that the men, after dinner, should withdraw and leave him the only Adam in a garden of Eves. His dancing fairies had living prototypes, as did his scowling dames. Gilbert's jibes at marriage, in his writings, do not go beyond the tradtional wit of mankind against the custom.

> Bridegroom and bride!
>   Knot that's insoluble,
>   Voices all voluble
> Hail it with pride.
> Bridegroom and bride!
>   Hail it with merriment;
>   It's an experiment
> Frequently tried.

That, from "The Gondoliers," is a typically Gilbertian wedding hymn, blown up by the breath of ecstasy and pricked, in the last two lines, by the needle of wit. In private, the librettist could not offer a young lady his congratulations upon her marriage without at the same time intimating that she was a fool. Marriage was an institution that might create beautiful young things, but they themselves—as long as they were not inmates of Princess Ida's Castle Adamant—should eschew it. Though he took a wife at thirty-one—Lady Gilbert is still happily alive and alert

—there was no issue; as daughter he adopted Miss Nancy McIntosh, who, at his insistence, was allowed to create the chief feminine rôle (Princess Zara) in "Utopia, Limited." His plays in prose and verse are studded with sentimental speeches glorifying the power of woman's purity; as early as 1873, a year before Hardy's troubles with "Far from the Madding Crowd," and more than twenty before "Jude the Obscure," he is the victim of Mrs. Grundy because, in "Charity" he dared to defend the "fallen" woman. His devil, in "Gretchen," is wiser than the puritans:

> Why, there's no harm in women.
> I didn't make them! They're my deadliest foe!
> Why, he who of his own unfettered will
> Cuts himself off from pure communion
> With blameless womanhood, withdraws himself
> From a holier influence than he finds
> Within these sad and silent solitudes.

And this is the selfsame Gilbert who, at other times, could envisage love itself with a realistic scrutiny that makes his operettas conspicuous for their lack of passion. His fondness for, his belief in, his defense of, the "young lady in the dress circle" (the Victorian symbol of a clean audience for clean plays), like all exaggerated purity, had an undoubted element of lust in it. What he did not express to his prunes-and-prism *puellae* he wreaked upon the heads of his over-ripe maidens. If convention or personality forbade him to make real love to—and for—his virgins, he could openly hate his viragos. Gilbert, who showed us what the Victorian darling looked like, told us also what she thought. And she did not think what she looked like.

He threw the truths at the faces of his older women; he drew them from the lips of his lasses. So doing, in either case he achieved a genuine victory over Victorian reticence.

Early in his career, indeed, he is accused of vulgarity and blasphemy. An innocent little piece written for the German Reeds and their audience of church-goers who would have been scared away from the Gallery of Illustration had it been called a theater, worried some critics with its questionable decency. In this piece, by the way, entitled "A Sensation Novel," Gilbert more than fifty years ago toyed with a technique that we should now label Pirandellian. The characters of an unfinished novel come to life out of the manuscript and begin a discussion of their existences in the book as contrasted with their desires and aims outside of it. It is a typically Gilbertian motif; the man was fascinated by the problems of contending selves and was himself the prototype of the many that he placed upon his scene.

Most amusing of the contemporary accusations against a pair who came almost to boast of their purity as purveyors of pleasure to London is a little-known attack—it amounts to no less—by none other than Mr. Dodgson, who as Lewis Carroll had an especial affection for children. Dodgson, it should be recalled, had several times broached to Sullivan the musical setting of "Alice in Wonderland." This was when the triumvirate of D'Oyly Carte, Gilbert and Sullivan was just getting under way; shortly "The Sorcerer," first production of the newly formed Comedy Opera Company, was to make its historic debut at the Opera Comique. No sooner had the operetta of the love-elixir been given than Sullivan was chided by the critic of the *Musical Standard* for having put his talents to low uses and Gilbert condemned for having made "the earnest, hard-working and serious clergy" the subject of "sneering caricature." But the final stroke was left for Dodgson, who, eleven years later, revived the censure of "The Sorcerer" on the occasion of the children's performance of "Pinafore." "Mr. Gilbert," wrote Dodgson in *The Theatre,* under the title "The Stage and The Spirit of Reverence," "seems to have a craze for making bishops and clergymen contemptible." (The early aspirant to the ministry, who found in his tales for children a relief from the rigors of theology and mathematics alike, remained the churchman.) "Yet are they behind other professions in such things as earnestness, and hard work, and devotion of life to the call of duty? That clever song, 'The Pale Young Curate,' with its charming music, is to me simply painful. I seem to see him as he goes home by night, pale and worn with the day's work, perhaps sick with the pestilent atmosphere of a noisome garret where, at the risk of his life, he has been comforting a dying man—and is your sense of humor, my reader, so keen that you can *laugh* at this man? Then at least be consistent! Laugh also at the pale young doctor, whom you have summoned in such hot haste to your own child; ay, and laugh also at that pale young soldier, as he sinks on the trampled battle-field, and reddens the dust with his life-blood for the honor of Old England!" Was the creator of the immortal Alice chiding Gilbert or trying to rival him?

Against the children's "Pinafore" he grew even more eloquent, and humorless. One passage "was to me sad beyond words. It occurs when the captain utters the oath 'Damn me' and forthwith a bevy of sweet innocent looking girls sing, with bright and happy looks, the chorus, 'He said Damn me! He said Damn me!' I cannot find words to convey to the reader the pain I felt in seeing those dear children taught to utter such words to amuse ears grown callous to their ghastly meaning. Put the two ideas side by side—Hell (no matter whether *you* believe it or not; millions do:) and those pure young lips thus sporting with its horrors—and then find what *fun* in it you can! How Mr. Gilbert could have stooped to write, or Sir Arthur Sullivan could have prostituted his noble art to set to music, such vile trash, it passes my skill to understand." Evidently, though "Bother it!" Mr. Dodgson might occasionally say, he never (No, never!) used a big big D---.

A Victorian, then, Mr. Gilbert may have been; but not a good, certainly not a representative one. There was not a virtue on which he prided himself that was not, in his own hey-day, contested. "New and original" was a favorite description of his for his own work, yet more than once he was accused of plagiarism. He was a litigious fellow and was often in court; nor was he always victorious. As he helped to make the career of more than one actress, so he was accused—and not entirely without justice—of arbitrarily obstructing the career of others, from purely personal motives. Old files of contemporary magazines reveal the story in full detail. Today, it is curious rather than anything else that he could have been accused of stealing the plot of "Engaged" (that most cynical of farces) from an unpublished manuscript by one William Muskerry; of purloining "The Gondoliers"; of lifting a goodly portion of "The Mikado" from Morton's "Our Wife, or The Rose of Amiens." His plots, his themes, after all, were in his own nature.

That nature—capable alike of old-fashioned, sentimental, still-born productions in prose and verse, and the vitality of the farces, the ballads, and the librettos—is peculiarly modern in its unrest, its sense of psychological plurality, its artistic unemotionalism. Beyond a doubt he was original in both the French sense and the English. As a stage manager he ruled with such an iron hand, he impressed the values of his text so deeply upon his actors, that to this day he dominates from the grave. His books of the opera have become, for the old guard, a sacred text that must not be tampered with even to the disturbance of a comma. Once upon a time, before the full story of the disagreement with Sullivan was known, he was considered as the sole culprit in a silly dispute over a carpet. Today it appears that he knew, better than Sullivan, his own limitations, and that, even as a commercial gentleman, he was wiser at times than D'Oyly Carte. In the matter of the Royal English Opera House and Sullivan's serious opera, "Ivanhoe," he was clearly more sure of sight than either of his partners.

He hated gush. He turned his sterner face toward the world. But when his Fairy Queen sang, she sang for him, too:

> Oh, amorous dove!
>   Type of Ovidius Naso!
>   *This heart of mine*
>   *Is soft as thine,*
>   *Although I dare not say so!*

The italics are mine; I am sure that they were Gilbert's, as well.

Henry Ten Eyck Perry

The Victorianism
of W. S. Gilbert

(1928)

It may seem odd to think of W. S. Gilbert as an important representative of Victorianism. He is not in the same class with Tennyson and Browning, granted; for he is not a poet at all, only a versifier. Still, his gifts of light satire and playful humor have given him a popularity at the present day at least as great as theirs, and he is of equal importance as an index of the spirit of his age. Tennyson and Browning took their Victorianism seriously; Gilbert did not openly attack contemporary civilization, like Samuel Butler, but he treated it more gaily than the great poets did. He was able to make mild fun of its shortcomings in adroit paradoxes and sly understatements at the same time that, with delightful whimsicality, he glorified its major premises. The lines that fall from the lips of his characters cannot safely be taken as literal expressions of his own point of view; but the bewildering variety of Gilbert's comic inventiveness does not obscure the fact that his basic ideas were those of a conservative Victorian.

Literature in the Victorian age was fundamentally conservative, and why should it not have been? Things were going well for England in the days of the great Queen. The Empire was being extended in all quarters of the globe; Canada, Australia, Africa, and India were rapidly growing in importance. There were no foreign wars of the magnitude of the Napoleonic conflicts, for the Crimean episode can hardly be considered more than a minor operation. The Reform Bills of 1867 and 1884 were hastening the advance of democratic government. Factories were increasing, and industrial prosperity followed in their wake. The invention of steamboats, railroads, and the telegraph was making travel and communication more easy. Education was growing by leaps and bounds; the spirit of religious toleration was abroad in the land. On the whole there seemed little cause for unrest or uneasiness as to the way the world was wagging.

Under the surface, to be sure, there were disquieting symptoms, apparent to the more thoughtful. Imperialism, Democracy, and Industrialism have their dangers, but these were not obvious in the first flush of success. The average Englishman, like the hero of *Locksley Hall,* may have felt some vague stirrings of distrust, but he was willing to quiet them for the sake of the bright hopes held out by the next "fifty years of Europe." W. S. Gilbert was such a person. He saw the absurdities, if not the perils, of much in the Victorian régime, but he was content to accept life as it was going on about him on its own terms. He valued British institutions for the good that they were achieving and criticized only their less significant features;

his adverse criticism is of the limited kind permitted by Englishmen to Englishmen, not to outsiders.

His treatment of the British navy is a case in point. The navy was England's greatest asset and, as such, must be properly respected. Gilbert permitted himself to laugh at the eccentricities of the First Lord of the Admiralty, who polished up the handle of the big front door so carefully that now he's the Ruler of the Queen's Navee. Sir Joseph Porter stuck close to his desk and never went to sea until he got his present office, so that he is quite unfitted for the position. But does the navy suffer on that account? Certainly not. Those in high place may be inefficient, but the back-bone of the service sees to it that all goes well. The captain of the *Pinafore* is a right good captain; he can manage his ship skilfully, and he is never known to quail at the fury of a gale. He is slightly ridiculed for his excessive politeness, but the gallant hero, a common seaman, escapes completely unharmed by criticism. This ideal young man delights in frequent proud boasts as to his nationality and profession: "A British tar is a soaring soul." "Josephine, I am a British sailor, and I love you," "I am an Englishman—behold me." Breathes there an Englishman with soul so dead who does not see in the disparagement of other nationalities, from Roosian to Itali-an, an indirect appeal to patriotic fervor?

Gilbert's pride in the British navy is reflected in his attitude towards the Queen under whose auspices it fought. The final triumph of the police over the Pirates of Penzance is effected in the name of loyalty and allegiance. Charged to yield in Queen Victoria's name, the Pirate King is baffled and succumbs, "because, with all our faults, we love our Queen," a triumph for the most personal kind of Victorianism. Then that the patriotism of the regular army may not be outdone by that of outlaws from justice, the pirates are revealed as noblemen who have gone wrong, which brings tears to the eyes of the very model of a modern major-general, "because, with all our faults, we love our House of Peers." Gilbert himself loves the whole structure of English society, with all its faults, just this side idolatry.

Its weaknesses were evident to him too, particularly those of the House of Peers, as he shows very clearly in *Iolanthe*. This opera, one of the very best of the librettos, contains his most outspoken criticism of those "paragons of legislation, pillars of the British nation." Lord Mounta-rarat sings of their lack of intellectual eminence in good Queen Bess's time and their doing nothing in particular when Wellington thrashed Bonaparte. In Victoria's reign they were no more able and with the rise of democracy, less important. When the fairies arrange that the peerage is to be thrown open to Competitive Examination and so recruited from persons of intelligence, the question is, "What's to become of the House of Commons?" The House of Peers has been a decorative luxury in the past, but when intellectualized it will cease to have an independent existence. Under the new order it will coalesce with the lower house, so that the present lords may fly away to Fairyland, unnoticed and unmourned. The House of Peers is an institution "not susceptible of any improvement at all," a state of affairs which reduces it to a nonentity and at the same time softens the satire directed against it. In this way the topsy-turvydom of *Iolanthe* becomes a perfectly innocuous, if utterly charming, realm.

One of its inhabitants, the Lord Chancellor, embodies Gilbert's view of another pillar of the British nation, the law. It is not subjected to such a harsh attack as it has received from many another satirist; for the Lord Chancellor merely insists with absurd pomposity that "the Law is the true embodiment of everything that's excellent" and lays his own rise in the profession to a rigorous prosecution of duty. He admits that he is working on a new and original plan in feeling that professional license has been carried too far, but the result has justified his honesty. The weakness of the law, according to Gilbert, lies in the conflict which its machine-like nature causes with the ordinary humanity of its practitioners. The Lord Chancellor is chiefly occupied with his function as guardian of the young wards in Chancery, and as he is a highly susceptible Chancellor, he finds the dictates of his heart interfering with the impartial administration of justice. He is never so inconsistent as the Judge in *Trial by Jury,* who dissolves the breach of promise suit that he is trying by marrying the Plaintiff himself, an act which may call his legal judgeship into question but indisputably proves that of beauty he's a judge—"and a good judge too."

Trial by Jury is a significant document in Gilbert's treatment of sex; the casual way in which the Judge succumbs to the charms of the Plaintiff suggests not only a carelessness as to the sanctity of law, but also a lack of violent physical attraction on either side. One need not take this lack too seriously, as the comic opera tradition demands a general pairing off of all the characters at the final curtain. Still there is an indication throughout Gilbert's work that he did not consider the relation between the sexes as a vital matter. His most pronounced views on the subject are to be found in the *Princess Ida,* an operatic per-version of Tennyson's poem on woman's position in the Victorian scheme of things. The Laureate had made the error of conceiving female celibacy a necessary adjunct of female education, and by doing so he had reduced Ida's ideal experiment to the absurd. Gilbert, with his keen perception of the ridiculous, at once saw the comic possibilities of the theme and made the most of them. For women to forswear the society of men seemed to Tennyson wrong and to Gilbert absurd, but both writers were agreed upon the unnaturalness of Ida's program. The God of Things as They Are rules Gilbert's world to such an extent that virginity was abhorrent to him and marriage a good in itself. Even love, though not so good as marriage, was a means to that desirable end and was to be tolerated or condescendingly approved.

Love must be upheld because it leads to marriage and children and the home, dearest of Victorian institutions; love as a spiritual factor in life is beyond Gilbert's ken, and the same holds true of his attitude towards beauty, art, and poetry. He is well within his rights in satirizing Reginald Bunthorne in *Patience,* for the insincerity of pseudo-aestheticism makes it an easy target. What Gilbert did not appreciate was the reality which Bunthorne was imitating when he altered his model from mediaevalism to pastoral simplicity. The idyllic poet, Archibald Grosvenor, possesses a true feeling for the arts, but he is ridiculed for his approach to perfection. Patience can only love the fallible, so that the solution for Grosvenor is to become common-place. The idyllic poet is certainly superior to the sham poet, but the idyllic poet must yield to the ordinary man. Grosvenor might be said to represent Gilbert's version of the Victorian Laureate; Tennyson had within him the potentialities of a great poet, but in adapting himself to his age he submerged his imagination and he won his Queen. Grosvenor in like manner won his Patience, and Gilbert gained his contemporary popularity by calmly accepting the common-place in a day when poetry was no more popular than was the ideal in sex or politics.

Gilbert finds funny those things which do not con-
form to the spirit of his time, and he did not dare the
apparent impiety of suggesting a better world. He never
transcends the limitations of time and space or devotes
any real attention to the relation of man to an unseen
universe. His supernatural beings are of such a gossamer
variety that their power over human affairs is trivial and
superficial, as when the fairies in *Iolanthe* occupy their
energies with reorganizing the already superfluous House
of Peers. In *Thespis; or, The Gods Grown Old,* the first
work on which Gilbert and Sullivan collaborated, the
mortals and immortals appear on something like equal
terms. Here the gods concerned are the Greek divinities,
who give up their rule in favor of a travelling theatrical
troupe. Thespis assures Jupiter that the pristine glory of
the gods is gone—in fact they're behind the times; and
he feels that he can run the world after a much improved
fashion. At the end of the year, however, bad matters
have become worse, and mortals are sending indignant
complaints to protest against the fact that Saturday has
been dropped from the calendar, that grapes yield nothing
but ginger beer, and that war has been abolished. These
rational changes are unpopular, especially the last and
most ideal one, for "now that nations can't fight, no two
of 'em are on speaking terms. The dread of fighting was
the only thing that kept them civil to each other." No
wonder that before Thespis is driven from Olympus he
despairingly sings:

> Now, here you see the arrant folly
> Of doing your best to make things jolly.
> I've ruled the world like a chap in his senses.
> Observe the terrible consequences.

An ideal scheme is similarly ridiculed in *The Sorcerer,* this time in the realm of marriage. Alexis "has made some converts to the principle, that men and women should be coupled in matrimony without distinction of rank," but the aristocracy has held aloof, so that he resorts to black magic to further his plan. Ultimately it recoils upon his own head, and he is the first to wish for a return to original conditions. All ends happily, but Gilbert has shown through the person of Alexis that the natural view of sex is more satisfactory than the transcendental one. There is much common-sense here, and still more in the ridicule of an ideal government in *The Gondoliers.* In Barataria all Departments rank equally, and everybody is at the head of his department. The inconveniences are obvious, and the inevitable logic is expressed in the Grand Inquisitor's well-known song:

> In short, whoever you may be,
> To this conclusion you'll agree,
> When every one is somebodee,
>   Then no one's anybody!

In politics, as in love-making, Gilbert seems to say radical changes are of no avail; whatever is, is right.

He definitely repudiates the philosophic ideal in such a play as *The Palace of Truth,* where a justification of falsehood is implied, and his partial notion of perfection is aptly summed up in the title, *Utopia, Limited.* This piece, written near the end of his partnership with Sullivan, does not contain the creative exuberance of his early work, but in it his creed is not obscured by unessentials. Here the Princess Zara returns to Utopia from England, "the greatest, the most powerful, the wisest country in the world," with "six representatives of the principal causes that have tended to make England the powerful, happy, and blameless country the consensus of European civilization has declared it to be." One of these imported flowers of progress organizes Utopia as a Company Limited, and such prosperity ensues that there is soon no work to be done by doctors, lawyers, or soldiers. The sanitary and legal improvements are epoch-making, and the army and navy are put "upon so irresistible a basis that all the neighbouring nations have disarmed—and War's impossible!" Indeed Utopia seems about to decay of dry rot until Party Government is introduced as a certain panacea, "because one party will assuredly undo all that the other party has done." From this time on, "Utopia will no longer be a Monarchy (Limited), but, what is a great deal better, a Limited Monarchy!"

This apotheosis of an ideal state until it becomes "England—with improvements" is characteristically Gilbertian. It implies that England is not perfect as it is, but that it is progressing on the right track to a heaven upon earth. The absurdities of Victorian existence are only slightly caused by its falling short of what it might be; for the most part they depend upon minor deviations from the established order. To Gilbert, contemporary life appeared on the whole good, so that he could sum up his attitude towards the world by complacently and comfortingly singing,

> And I am right,
> And you are right
> And all is right as right can be!

This view of life has both its strength and its weakness. It is well to be in sympathy with the world about one, but it is dangerous to imagine that complete perfection is just around the corner. The true artist is concerned with the abstractions of Truth and Beauty and cannot be satisfied with earthly, imperfect realizations of his dreams. Complacency is a death-blow to great art, and complacency was the outstanding characteristic of the Victorian age. Gilbert had his share of this quality; it underlies all his literary work. That is why, although his comedies occasionally appeal to the critical faculty, they always leave us with a pleasant feeling of universal well-being. And that is why, delightful as Gilbert's phantasies are, they pale before the works of that author to which they have so often been compared. When Gilbert is termed "a *Victorian* Aristophanes," the much abused adjective takes on a renewed sting.

Arthur Quiller-Couch

W. S. Gilbert

(1929)

I

I had parted, at the Cambridge Post Office, with a young friend of parts who 'deplores' (as he puts it) our whole heritage of English poetry and holds with reason that it ought to make a fresh start. Musing on this assurance of his, on my way to the Botanic Garden, and resigning myself, as my custom, to grieving

> when even the Shade
> Of that which once was great is passed away,

I encountered two long lines of men on opposite sides of the thoroughfare; the one drawing, or seeking to draw, Unemployment Pay; the other taking, or seeking to take, tickets for Gilbert-and-Sullivan Opera.

'Ah, there,' thought I, 'after all, the last enchantment

of the Victorian age has captured you, my lads, and holds you by the Achilles tendon!' For I recognise your faces. You are the same that, the other day, were affecting to despise

> Come down, O maid, from yonder mountain
>   height—

or

> O lyric love, half angel and half bird!

But as soon as it comes to 'Tit-Willow!' or 'The Policeman's lot is not a happy one,' you are held and 'laid by the heel.'

Now I wish to enquire into this and the reason of it; and, believe me, not sardonically. My first introduction to Gilbert-and-Sullivan Opera dates back just fifty years, to an amateur performance of *H.M.S. Pinafore* that enchanted a child. The first play I ever saw in a London theatre was *Patience,* in the course of its first run at the Opéra Comique. As an undergraduate I have taken as much trouble as any of you to listen to *The Sorcerer, Princess Ida, The Mikado;* and my own two favourites, *Iolanthe* and *The Gondoliers,* still conjure up by association all manner of happy memories. I yet can surrender myself (at intervals) to Gilbert-and-Sullivan with an abandon you may ascribe to the natural gaiety of declining years, or to sentimentality—which you will. Let that pass: for, with your leave, the question affects not *me* but *you.* Why do you who expend so much cleverness in deriding the more serious contemporaries of W. S. Gilbert and Arthur Sullivan, yet experimentally confess to this one most typically late-Victorian enthusiasm which binds your spiritual contemporaries with your fathers and grandfathers?

You at any rate will not plead—you, who follow so eagerly all the many experiments of our Festival Theatre in substituting mechanics for drama—that you cling to a tradition of the provinces. That provincial audiences flock to these Operas even as you do; that amateurs throughout England spend their winters in rehearsing one and another of them; that regularly, in the week following Easter, the railways convey down baskets of regulation wigs and costumes from Covent Garden to remote towns and Village Institutes—all this is certain. And I doubt not that the executors and holders of the Gilbert-and-Sullivan copyrights have worked out commercial reasons for feeding the provinces with these Operas while denying them to the Metropolis. But as little do I doubt that, for some while to come, a noble presentation of the whole cycle in London would draw packed houses. This abstention is a mystery to me, but it does affect the argument; the first point of which is that all over England, after forty-odd years, generations of young and intelligent people keep renewing their delight in Gilbert-and-Sullivan Opera.

II

Now this, when we consider how typically late-Victorian these Operas are—how limited in range of idea, even of invention—how much of their quiddity (in *Patience*, for example) belongs to its hour in a past era; may well give us a shock. It might also give me occasion to ask, why some of you, and those not the least intelligent, haunt these Operas, although in clever debate you think it not unseemly to deride Meredith for a mountebank and Tennyson for a maiden aunt?

But I seem to know you too well to believe that in your heart of hearts you cherish any such foolish opinions, at any rate ineradicably, or truly believe Gilbert and Sullivan to be the lone Dioscuri of our late-Victorian night. Let us start on the plain common ground that, after forty years or so, their work continues to delight young and old, and try to account for it.

III

The appeal of Music being, by virtue of its indefiniteness, so much more elusive of date than the spoken or written word, and especially if the subject be at all 'topical,' shall we hold that Gilbert survives mainly through Sullivan's music? Vaguely we may feel Sullivan's melody to be as Victorian as are Gilbert's plots and tricks and whole theatrical concept; but these, having to be framed in words and on lines of logic—and topsy-turvy logic is yet logic and the basis of Gilbert's wit—can be brought to tests which music airily eludes. They are written in words and can be attacked in words; and must continue to suffer this comparative disadvantage until critics of music find a method of expressing their likes and dislikes by musical notation.

But no; this explanation will not serve. For Gilbert, very much of his period and exposed to all the perils which must beset any man who would attract a theatrical audience by wit and song, was yet (if you will search his libretti) extremely wary of topical allusions that might date him. In *Patience,* to be sure (one of his earliest), he shot at, and winged, a passing mode. But excepting a passing allusion to the late Captain Shaw of London's Fire Brigade and a somewhat pointed one in *Utopia, Limited* to the light refreshment provided for débutantes at Queen Victoria's Drawing-Rooms, you will seek his work in vain for topical references. To be sure, in *H.M.S. Pinafore* (his earliest success) he poked obvious fun at Mr. W. H. Smith, First Lord of the Admiralty: but there exists a most illuminating letter of his in which he hopes he has removed all suspicion of personal offence by indicating that the victim was a Liberal!—a letter which should be a *locus classicus* for research into the ultimate obtuseness of wit. Dealing with his times as he knew them, he could not of course foresee that events would in time blunt the application of one of his neatest shafts—the Sentry's song in *Iolanthe*. But I think we may agree that in this slow-moving country of ours Gilbert's raillery has worn as well as the absurd institutions against which he not too seriously aimed at. They are accustomed to that sort of thing, and have allowed him to wear just as well as they have worn.

I suggest that if you mark and note this avoidance of topical allusion in Gilbert, you will come to the conclusion with me that the man considered himself as one writing for posterity, as carefully at least as Horace Walpole did in composing his familiar letters to Horace Mann. But on this point I shall presently have more evidence to bring. For the moment let his forty-odd years' success stand for presumptive evidence that—Sullivan apart—Gilbert wrote with intent to last.

This intention apart, it were unjust to hold that Gilbert lives by the grace of Sullivan. Offenbach's music was as tunable as Sullivan's and belonged to its age as closely. But Offenbach lacked good librettists, and for this reason you do not stand in long files to buy tickets for Offenbach. You may say that you do not for the more obvious reason that his Operas are never presented in England now-a-days; but the true reason, if you search for it, is that Offenbach never found his Poet, his twin mind. Now Gilbert and Sullivan both lived by the grace of both. Habitually, in actual practice, Gilbert wrote first, plot and lyric, and Sullivan followed; which is the only right order in the making of an Opera, and was convincingly the right order in the making of these men's Operas. For the contribution which Sullivan brought was not only his genius for melody, nor a wit that jumped with Gilbert's, nor a separate and musical wit which revelled in parody. Priceless as these gifts undoubtedly were, above them all (I think) we must reckon the quite marvellous sense of *words* in all his musical settings. You may examine number after number of his, and the more closely you examine the more will you be convinced that no composer ever lived with an exacter appreciation of words, their meaning, their due emphasis, their right articulation. A singer must be a fool indeed if you do not hear through Sullivan's notes the exact language of any song. Take, for example, the well-known Sentry song in *Iolanthe* and attempt to unwed the wit of the air from the wit of the thought and words; or take the Lord Chancellor's song in the same play—

> The law is the true embodiment
> Of everything that's excellent,
> It has no kind of fault or flaw—
> And I, my Lords, embody the law.

and note how Sullivan subdues the air to something almost commonplace and almost silly, but just so as to bring out the intention of demure absurdity, with allowance for every syllable and room for the gesture in the fourth line. Yet should you think he is subduing himself to anything but his artistry, turn to the great duet in *The Sorcerer,* or to the robust Handelian burlesque that winds up 'He remains an Englishman' in *H.M.S. Pinafore,* and mark how riotously his own wit takes charge when Gilbert's gives it the rein.

IV

Gilbert had the advantage of setting the themes and dominating the stage-management of the Operas. But before we call his the master-spirit (which by no means implies that it was the more valuable) in the combination, let us take a little evidence from the actors and singers they commanded. Remind yourselves that these two men, when they started the old Opéra Comique, off the Strand, had to work with the cheapest material. The 'brassiness' of the orchestra during the first run of *Pinafore*—the combined incompetence in *Patience* of the vocalists as actors and of the actors as vocalists—would be incredible today even if faithfully reproduced to eye and ear. In that first run of *Patience* one or two of the cast could act a little, one or two could sing a little; Miss Rosina Brandram alone, asserting that there would be too much of her in the coming by-and-by, could do both.

But these two men, combining upon an idea, turned even shortness of means to their service. They found themselves in the position long and vainly required by a neighbour of mine, a great gardener—'I want an intelligent fellow ready to plant a cabbage upside down without questioning.' Having at first a stage so inexpensive, a cast which had to listen and obey, they imposed their idea, or ideas, with a tyranny to which countless anecdotes bear witness.

The most of these anecdotes are of Gilbert: but Sullivan, if less irascible in rehearsal, appears to have been almost as ruthless. Here is the musical procedure, as related by George Grossmith—who knew it if any man did:

> The music is always learned first. The choruses, finales etc., are composed first in order; then the quartets, the trios; the songs last. Sometimes, owing to changes and re-writing, these are given out to the singers very late (so late that the singer sometimes found less difficulty in learning the new tune than in unlearning the old one). The greatest interest is evinced by all as the new vocal numbers arrive. . . . Sullivan will come suddenly, a batch of MS under his arm, and announce that there is something new. He plays over the new number—the vocal parts only are written. The conductor listens and watches and, after hearing them played over a few times, contrives to pick up all the harmonies, casual accompaniments etc. Sullivan is always strict in wishing that his music shall be sung exactly as he has written it. One of the leading performers was singing an air at rehearsal, not exactly dividing the notes as they were written, giving the general form as it were. 'Bravo!', said Sullivan, 'that is really a very good air of yours. Now, if you have no objection, I will ask you to sing mine.'

But the little finger of Gilbert at rehearsal would be thicker than Sullivan's loins. He kept at home a small model stage, made to scale, and a box or boxes of tiny bricks varying in height and colour. These he would group and re-group in endless patient stage-management until satisfied just where and just how at any given moment any actor should be standing. Then he would come to the theatre and, moving everybody about as on a chessboard, start to bully them into speaking to his exact wish. To quote Grossmith again:

> The music rehearsals are child's play in comparison with the stage rehearsals. Mr. Gilbert is a perfect autocrat, insisting that his words shall be delivered, even to an inflexion of the voice, as he dictates. He will stand on the stage and repeat the words, with appropriate action, over and over again until they are delivered as he desires.

Add that Gilbert, on top of a detestable temper, had a tongue like a whip-lash: and—well, you see, as any of you who wish to be artists must learn in some way, sooner or later, that there is not only a pleasure in poetic pains but a tax upon human pains for poetic pleasure.

V

Now, if I have established that Gilbert's is a dominant, even tyrannical brain in these plays which you find so delightful, let us go on to deal with them a little after the manner of Aristotle. Obviously they obey Aristotle in preferring plot to character, even though by inversion: for, his plots being always legal rather than moral in their topsy-turviness (Gilbert, you know, was a barrister and made his first success as a playwright in *Trial by Jury*), his characters behave always on a topsy-turvy legal logic—

a logic as mad as Lewis Carroll's or madder; they transfer their affections, or reverse their destinies, by insane rational process—

> Quiet calm deliberation*
> Disentangles every knot.

A captain in the Royal Navy turns out to have been changed at birth with a common seaman: it follows that, the revelation made, they change places and stations. A promising lad has, by a lapse of terminological exactitude, been apprenticed to a pirate instead of to a pilot; a love-philtre works the wrong way (as it did in *A Midsummer-Night's Dream*); a drummer ascends the throne of Barataria on the affidavit of a foster-mother in eight lines of *recitative*.

Within these limits of absurdity you will notice that all the Operas have limits also in ethic, and are built on an almost rigid convention of design. There is usually an opposition of the Victorian real against the fanciful: of a House of Peers, for example, in robes, against a chorus of fairies under Westminster clock-tower: of a body of Heavy Dragoons against Bunthorne and his lackadaisy maidens. There is almost always a baritone singer, more or less unconnected with the story, introduced with some sort of patter-song—the First Lord's song in *Pinafore* (which, by the way, started its success), the Major-General's in *The Pirates*, the Lord Chancellor's in *Iolanthe*, the Grand Inquisitor's in *The Gondoliers*, and so on. There is also a lady with a contralto voice, who deplores her mature years. The more you examine the Operas to compare

* Quiller-Couch writes "peaceful contemplation" for "calm deliberation."—Ed.

them, the closer you will get to a severe and narrow model. And the model in its ethical content is no less straitly laced. It invites you to laugh at the foibles of kings, soldiers, lawyers, artists, and faddists of all sorts. But it touches no universal emotion, no universal instinct even (such as conviviality). Still less does it allow us to think of the base on which Society is built, or admit a thought on it to intrude in any way upon our tom-fooling. We all belong to the upper or upper middle class, or to the class which apes these two. We are all conscious of class distinctions, are a little too consciously snobbish even while we enjoy the exposure of snobbery. The general moral, in fact, is that of the song which he characteristically entitled *King Goodheart*:

> There lived a King, as I've been told,
> In the wonder-working days of old,
> When hearts were twice as good as gold
>   And twenty times as mellow.
> Good temper triumphed in his face,
> And in his heart he found a place
> For all the erring human race
>   And every wretched fellow.
> When he had Rhenish wine to drink
> It made him very sad to think
> That some, at junket or at jink,
>   Must be content with toddy:
> He wished all men as rich as he
> (And he was rich as rich could be),
> So to the top of every tree
>   Promoted everybody. . . .
>
> That King, although no one denies,
> His heart was of abnormal size,
> Yet he'd have acted otherwise
>   If he had been acuter.

The end is easily foretold,
When every blessed thing you hold
Is made of silver, or of gold,
　　You long for simple pewter.
When you have nothing else to wear
But cloth of gold and satins rare,
For cloth of gold you cease to care—
　　Up goes the price of shoddy:
In short, whoever you may be,
To this conclusion you'll agree,
When every one is somebody,
　　Then no one's anybody!

VI

That, you may say, is all very well—or would be well
enough if Gilbert could be cleared as a writer who genuinely sympathised with some things, or with one class, and
just happened not to sympathise with others. That is common enough with authors, and especially with comedians
and writers of light verse. Their business being to apply
the touch of common sense to human affairs, one may even
allow a certain hardness to be a part of their outfit [I am
ungrateful enough even to find a certain hardness of surface in that favourite of us all, C. S. Calverley]. But Gilbert had a baddish streak or two in him; and one in particular which was not only baddish but so thoroughly cad-
dish that no critic can ignore or, in my belief, extenuate
it. The man, to summarize, was essentially cruel, and delighted in cruelty. I lay no heavy stress on his addiction—
already glanced at—to finding fun in every form of torture
and capital punishment. This indeed persists in his work
from *The Bab Ballads* right through the plays:

Oh! listen to the tale of little Annie Protheroe;
She kept a small post-office in the neighbourhood
    of Bow,
She loved a skilled mechanic, who was famous in
    his day—
A gentle executioner whose name was Gilbert Clay.

I think I hear you say, 'A dreadful subject for your
    rhymes!'
O reader, do not shrink—he didn't live in modern
    times!
He lived so long ago (the sketch will show it at a
    glance)
That all his actions glitter with the limelight of
    Romance.

In busy times he laboured at his gentle craft all
    day—
'No doubt you mean his Cal-craft' you amusingly
    will say—
But, no—he didn't operate with common bits of
    string,
He was a Public Headsman, which is quite another
    thing.

And when his work was over, they would ramble
    o'er the lea,
And sit beneath the frondage of an elderberry
    tree;
And ANNIE's simple prattle entertained him on
    his walk,
For public executions formed the subject of her
    talk.

And sometimes he'd explain to her, which charmed
    her very much,

How famous operators vary very much in touch,
And then, perhaps, he'd show how he himself
        performed the trick,
And illustrate his meaning with a poppy and a
        stick.

It persists (I repeat) through *The Bab Ballads* and into
play after play; until, if you are tired and seek a *terminus
ad quem,* I suggest this, from *The Mikado,* where an
artless maiden sings:

He shivered and shook as he gave the sign
    For the stroke he didn't deserve;
When all of a sudden his eye met mine,
    And it seemed to brace his nerve.
For he nodded his head and kissed his hand,
    And he whistled an air did he,
        As the sabre true
        Cut cleanly through
    His cervical vertebrae!
        When a man's afraid
        A beautiful maid
    Is a cheering * sight to see.
        And it's O, I'm glad
        That moment sad
    Was soothed by sight of me!

Or—

To sit in solemn silence, in a dull dark dock,
In a pestilential prison, with a life-long lock,
Awaiting the sensation of a short, sharp shock
From a cheap and chippy chopper on a big black
        block.

* Quiller-Couch writes "charming" for "cheering."—Ed.

On this cheap and chippy chopper business I merely observe that Gilbert revelled in it; as anyone else may, so long as I am not asked to join the party.

But Gilbert's cruelty took an uglier twist upon one incurable and unforgivable vice—that of exposing women to public derision on the stage just because they are growing old and losing their beauty. We can forgive Horace or Catullus (if hardly) for venom against their cast-off mistresses. We should all think the better of them had they refrained. But the revulsion, even the vituperation, of a wearied amorist—unpleasant as one may think it—consists with our experience of men and women. It is *humanly* vile. What disgusts one in Gilbert, from the beginning to the end, is his insistence on the physical odiousness of any woman growing old. As though, great Heaven! themselves did not find it tragic enough—the very and necessary tragedy of their lives! Gilbert shouts it, mocks it, apes with it, spits upon it. He opens with this dirty trump card in *Trial by Jury,* where the Judge tells how, as a briefless Barrister:

> I soon got tired of third-class journeys,
>   And dinners of bread and water;
> So I fell in love with a rich attorney's
>   Elderly, ugly daughter.
>
> The rich attorney, he jumped with joy,*
>   And replied to my fond professions:
> 'You shall reap the reward of your pluck, my boy,†
>   At the Bailey and Middlesex Sessions.
> You'll soon get used to her looks,' said he,
>   'And a very nice girl you'll find her—

* Quiller-Couch writes "wiped his eyes" for "jumped with joy."—Ed.
† Quiller-Couch substitutes "enterprise" for "pluck, my boy."—Ed.

She may very well pass for forty-three
    In the dusk, with a light behind her!'

He follows it with 'Little Buttercup' in *Pinafore,* in
Patience with

Fading is the taper waist—
    Shapeless grows the shapely limb,
And, although securely laced,
    Spreading is the figure trim!
Stouter than I used to be,
    Still more corpulent grow I—
There will be too much of me
    In the coming by-and-by!

—in *The Mikado* with

The flowers that bloom in the Spring, tra la,
    Have nothing to do with the case:
I've got to take under my wing, tra la,
*A most unattractive old thing, tra la,
With a caricature of a face.

—and so he proceeds until the end, in *The Mountebanks,*
to a scene which almost drove one from the theatre in
nausea.

But I dare say the best rebuke of this was the gentle
one administered by his favourite actress, Miss Jessie Bond.
When she told Gilbert she was going to marry, he burst
out, 'Little fool!' 'I have often,' she answered, 'heard you
say you don't like old women. I shall be one soon. Will

* Quiller-Couch writes "This" for "A."—Ed.

you provide for me? You hesitate. Well, I am going to a man who will.'

VII

Mr. Rudyard Kipling has observed somewhere that in the life of every happily married man there must come a moment when the sight of his wife at the head of the table suggests the appalling thought that this must go on for ever. Without going so far as this, one may say that even in the happiest marriage one or both of the partners has an occasional sense of some ambition missed. So it happened, we know, in the immensely successful partnership of Gilbert and Sullivan, and it led to frequent quarrels, endeavours on Sullivan's part to break away, finally to estrangement, though happily to no such deadly feud as closed the almost equally successful partnership of MM. Erckmann-Chatrian. Sullivan dreamed that he was capable of High Opera; and so perhaps he was, had he attempted it sooner. But few men can usefully resolve to embrace a new and higher career on their silver wedding-day, and when Sullivan produced *Ivanhoe* at the Royal English Opera House in 1891 it was evident that his resolve had come too late.

But Gilbert, who had bound him to his task, in latter days so sorely against his protestations, also cherished a soaring dramatic ambition. Of men so irascible as he it may usually be observed that they have a bee in their bonnet. (I may use that expression because Gilbert once wore a bonnet as officer in the Gordon Highlanders Militia and had a photograph taken—reproduced in his *Biography*—in the full costume of that gay regiment.) And the very queer bee in Gilbert's bonnet was a violent antipathy against the name and fame of Shakespeare, particularly against the public appreciation of *Hamlet*. It sounds incredible, but there it was. He not only lampooned the great tragedy in a play, *Rosencrantz and Guildenstern*: he never could get away from Hamlet and Ophelia; he had to go on and be-fool their story, as in *The Mountebanks,* in a silly duet— and again to drag the very weeds and the mud out of Ophelia's end:

> When she found he wouldn't wed her,
> In a river, in a medder,
> Took a header, and a deader
> > Was Oph-e-li-a!

Levity, vulgar and blatant!—Yes, and almost we might call it incredible in the man, even if explicable by that same strain of insensitiveness which deadened him to all charity for women past their first youth. It has indeed a like suggestion of impotence.

But insensitiveness will not cover this fault, which actually lay very near the raw. Reading his 'Life' and his plays together, we perceive that this neat rhymer, neat wit, neat barrister, neat stage-manager, nursed at the back of his head a conception of himself as a great and serious dra-matist—even as Sullivan, with better excuse, nursed the conception of himself as a great composer in Oratorio. Nor did Gilbert fail to realise this conception for want of try-ing. He has left a number of 'serious' dramas behind him —dramas in prose and verse—all more or less unsuccessful on the stage. He even essayed one on the Faust theme, fated to allure and defeat all but great souls. He could not see that whilst genius may be versatile and many-sided, there are certain talents which naturally *exclude* greatness.

In his workshop, maybe, he was happy to deem himself possessed of high seriousness. When his efforts came to be produced, the public quite accurately divined that he was not. The discovery cost a not very critical generation of audiences no great effort; but it bit into Gilbert's self-esteem, and he bit upon the wound.

VIII

Most of us in ordinary life have known men who, apt to make fun of others' foibles, show extreme anger or sulkiness when the slightest fun is retorted upon their own. Gilbert was such a man: a professional cynic and ruthless (as almost all reported anecdotes attest) in wounding with a jest, but extremely touchy—nay, implacably vindictive—when his own withers were wrung, however lightly.

But before he turned to libretto Gilbert in his lighter plays, unrewarded by applause, did perhaps as much as his friend Robertson, and more than his friend Byron, to break up by solvent the turgid tradition of mid-Victorian drama and expose its theatricalities. It is usual to ascribe the revolution to Robertson. But Robertson, although he showed a glimmering light towards such reality as exists in 'realism,' did not—being himself a sentimentalist—probe the real disease of sentimentality. It was Gilbert who probed it and applied the corrosive; and the corrosive proved too strong at first for the public taste, perhaps because it confined itself to destroying the fatty tissue without any promise of healing. At any rate his satirical comedies, deliberately intended to provoke mirth, fell flat; and this no less to their author's bewilderment than to his exasperation.

Let us take *Engaged,* to my mind the best of these,

and anyhow characteristic; and let us select one short typical passage. The heroine (or one of them), Miss Treherne, is speaking:

'Cheviot, I have loved you madly, desperately, as other woman never loved other man. This poor inexperienced child'—a second heroine—'who clings to me as the ivy clings to the oak, also loves you as woman never loved before. Even, *that* poor cottage maiden, whose rustic heart you so heedlessly enslaved' —a third heroine—'worships you with a devotion which has no parallel in the annals of the heart. In return for all this unalloyed affection, all we ask of you is that you will recommend us to a respectable solicitor.'

In those few lines we detect the Gilbertian imbroglio, with the Gilbertian treatment which afterwards served him so well. Yet the public took *Engaged* coldly. To its mind the play wanted a 'something.'

What? . . . But already we have the answer. Venables anticipated it when he congratulated Thackeray on the success of *The Four Georges,* delivered as lectures in Willis's Rooms, 'Capital, my dear Thack! But you ought to have a piano.'

Later on, in Sullivan, Gilbert found his piano, and something more.

But I doubt if, in his own development, he ever progressed an inch deeper in meaning than anything you can find implicit in the passage I have quoted, or (stage-craft apart) any technical skill in lyric or even in plot that he had not anticipated in *The Bab Ballads.* I find—since we talk of pianos—some symbolic truth in the vignette drawn by his own hand and reprinted in successive editions on

the title-page of those lays. It represents an infant thumping a piano. You may even read some prophecy in the title
of his first real operatic success—*Pinafore*.

IX

At any rate you may assure yourselves, by examination
of the libretti, that Gilbert, having found his piano, stuck
to variations upon a few themes of the *Ballads* and to the
end of his career returned to them for his plot. By deft
rehandling of their themes, with their originally conceived
topsy-turvies and logical reductions to absurdity, he won
his success in the partnership; and it is at least some vindication of your elders' intelligence, Gentlemen, that they
delighted in this play of mock logic, as they had already
fallen to it genially, in their nurseries, over *Alice in
Wonderland,* a province of it in which all had been kindly.

For *The Bab Ballads*—if you are wise, you will treat
them as wise men treat *Tristram Shandy*. You will not
argue, but either like them or leave them alone. I do not
compare them as achievements, but simply as they are
unsusceptible to criticism; and, however wrong I may be
about Gilbert, I have read enough miss-the-mark criticism
of Sterne by eminent persons, from Thackeray down, to
assert that there are some writings for which criticism has
found little guidance between 'I Like It' and 'I Like It
Not.'

For my part I rejoice in *The Bab Ballads,* and find
them on the whole considerably superior to the lyrics with
which Gilbert diversified the Operas. Nor can I easily believe that, being the man he was, he deliberately and artis-
tically keyed down his wit to the requirements of the music
and of stage-presentation. He may have done so half con-

sciously. The possibility, however, suggests a question on which we may conclude.

X

An examination of Gilbert's and Sullivan's success in sometimes wedding, sometimes alternating, words with music to produce a genuine, if narrow, form of Light Opera may be of some use to those who accept, as to those who on its results feel a little doubtful about accepting, the Wagnerian and post-Wagnerian claims for Grand Opera. I feel some timidity in advancing so much as a foot over this ground; since of all hierophants those of music are the most scornful of intruders who would ally their pet art with others that make life enjoyable. I observe also that the majority of these apostles of harmony are as intense in vendetta as incapable of explaining what it is all about; so that one wavers in amaze between the 'interpretations' in the programme of any Symphony Concert and the Billingsgate in which these critics pursue their sacerdotal loves and hates.

But I suppose that, after all, it works out to this:

(1)   Grand Opera, like any other opera, is an artificial thing; a lovely form of art if its components of drama, words and music be intelligently blended, yet always so artificial that the audience's imagination and intelligence must be invited together to assist in their own captivation.

(2)   If these three elements (to omit scenery) of drama, words and music could be captured, each at its highest, *and perfectly blended,* we should have perfection in one combined form of art.

(3)   But this combination implies that each con-

tributory has its due place, each giving its best and yet subduing it to the others' best, at the right moment: that suppose, for example, one could enlist Shakespeare and Beethoven together for an Opera of *Lear,* or Molière and Mozart for a *Don Giovanni,* still the composing authors must each submit his genius to the total result.

(4) Now the trouble is that such things don't happen in this world.

(5) But suppose the theory sound. Of all men of genius Wagner was perhaps the worst equipped with those concomitants which his theory demanded. Therefore, being one of the most arrogant of men, he put music in supreme command and tortured our divinest of gifts—the modulated speaking voice for which Sophocles and Shakespeare wrote—to speak *through* music; which is to say, largely *against* it. It is not for me to do more than marvel at the genius for orchestration which stunned or mesmerized sensible men into accepting a megalomaniac theory which, cooly examined, bears about as much identity with any notions of the great masters of poetry, painting, music, as did the dismembered carcasses before the tent of awaking crapulous Ajax with the tall captains from whose imagined slaughter he had reeled to bed. The temperate voice of the eighteenth century may whisper something salutary at this point: for, after all, Joshua Reynolds *could* paint.

> I believe—says Reynolds—it may be considered as a general rule, that no art can be grafted with success on another art. For although they all profess the same origin, and to proceed from the same stock, yet each has its own peculiar mode of imitating nature and of deviating from it, each for the accomplishment

of its own particular purpose. These deviations, more especially, will not bear transplantation to another soil.

Now Reynolds may easily be wrong if we apply this observation to opera in general, as presumably Hazlitt would have applied it. 'The opera,' says Hazlitt, 'is the most artificial of all things . . . it is an illusion and a mockery. . . . A headache may be produced by a profusion of sweet smells or sweet sounds; but we do not like the headache the more on that account. Nor are we reconciled to it, even at the opera.'

But the Attic Theatre proved, centuries ago, that speech and music, with dancing and scenery, could be brought together to produce one of the very highest forms of art, *provided that each of the contributories were kept in its proper place.* Aristotle recognised this, of course; and, to use our immediate subject for an illustration, Gilbert and Sullivan prove that the difficulty of bringing together accomplished pedestrian speech and accomplished music can be solved *ambulando,* if the rule of keeping them in their proper places be observed more or less as the Greeks observed it. As I have said, a combination of supreme poetry with supreme music and a variety of the other arts at their very best is not granted by the gods to the generations of men; but it seems evident that in some happy moments the cooperation of poet and musician, neither of the first eminence, may almost chemically produce a new thing which, if not transcendent, is extremely pleasing, at once novel and reasonably permanent in its appeal. Opera is an artificial thing. It is not made less artificial on a theory of 'realism' which disguises nature under a new artificiality such as the *leit-motif,* this *leit-motif* being actually as much of a convention as the labels enclosing words which primitive painters and caricaturists drew as issuing from the mouths of their figures. It is, I suggest, greatly to Sullivan's credit that with his incomparable talent for articulating speech in music, he resisted all temptation of that talent to obscure or deafen by music the spoken words which must be the backbone of all drama since they carry and advance the plot.

And—for a last word—it may even be that your delight in Gilbert and Sullivan testifies to a natural unconscious revolt against the theory of opera so prevalent in our time. We know from the history of the Theatre—from the tyranny, for example, laid upon it so long by the theories of Castelvetro and his followers—that a barbarous mistake can be ferociously enforced by pedantry. Against such pedantry a child-like instinct may sometimes usefully assert itself, insisting 'But the Emperor *has* no clothes!'

G. K. Chesterton

Gilbert and Sullivan

(1930)

No institution was so supremely typical of this section
of the Victorian era as that product of the partnership of
Gilbert and Sullivan, commonly called the Savoy Opera.
Nowadays everybody is talking about the Victorian era,
especially those who would persuade us that their minds
are wholly fixed on the future. Unfortunately, it is also
true that those who defend the Victorian era are quite as
unjust to it as those who attack it. They both make the
mistake of supposing that, because it was a phase of the
English character, it was solid or stolid; whereas the English character is moody and very subtle. On the one hand
the futurists, with the ignorance naturally produced by
exclusive contemplation of the future, talk of the Victorian Age as merely limited and timid, a system of restrictions and respectabilities. The truth is, of course, that it
was emphatically the Liberal Age, perhaps the first and
perhaps the last; certainly believing much more in the in-

trinsic claim of Liberty than does the age of Mussolini and
Mr. Pussyfoot Johnson. On the other hand, the reaction-
aries are driven by reaction to represent it as a civilization
ideally domestic, and founded on the sacredness of the
family. The truth is that it was in many ways the very
opposite of this. For instance, the English of this period
were the only people in the world who prided themselves
upon sending their boys far away from home, to be herded
in undomestic institutions and taught to be rather ashamed
of being fond of their own mothers. Some, by a similar
reactionary illusion, have even described the Victorian
Age as an age of Religious Faith. If one thing is certain, it
is that it was supremely the Age of Religious Doubt.

The true definition or distinction, I fancy, is something like this. The Victorian epoch was the epoch in
which most respectable people still believed in liberty, because they still believed that no liberty would ever in *practice* invade respectability. Men believed that the consoli-
dated commercial civilization of England, with its great
wealth and its world-wide base, was already cast in a mould
of manners and morals that could not really be shaken by
any speculations. To take a personal example; the great
Professor Huxley was as much of a sceptic or agnostic in
theory as his grandson Mr. Aldous Huxley. But if you had
told old Huxley that some of the young Huxley's literary
works could be published and printed, he would have refused to believe it. Yet the grandson is in some ways more
in sympathy with dogmatic Christianity than the grandfather. In short, the Victorian Age was one in which freedom of thought went with conservation of convention;
that is why men like Dean Inge revere and regret it. The
cheap way of putting it would be to say that one could
attack the Deity without affecting the Deanery. But that
would be unjust to the subtle sincerity in the Victorian

and in the Dean. It was an age when a conservative could safely be a sceptic; but in these later days we must believe in order to conserve.

One result of this curious condition was this. The Victorians excelled in throwing off fancies, which were rather dreams relieving the general system than visions breaking it up. They were holidays of the intellect rather than (in the modern sense) emancipations of it. Alice in Wonderland is not Alice in Utopia; she is not in an ideal country which challenges or satirizes her own country. Lear's landscapes and travels are really in the other end of Nowhere; not in Somewhere disguised as Somewhere Else. In this sort of bourgeois Saturnalia there could even be a great deal of satire; but not satire that could ever be mistaken for sedition. Perhaps that is what the Victorians really meant by talking so much about evolution; that the one thing quite inconceivable to them was revolution. They would never turn the world topsy-turvy in fact; but they would travel in topsy-turvydom in fancy; and they found it, as they did their annual journeys to Brighton or Margate, bracing and quite a change.

This special type of escape is well exemplified in Opera. *Le Mariage de Figaro* was a light opera; but it helped to produce the French Revolution; which was not a light opera. *H.M.S. Pinafore* in many respects made as much fun of British pride and prejudice as *Figaro* made of the pride and prejudice of the old régime. But we may safely bet that it never crossed the mind of any human being that *H.M.S. Pinafore* would ever produce, I will not say a revolution, but even the tiniest mutiny on the most minute gun-boat. The Victorians, for various reasons, felt secure from all practical results; and therefore their satire was all in the air and lacked both the malice and the force of more militant peoples. And, as I have said, there never was a more marked example than this great achievement of the Savoy Operas, which held the field for so long as a genuine creation of the national humour and hilarity; and which was the result of two men of genius, and as some held of serious genius, consenting to dedicate their lives to playing the fool. But they were British buffoons; they were only *playing* the fool; anything more practical they would have regarded as acting the lunatic.

Mr. Maurice Baring has truly remarked that we, who grew up in the great days of the Savoy Operas, never realized how great they were till they ceased. With all the growth of theatrical technique and experiment, even with a certain amount of wit and intelligence lingering in the world, it has been found in fact impossible to do anything like the same thing again. Doubtless it was largely the coincidence that brought together two talents suited for a special tone and style of work. I must speak here mainly of the literary talent; for though even I could appreciate the popular fascination of Sullivan's work, I do not even know enough of music to describe my own pleasure in musical terms. But certainly, in any case, the work as a whole was very remarkable. A distinguished foreign musician said to me that it would be easy to find here or there, on the Continent, one or two particular comic operas as good or better; but of the Savoy Operas there are at least ten, if not twelve, of the first rank of invention; and we had come to count on their going on for ever, like the seasons of summer or of spring.

Some of Sir Arthur Sullivan's admirers, or perhaps some of his detractors who cunningly posed as his admirers, were in the habit of lamenting that he had lent himself (they sometimes said sold himself) to a lifetime of light opera music, when he was originally capable of doing something more serious. Curiously enough, the judgment upon Sir William Gilbert, his great colleague, must be almost the reverse. Sullivan began with work that was more serious and may have been better; Gilbert began with work that was broadly comic and was quite certainly his best. I know he had written some sentimental plays like *Broken Hearts,* and probably fancied himself as a pathetic writer; but that was perhaps no more than the recurrent anecdote of Grimaldi longing to create Hamlet. Gilbert was a mocker, if ever there was one; he knew much better what he wanted to deride than what he wanted to defend; on the negative side he was really a satirist, on the other side he would never have been dogmatic enough to be anything but a sentimentalist. The point that is not adequately grasped is that his satiric power appeared long before the Savoy Operas; and was at its wittiest when it was most wildly satiric. Nobody knows anything about W. S. Gilbert who does not constantly compare the Savoy Operas with *The Bab Ballads.* Unfortunately, while managers still find it worth while to revive the Operas, publishers and reviewers do not at the same regular intervals republish and review the *Ballads.* If they did, we should know all about the Savoy Operas; exactly why they succeeded and exactly where they failed. They succeeded because Gilbert had already accumulated in *The Bab Ballads* a dazzling treasure-house of fantastic and paradoxical ideas. They failed because even a man of genius cannot always repeat his best idea twice. He has very often forgotten what it was.

Oddly enough, there is a sort of symbol of this repetition and relative deterioration in his experiment as a caricaturist, as well as a satirist. To the first edition of *The Bab Ballads* he appended delightfully indefensible little pictures, grotesque and grimacing, figures with bodies like eggs and mouths like frogs' and little legs like dancing

insects'. They were amateur drawings; but they were artistic drawings, in being apt and fitted exactly to their purpose. Afterwards, in a later edition and in a disastrous
hour, in some dark moment of mental decline, he actually
erased these right little tight little goblins, and laboriously
went over the design again with a timid and tottering line,
in the attempt to give some resemblance to real human
figures; an attempt not merely amateur but amateurish.
He actually said, with all solemnity, that perhaps the
original figures were a little too grotesque; and this represented his attempt to make them a little more serious. Serious, if you please, as a quality slightly lacking in Calamity
Pop Von Peppermint Drop or Mrs. MacCatacomb de
Salmon-Eye. The truth is that Gilbert had made the joke
and forgotten the joke. It is a thing that does sometimes
happen to humorists. And it is a thing that did most definitely happen to Gilbert, as can specially be noted by a
comparison between *The Bab Ballads* and the Savoy
Operas. Every single Savoy Opera is a splendid achievement as compared with every other attempt at such an
opera in modern times. But every single Savoy Opera is a
spoilt Bab Ballad.

There are several obvious cases in which this double
operation occurred. I mean that Gilbert first went back to
one of his ballads for an idea, and then came back with
the wrong idea, because he had forgotten the right one.
For instance, in some of his best operas, notably in *H.M.S.
Pinafore* and *The Gondoliers,* he seems obsessed with the
notion that there is something very funny about the idea
of two babies being mixed up in their cradles, and the
poorer infant being substituted for the richer. But there
is nothing particularly odd or original, or even amusing,
about the mere idea of a substituted baby. That baby has
been a stock property of many tragedies and numberless

melodramas. To blast it with a yet more withering bolt of criticism, it has even happened in real life. The truth is that Gilbert vaguely remembered having put the joke into a very good ballad, where it is a very good joke; but, in searching for it again, found the ballad but could not find the joke. He did not notice what it was that was really funny in his original fancy. The real ballad, which contained the real joke, which entirely withered in being transplanted to the opera, is the admirably severe and simple poem of "Private James and Major-General John." I hope that all readers will remember it; I fear that most readers have forgotten it. Perhaps they dimly recall that the Major-General was of a disdainful disposition:

> "Pish" was a favourite word of his,
> And he often said "Ho! Ho!"

James, the private soldier was a sadder and more obscure being: "No characteristic trait had he of any distinctive kind." But this gloomy ranker suddenly addresses the General out of the ranks and says that he has been visited by an intuition:

> A glimmering thought occurs to me
> (Its source I can't unearth),
> But I've a sort of a notion we
> Were cruelly changed at birth.

Major-General John ungraciously sneers at the suggestion, though reminded that "No truly great or generous cove . . . would sneer at a fixed idea that's drove in the mind of a Private James"; whereupon the General, his better nature prevailing, abruptly admits that the facts are probably as suggested:

> So General John as Private James
> Fell in parade upon;
> While Private James, by a change of names,
> Was Major-General John.

Now that is the pure and holy spirit of Nonsense; that divine lunacy that God has given to men as a holiday of the intellect; has given to men and, if we may say so, rather especially to Englishmen. It may be hard to talk about the point of something when its point is its pointlessness. But essentially the point of that nonsense rhyme is not in the rather stale and vulgar notion of mixing up the babies. The point is in the outrageous abruptness with which the brooding James mentions his intuition, entirely unsupported by reason; and the equally absurd abruptness with which it is accepted. That is a very funny idea, and yet it was not the idea which its own author thought funny. That error accounts for many of the defects which disfigure the general brilliance and fancy of the Gilbertian Operas. A man can borrow from himself; but a man does not really know himself. And Gilbert, when he borrowed what he thought was most grotesque, did not really know what was most Gilbertian.

It would be easy to give many other examples of the same truth; that the Gilbertian Operas, vivacious and inventive as they are, are not the first sprightly runnings of the Gilbertian fancy; and that he sometimes fished out the wrong things from those upper streams. In *H.M.S. Pinafore,* with the assistance of Sullivan's lively music, he makes an excellent musical comedy chorus of ladies of the refrain, "And so do his sisters and his cousins and his aunts." But in its very joviality it has lost the joke; the original joke suggested by the wooden solemnity of the stiff lines about Captain Reece:

> The sisters, cousins, aunts and niece,
> And widowed ma of Captain Reece,
> Attended there as they were bid:
> It was their duty, and they did.

Similarly, I think, his parade of coronets and the costumes of the Peerage in *Iolanthe* is partly a reminiscence of the beautiful inconsequence of the poem called "The Periwinkle Girl" and the two Dukes who "offer guilty splendour" to that discriminating young woman. But he leaves out the fine and delicate point about the adoring Dukes; which is the contrast between these exalted yet degraded aristocrats and the honest worth of the humble youth, who could claim no better social position than that of an Earl:

> Her views of earldoms and their lot
> All underwent expansion—
> Come, Virtue, in an earldom's cot!
> Go, Vice, in ducal mansion!

But perhaps the strongest example of all is to be found in *Patience;* which contains a typical example of this readiness to spoil a joke in order to repeat a joke. All the business about the one poet persuading the other poet to give up his poetical hair and habits, and put on the uniform of a stockbroker, is obviously copied from the notion of a similar rivalry in the magnificently absurd ballad of "The

Rival Curates." In that touching story one curate, accounted the mildest for miles round, hears the hissing and poisonous whisper that there is another curate who is yet milder. He therefore sends assassins to force the meek usurper to assume a gay demeanour, and smoke and wink at the girls. But the seed of sublime nonsense is in the notion of men fiercely competing as to which of them is the more insipid. It is inherent in the idea of a mild curate being jealous of a milder curate. It evaporates altogether with the change to a wild poet being jealous of a wilder poet.

So much should be said to make clear that, if we are considering the Gilbertian literature as literature, and alone, the still fashionable Savoy Operas are not the first or the best work of Gilbert. But they are so very much better than any work of anybody else that has been done in the same medium then or since, that it is no wonder that his genius, when it had been so exactly fitted to the genius of Sullivan, produced something that was in every way unique; and not least unique in being united. It may be equally true, on Sullivan's side, that his earlier musical expression was yet more individual and promising than that which he showed in the great partnership; it is a point upon which I cannot judge even as tentatively as I judge the literary comparison. Some may tell me that The Lost Chord is more completely lost than Lost Mr. Blake, that glorious but I fear largely forgotten sinner. But even if these two masters had each brought to the work only half his mastery, there was enough when taken together to make up a masterpiece. It is a masterpiece of a very singular and significant kind, both as a type of the things of its period and as a contrast to them.

Perhaps the first point to note is that Nonsense was here treated as almost a sacred thing, in the ancient sense of a thing fenced off and protected from intrusion. The history of what may broadly be called Pantomime, in modern England, based on the old Harlequinade with its clown and poker and policeman, ranging through various phases such as the fairy plays of Planché, and now transformed like one of its own transformation-scenes (not to say dissolving like one of its dissolving-views) into the form or formlessness of the Revue—-that tradition of the Pantomime had many moods and changes, but it always possessed, both before and after Gilbert, a certain vague implication of infinite possibilities or impossibilities. It was a spirit not only of hilarity but of hospitality. In the old as in the new fairy-palace, all the doors of the stage stood open. In the Gilbertian fairy-palace all the doors were shut. They were shut so as to enclose and secure the separate dream of an individual artist; something that was nonsensical from the standpoint of reality, but was none the less serious from the standpoint of art. The atmosphere of the old Pantomime and of the new Revue implies, if not that everybody may turn up, at least that anybody may turn up. Incongruous figures from the ends of the earth may appear against any scenery, however conventional or local. The man in the top-hat in front of the Ogre's Castle, the man with the red nose in front of the Gates of Fairyland, was incongruous and was justified by his incongruity. He did not have to match his surroundings, but only to sing for his supper. This naturally led to the limelight being concentrated on the actor and not on the scenery; not indeed on the scene; or even on the play. This led to songs and speeches quite separable from the play, and much more connected with the world outside the theatre; songs that could be sung in the streets; topical songs; political songs; songs that one man could pick up from another without even seeing the play at all. It also led to gags; to infinite, incessant, irresponsible gagging. The player was ten times as big as the play. The Ogre and the Fairy were nothing; but Dan Leno and Herbert Campbell were everything.

W. S. Gilbert was accused, rightly or wrongly, of being a splenetic, acrid and fault-finding individual. However this may be, in the creation of his art, these vices, if they were vices, were also virtues. He would not permit anything really incongruous to mar the complete congruity of his own incongruity. He stopped all gags so despotically that one can only say that he gagged the gaggers. He would not allow a word of contemporary political or social allusion, beyond the few which he touched upon very lightly himself. His whole conception, right or wrong, was to make a compact artistic unity of his poetical play; and the fact that it was also a nonsensical play was not a reason, in his eyes, for anything being thrown into it; but, on the contrary, for everything else being kept out of it; because its very frivolity was fragility. It was not a potato sack into which the clown could poke anything with a poker; it was a coloured soap-bubble which would burst if tickled with a straw. In this matter of keeping the artistic unity of a comic play as a whole, Gilbert has rather an important position in the history of modern artistic experiments. It is all the difference between the levity of *Three Men in a Boat* and the levity of *The Wrong Box*. For the main point about the Wrong Box is that it is emphatically the Right Box; it is a box, in being a compact enclosure into which nothing *really* incongruous is allowed to enter; and Stevenson hits the right nail on the head every time, when he is hammering the box together. The scenery of the Gilbertian Operas has exactly the same quality of harmonious chaos or carefully selected senselessness.

Thus *The Mikado* is not a picture of Japan; but it is a Japanese picture. It is a picture deliberately limited to certain conventions of colour and attitude; it is, as is truly claimed in the first words of its first chorus, something to be seen "on many a vase and jar, on many a screen and fan." And it will be noted that its author was as autocratic as any Emperor of the Far East about the exclusion of sky-breakers and barbarians from other lands. There is not a single European character or costume in the whole of *The Mikado;* and there could not be, without destroying the whole fantastic conception and colour scheme. Imagine an old popular Pantomime about Japan, or for that matter a modern Revue about Japan; and the very background of Japan would be regarded as an opportunity for introducing everybody, or anybody who was not Japanese. A popular test was almost immediately provided by *The Geisha;* the most famous, or rather the least utterly forgotten, of the string of Musical Comedies which so rapidly attempted, and so completely failed, to fill the place of the old Savoy Operas. In *The Geisha,* which does glimmer faintly among my boyish memories, the scene was also laid in Japan. But it was only laid in Japan in order that Mr. Hayden Coffin, or some such gentleman in a naval uniform, should instantly land from a British battleship in company with an equally British young lady and attended by a comic Chinese cook. In that Japan the ports were all open; in Gilbert's Japan the ports were all closed; because it was the undiscovered island of a dream. Similarly in a play like *The Gondoliers,* the Venice is not really Venetian; but it is really artificial; one might say as artificial as Venice. The author will introduce a Spanish Inquisitor in a black cloak, because he fits into the same sort of Mediterranean masquerade. But wild horses would not have driven him to introduce an English policeman, such as lends a final inconsequence to the chaos of the Harlequinade. The thing may not be taking place in Venice;

but it is not taking place in Britain; it is taking place in Barataria, the imaginary kingdom, the island of Sancho Panza's dream. And the Two Kings are not Pantomime Kings, or mere knockabouts with wooden sceptres and crowns; all the setting is fitted to a certain frosty eighteenth-century elegance; the mockery of a Venetian romance. The same scheme of decorative unity could be shown as running through each of the operas in turn. The scene of *H.M.S. Pinafore* is in the harbour, but it is never off the ship. Only one landsman is allowed on board; and he in order to emphasize the jest that the First Lord of the Admiralty is not a landsman, but out to be a sort of seaman. It is amusing to think what vistas of varied scenery a modern producer of Revue or Pantomime would see in such a story; what grand receptions at Sir Joseph and Lady Porter's town house; what riotous scenes in taverns to celebrate the adventures of Jack Ashore. But in the strict simplicity and concentration of the Gilbertian theme, Jack is never Ashore. He has taken the background of deck and rigging and blue sea; and he sticks to the note and the theme. It is perhaps amusing to reflect that the author of *The Bab Ballads* was the only Englishman who understood and observed the unities of the Greek Tragedies.

The next thing to notice is this; that it was precisely because he did keep this comic convention, as strictly and even sternly as if it were Chinese etiquette, that he was able to be a satirist of our own society; almost as airy and impartial as a voice from China. The gag, the topical allusion, the ordinary vulgar joke about the things most notorious in the newspapers, could never be thus deadly because it could never be thus delicate and detached. There was always something rowdy about it, because it was not only an appeal to the gallery, but a direct demagogic appeal instead of an indirect dramatic appeal. It was an appeal to people's momentary political feelings, and not to their permanent artistic tastes. Now I am very fond of demagogy in the right place, which is exactly where it is not allowed: in Parliament and the places of open debate, which are supposed to express the feelings of the democracy. But in a satire, especially an ornamental and elegant satire, there can never be any place for demagogy; satire and demagogy are direct opposites. For it is the very definition of demagogy that it deals with the obvious; sometimes with obvious and very valuable virtues; often with obvious and very noble ideals. But it is the very definition of satire that it is not obvious, and deals with points of view that are not obvious. And it needs a sort of unreal exactitude of setting and habit which is different from the rowdy reality of life. For instance, I do not in the least share the sickly and chilly reaction against the traditional passion of patriotism. I do not object to patriotism, at some passionate crisis, breaking out of the framework of art. If a popular actor happens to be acting Fauconbridge on the night of a great national crisis, when war is declared, I do not in the least object to his swaggering sword in hand down to the footlights, and bellowing to the gallery, without the slightest reference to the play:

> Come the three corners of the world in arms,
> And we shall shock them. Nought shall make us
>   rue,
> If England to itself do rest but true.

I do not mind that, because I happen to hold the horrid heresy that the nation is more important than the drama;

and even that England is more important than Shakespeare
—a view in which Shakespeare would have warmly con-
curred. And if I do not mind this being done to Shakespeare, I naturally do not mind what anybody does to *The
Geisha;* and should not in the least object if the gentleman
in the naval uniform became on such an occasion a regular
gatling-gun of gags, about British bulldogs assisting God
in saving the Union Jack. This is demagogy; but it is also
humanity; and it matters the less that it knocks the whole
play out of shape, because the play was in any case shape-
less. But for the purposes of satire we do emphatically
want a shape; something sharpened and pointed and above
all polished. If we want people to look at the unfamiliar
side of patriotism, at the unpopular side of demagogy, we
need a certain conventional calm over the whole proceedings, that people may have the patience to criticize themselves. If we want to point out what can really be stupid
and irrational and dangerous about a vulgar and conceited
patriotism, we need a sort of ritual of satire that the irony
may have a chance. Thus we find it is against the almost
monotonous background of blue waves and bulwarks, in
the unreal rigidity of *H.M.S. Pinafore,* that the sailor
is permitted to burst forth into that sublimely logical
burlesque:

> He is an Englishman!
> And it's greatly to his credit.

And reaching the ironic heights of:

> But in spite of all temptations
> To belong to other nations,
> He remains an Englishman.

That knocks at one blow all the stuffing out of the stuffy and selfish sort of patriotism; the sort of patriotism which is taking credit instead of giving praise. It lays down for ever the essential and fundamental law; that a man should be proud of England but not proud of being an Englishman.

But the point is that we cannot get these detached or distinguished points of view listened to at all, in a general atmosphere of the rowdy, the fashionable or the obvious. They require something like an unusual atmosphere or a rather remote symbolism. A man might make any number of highly justifiable jokes about, or against, Mr. Lloyd George or Mr. Winston Churchill or Lord Birkenhead or Lord Reading; and the jokes might involve real criticism of our political inconsistencies or legal fictions. But in practice, the effect would simply be that everybody would howl his head off at the mere mention of Winston or Lloyd George. The people would not wait for the jokes; the names would be jokes enough. They certainly would not wait for the criticism; being altogether in too hilarious a mood of the public meeting. But Gilbert can criticize a hundred of such inconsistencies and fictions, if he puts the scene entirely in Japan or calls the politician Pooh-Bah.

It is certainly rather grotesque that the satire should have been understood so little that certain British officials gravely discussed whether the performance of *The Mikado* might not offend our allies in Japan. There is not, in the whole length of *The Mikado,* a single joke that is a joke against Japan. They are all, without exception, jokes against England, or that Western civilization which an Englishman knows best in England. I doubt whether it is an ancient and traditional Japanese habit to scribble on the window-panes of railway carriages; I think it improbable that any native Japanese peasants were "sent to hear sermons by mystical Germans who preach from ten to four," it may be questioned whether even the habit of autograph-hunting is confined to the islands of the Rising Sun; it seems probable that "the judicial humorist" is more often an English judge than an Oriental official; and "the people who eat peppermint and puff it in your face" were not, I imagine, first encountered by W. S. Gilbert in the streets of Tokyo. But it is true to say that this sort of English caricature requires a Japanese frame; that, in order to popularize a criticism of our own country, it is necessary to preserve a sort of veil or fiction that it is another country; possibly an unknown country. If the satirist becomes more of a realist, he enters the grosser native atmosphere in which he is expected to be a eulogist. The satire bears no sort of resemblance to an Englishman criticizing Japan. But it has to assume a certain semblance of a Japanese criticizing England. Oliver Goldsmith discovered the same truth, when he found he could only talk truthfully to his countrymen in the stilted language of a Chinaman.

In a word, the style must not be too familiar when the moral is unfamiliar. The story is told of W. S. Gilbert that he indignantly rebuked a leading actor who had introduced a gag, that is a joke of his own, into the dialogue. The actor defended himself by saying, "Well, I always get a laugh for it"; and Gilbert answered, "You could get a laugh any time by sitting down on your hat." What is true about a man sitting on his hat and getting a laugh is equally true about a man waving his hat and getting a cheer. It is always possible to appeal to the audience with success, if we appeal to something which they know already; or feel as if they knew already. But if we have to get them to listen to a criticism, however light, which they have really never thought of before, they must have a certain atmosphere of repose and ritual in which to reflect on it. How many of Gilbert's best points were in a sense rather abstruse points. They asked the listener to think about phrases which he had always used without thinking; they pointed out something illogical in something that had always been thought quite sensible. Men cannot so re-examine their own phraseology and philosophy except in a world more detached, and perhaps more dehumanized, than that in which they roar at an old chestnut or cheer at a patriotic toast. To take only one example; there has crept into our common speech and judgment a very evil heresy, one of the dingy legacies of Calvinism; the idea that some people are born bad and others born so solidly good that they are actually incapable of sin; and can never even be tempted to cowardice or falsehood. So long as this is re-peated as a sort of hearty and jolly compliment, in the form of saying, "William Wiggins, Sir, could not tell a lie if he tried," it all passes off well, in the atmosphere of the fashionable toasts and the familiar jests. But that notion of the impossibility of lying is itself a lie. It is one of the worst lies produced by one of the worst heresies. And Gil-bert struck that heresy to the heart, and nailed the logic of that lie as with a nail hammered through its head, in two or three lines of the lightest and most buoyant lyrical chorus:

> We know him well,
> He cannot tell
> Untrue or groundless tales,
> He always tries
> To utter lies
> And every time he fails.

That is a pure piece of logical analysis and exposure; a great deal more philosophical than many that are quoted among the epigrams of Voltaire.

It is true that Gilbert had no particular positive philosophy to support this admirable negative criticism; he had even less than Voltaire. For that reason he did sometimes fall into mere expressions of prejudice; and sometimes into expressions of bad taste. But the point here is that the satire was often a really intellectual satire; and that it could hardly have been expressed except under certain formal and even fictitious conditions, which make it possible to appeal to the intellect without arousing the prejudices, or even the more obvious and vulgar of the really healthy sentiments. People would hardly have followed the real satire of *H.M.S. Pinafore* if it had been filled with real and rousing patriotic songs; as an ordinary writer of pantomime or musical comedy would certainly have tried to fill it. This is not to say that anti-popular satires are necessarily better than popular songs. It is only to say that the artist is generally a man who does one thing at a time.

It would be easy to give numberless examples in which the Gilbertian wit did criticize things that need to be criticized, and even did so by the right negative standard of criticism; but it would still be true that there was an absence of the positive standard of perfection. The real power of the Sophist over the Philistine, of the pretentious person over the plain man, could hardly be better conveyed than in the limpid and flowing lines of the song about the man who had a Platonic love for a potato:

> And everyone will say,
> As you walk your flowery way,
>   "If he's content with a vegetable love
>   Why, what a very singularly pure young man
>   Which would certainly not suit *me,*
>   This pure young man must be."

But there is no heroic indignation behind the sarcasm, as in some of the great satirists; for nobody can feel a moral enthusiasm for three fatuous Guardsmen and an impossible milkmaid. There was no such prophetic satire as Aristophanes or Swift might have shown; and certainly no sort of prophecy of the path which the pure young man eventually followed, or the way in which Platonic love came to mean something different from admiration of a potato.

This relative lack of moral conviction did mark Gilbert as a satirist, and did to some extent mark all his epoch as an epoch. There were many men of conviction still active; Newman was still teaching and corresponding in his old age; Gladstone was still blazing away with his discovery of the case for Ireland; but Newman stood for something still almost alien; and perhaps even the case for Ireland was the first wedge of such alien things that broke up the Victorian solidity of England. The older Victorian prophets had been earnest enough; and though Matthew Arnold "was not always in all ways wholly serious," Ruskin was never anything else. But in the case of the mocker, it was already true (as he himself hinted) that the mockery had become something like a hollow mask. The original forces that had sustained the hope and energy of the nineteenth century were no longer at their strongest for the rising generation. The light of the great legend of the French Revolution had been darkened by the success of Prussian materialism in 1870; the men who had taken the humanitarian ideal simply and naturally were dropping out; like Dickens, the greatest of them, who died in the same year as the fall of Paris. Nor had any other or older ideas as yet taken hold so solidly of the human mind as to permit of natural laughter or of noble scorn. Hence there were not in this epoch any great convinced satirists, as Vol-

taire and Beaumarchais were on the one side, or Father
Knox or Mr. Belloc are now on the other. The typical
satire of this period remained what Gilbert himself loved
to preserve it, an airy, artistic, detached and almost dehumanized thing; not unallied to the contemporary cult of
art for art's sake. Gilbert was fighting against a hundred
follies and illogicalities; but he was not fighting for anything, and his age as a whole was no longer certain for
what it was fighting. The moral of *The Pirates of Penzance* is in some ways exceedingly like the moral of a play
by Mr. Bernard Shaw; but there is not the moral fervour
behind it which really belongs to Mr. Bernard Shaw even
when his moral is most immoral. For Mr. Bernard Shaw,
like Mr. Belloc, belongs to a later period when the contro-
versy has fallen back upon ultimates and reached the ends
of the earth. It is not in these new struggles of our own
time that we can find the clue to that curious and half unreal detachment, in which some of the Victorians came at
last to smile at all opinions including their own. Perhaps
the finest form of it is in a certain light version of the
Vanitas Vanitatum, such as Thackeray so often suggested;
and which is really not unlike a certain almost empty radi-
ance in some of the later lyrics of the Renaissance. This
would seem to have been the most serious mood of W. S.
Gilbert; and it makes one entirely apt appearance in his
most serious play. For one of his comic operas was very
nearly a serious play. *The Yeomen of the Guard* is deliberately pathetic; and it marks exactly what I mean, when I
say that if Gilbert had been serious he could only have
been pathetic. He had not the positive moral resources to
be heroic or mystic or dogmatic or fanatical. *The Yeomen
of the Guard* is in a Renaissance period and setting and it
contains one serious lyric really worth quoting, as having
caught the spirit of the end of the sixteenth century; and

perhaps in some sense of the end of the nineteenth. When the hero is going to execution, under Henry VIII, for his sixteenth-century scientific curiosity, he sings words which do prove, perhaps paradoxically, that the veteran song-writer could really write a song:

> Is life a boon?
>   If so, it must befall
>   That Death, whene'er he call,
> Must call too soon.
>   Though fourscore years he give,
>   Yet one would pray to live
> Another moon!
>   What kind of plaint have I,
>   Who perish in July?
>   I might have had to die
> Perchance in June!
>
> Is life a thorn?
>   Then count it not a whit!
>   Man is well done with it:
> Soon as he's born
>   He should all means essay
>   To put the plague away;
> And I, war-worn,
>   Poor captured fugitive,
>   My life most gladly give—
>   I might have had to live
> Another morn!

That is not unworthy of what it imitates; and might really have been thrown off by Raleigh, when he gave The Lie to all the vanities of this world, or by Chastelard, when he refused on the scaffold all the ministrations of religion and recited, standing alone, the great ode of Ronsard to Death.

Charles E. Lauterbach

Taking Gilbert's
Measure

(1956)

William Schwenck Gilbert wrote for the comic journal *Fun* from 1861 until 1875. His contributions included
humorous verse, drama, drama criticism, commentaries on
contemporary events and customs, quips, and illustrations.
About all that has survived of *Fun* of perennial interest
is "The Bab Ballads," [1] which first appeared in its columns. These, too, are about all that are remembered of
Gilbert's writings, excepting of course the librettos of the
Gilbert and Sullivan operas.

Gilbert described "The Ballads" as "much sound and
little sense." [2] By a curious quirk of circumstance it was
this non-sense, not his sense, which made him famous. He
might well be called the King of Topsy-turvy-dom, as his
biographers suggest, thus ranking him with those illustri-
ous monarchs of whimsey King Borria Bungalee Boo, the

Three Kings of Chickeraboo, and the King of Canoodle-
dum. But is is questionable science to "psychologize" him
as sadistic and infantile because of the behavior of his
nonsense characters.[3] It is more probable that his good
common sense led him to a vein of popular interest which
he then mined for all it was worth.

It might be supposed that continued indulgence in
utter nonsense would become monotonous. There are at
least two reasons why Gilbert's doesn't. One is the wide
range of his inventiveness. Kings, princes, generals, lieutenant colonels, majors, captains, bishops, curates, ogres,
ghosts, precocious infants, and modest maidens throng
his pages without a vestige of logic or a shred of dignity.
His characters possess a sort of primitive universality that
keeps them from growing stale. That the clever "Bab"
drawings contribute to their effectiveness is generally
acknowledged. They also cancel his anonymity wherever
they appear and identify much of his unsigned writing.

Another circumstance which prevents "The Ballads"
from becoming wearisome is the great variety of verse
and stanza form in which they are written. The predominant meter is iambic but the anapaest also appears, as in
"Old Paul and Old Tim":

> He took care to abstain from employing his fist
> On the old and the cripple, for they might resist.

Nor is the trochee slighted. It is in trochaic dimeters and
trimeters that Georgie of "The Fairy Curate" resolves to
join the clergy, in which noble calling

> People round him
> Always found him
> Plain and unpretending;

> Kindly teaching,
> Plainly preaching—
> All his money lending.

The length of verse varies from this airy dimeter to the protracted Ogden Nashery of "Lost Mr. Blake."

> She was an excellent person in every way—and won the respect even of Mrs. Grundy,
> She was a good housewife, too, and wouldn't have wasted a penny if she had owned the Kohi-noor,
> She was just as strict as he was lax in her observance of Sunday,
> And being a good economist, and charitable besides, she took all the bones and cold potatoes and broken piecrusts and candle ends (when she had quite done with them), and made them into an excellent soup for the deserving poor.

The length of the stanza is as variable as the verse form, ranging from the couplet of "Ferdinando and Elvira" through stanzas of three lines, four lines, five lines, and so on, to the twelve-line stanza of "The Fairy Curate." All of which helps keep "The Ballads" out of the rut and makes each one a refreshing adventure.

Gilbert is quoted by one of his biographers as having once said that he had been "paid, and well paid for every verse he ever wrote." [4] Goldberg has casually mentioned that Gilbert's pay under Hood "was at the moderate rate of one pound a column." [5] Just how well he was paid, for his verse and prose, as well as for his illustrations, can be determined from the "Proprietor's Copy" of *Fun* held by the Henry E. Huntington Library.[6] This file contains marginal notes giving the names of all authors and artists for every item published and a statement of account of the amounts paid (except for occasional contributions by the proprietors, which are not charged).

Each account is a weekly statement and shows the total amount each author and artist received for all his contributions to *Fun* for that week. When the contribution was a single item the amount in the statement is the payment he received for that item. But if he made more than one contribution, the amount received for an individual item is hidden in the total. For example in the March 3, 1866, number Gilbert has three separate contributions, including "The Yarn of the *Nancy Bell*." For the three items he received a total of £2.12s. What did he receive for writing "The Yarn of the *Nancy Bell*"?

The solution to this problem was not at once apparent. It involved the question of how *Fun* paid its contributors and on this point Goldberg's casual remark was the only evidence available. A tabulation of the data confirmed his statement that the basic rate of pay for all contributors was one pound for a column of letter press (art work was paid separately). This rate applied whether the material was prose or verse, and also regardless of who the author might be. George Augustus Sala, a writer of some repute, received no more for his literary offerings than the most obscure contributor. Thus a half-column was paid 10s, a quarter-column, 5s. But items of lesser space still presented difficulty.

Further study of the weekly accounts revealed that no contribution ever received less than 6d., no matter how short it was, even if it was only a single line. Since there are 240 pence in a pound, and since it was found that a column measured 240 millimeters (with only slight deviations), the solution to the problem became manifest. The fraction of a pound and the fraction of a column correlated exactly, with the exception that 6d. was a minimum unit. This was "measure pay," an expression which occurs twice in connection with Gilbert's accounts and several times elsewhere.[7] In Gilbert's case the expression "measure pay" was used when the question of putting him on salary arose. He is credited with two pounds with this notation, "I have not seen him yet—this is *measure* pay." The term was not intelligible until it became apparent that a contributor's pay was actually measured. It was a matter of literature at so much a yard!

"Measure pay" almost completely deprived the editor of any discretion in the matter of remuneration. Since 6d. was the smallest unit of pay, he could stretch a point now and then when the measure was close. Otherwise he seldom departed from the rule. The way the method worked out in practice is illustrated in the contributions of Arthur Sketchley.[8] He frequently contributed two columns of prose and his reward was invariably two pounds. Sometimes the second column was a unit or two short and the editor ran a filler for which, of course, he had to pay extra at the regular rate. But there was no deduction from Mr. Sketchley's two pounds. A few weeks later, however, with the same situation—a skimpy column which required a two-line filler—Mr. Sketchley was docked 6d. and paid only £1. 19. 6. And two weeks later still, the identical situation again arising but the editorial euphoria having evaporated, Mr. Sketchley received only £1. 19. 0. for his wit!

On the basis of "measure pay," Gilbert did not receive any more for his "Ballads" (verse) than William Jeffray Prowse [9] did for his "Sporting Intelligence" (prose). But if "measure pay" is converted into rate of pay per word a more exact comparison can be made between Gilbert and other contributors, and between prose and verse contributions. Comparing Gilbert's word rate of .560d. for verse [10] with that of some of his associates on *Fun* who also wrote verse, we find that Tom Hood for a group of miscellaneous poem (36 items, 8,506 words), received .529d.; Henry Sambrook Leigh (58 items, 9,505 words), .482d.; William Jeffray Prowse (17 items, 5,271 words), .456d.; and Clement William Scott (38 items, 8,224 words), .556d. These rates are roughly one cent a word, or about what an author can expect to receive from some of the better pulp magazines of today.

For writing the prose series "Men We Meet" (10 items, 14,487 words), including such articles as "Some Engaged Men," "Wigs and Whiskers," "Concerning Some Bores," etc., Gilbert's word rate was .385d.; Tom Hood, Jr., for "Town Talk" (11 items, 10,862 words), received .263d.; Ambrose Gwinnet Bierce, for "Fables of Zambri, the Parsee" (12 items, 8,390 words), .401d.; William Jeffray Prowse, for "Sporting Itelligence" (15 items, 11,685 words), .291d.; George Augustus Sala, for a group of selected articles (11 items, 12,245 words), .357d.; and Arthur Sketchley (George Rose) for "The Brown Papers" (12 items, 21,883 words), .250d.

These differences in word rate do not necessarily reflect *quality*. They reflect *style*. The writer who used the longest words received the highest rate. Bierce, as already noted, received a word rate of .401d. for his prose, the highest in the list. This correlates nicely with his Latinate style.

This anomaly of variable rates may be further illustrated by a comparison of "The Bumboat Woman's Story" with "The Fairy Curate." The former, 885 words using one and one-half columns, set in long compact hexameters, paid at the rate of .358*d*. per word; the latter, 487 words using two and one-twentieth columns, consisting of dimeters and trimeters, paid 1.000*d*. per word. These dimeters could have been set up as tetrameters without much artistic loss:

> People round him always found him
>   Plain and understanding;
> Kindly teaching, plainly preaching—
>   All his money lending.

But to do so would have resulted in a reduction in pay of thrity-three per cent. It is amusing to surmise that Gilbert may have been well aware of this situation and may have used it to his own advantage. It was one way of getting a "raise." However, "The Bab Ballads" were being featured in *Fun* at this time, so the stratagem may have had full editorial sanction. Perhaps it was just a way of smoothing the ruffled feathers of a gamecock always looking for a fight. Henry Sampson, who succeeded Hood as editor, had the temerity to criticize one of the "Ballads," the cock "flew the coop," and the magic symbol "Bab" never appeared in *Fun* again.

Size of type also affected measure pay and the word rate. Again we may take an example from Gilbert. In May, 1865, he wrote an article of 525 words entitled "Literature," which consisted of prose set in seven point roman; verse, in seven point roman; and a footnote, in six point roman. The verse paid at the word rate of .544*d.;* the seven-point prose, .292*d.;* and the six-point footnote, .198*d.* Apparently an author never knew exactly what he would receive for a contribution until it was in type. It was then measured and the amount due credited in a ledger. Presumably payment was made once a month. This amounted to pay on publication, not pay on acceptance.

For illustrating the seventy-nine ballads with 228 cuts, Gilbert received £82, which averages 17s. 3.2d. per cut. These cuts ran three or four per ballad and varied in size. According to the Proprietor's Copy, then for all his contributions to *Fun* Gilbert received the sum total of £181 17s. 0d.

So *Fun* took Gilbert's measure and appraised "The Ballads" at a pound a column which turns out to be the unimpressive figure of a cent a word. The critics, too, were taking his measure. *The Athenaeum,* shortly after the appearance of the first volume of "Babs," found them dull, dreary, and wooden, the jokes entirely destitute of humor. "[They] do not contain a single thread of interest, nor a spark of feeling. The illustrations are painful, not because they are ugly, but because they are inhuman." [11] After such definitive damnation it is wonder that they survived at all.

But time has a way of confounding the smartest critics. About three-quarters of a century later Deems Taylor called "The Ballads" "the most widely read comic verse in the English language." [12] Shillings and pence alone do not mark the measure of a man.[13]

Notes

1. Gilbert's biographers mention that "Bab" was his nickname in infancy and childhood. See Sidney Dark and Rowland Grey, *W. S. Gilbert: His Life and Letters* (London, 1923), p. 4; and Isaac Goldberg, *The Story of Gilbert and Sullivan* (New York, 1928), p. 88. It may be noted that "bab," meaning "babe," is a dialectal word quite common in many English counties at that time. So "Bab" may be assumed to have been a term of endearment used when Gilbert was a "babby," which he appropriated as a pen

name when he "grew up" (which Pearson declares he never did).

2. W. S. Gilbert, *The "Bab" Ballads* (London, 1869), title page.

3. Hesketh Pearson, *Gilbert and Sullivan* (New York, 1935), p. 51 passim; Arthur Quiller-Couch, "W. S. Gilbert," in *Studies in Literature, Third Series* (Cambridge, 1929), pp. 217-40.

4. Dark and Grey, p. 9.

5. Goldberg, p. 61.

6. *Fun,* "Proprietor's Copy," May 20, 1865, to August 9, 1893. I am indebted to Edward S. Lauterbach for bringing this file to my attention.

7. *Fun,* Jan. 28, 1871, account; Feb. 11, 1871, account; May 31, 1875, p. 53; Aug. 14, 1875, p. 72; Aug. 28, 1875, pp. 93 and 94, marginal notes.

8. Arthur Sketchley (1817-1872), pseudonym for George Rose, dramatist, novelist, and humorous entertainer, author of what may be collectively termed "The Brown Papers," many of which appeared in *Fun* and eventually numbered thirty volumes.

9. William Jeffray Prowse (1836–1870), poet and sports editor. His pseudonym in *Fun* was "Nicholas." In *British Authors of the Nineteenth Century,* Stanley J. Kunitz and Howard Haycraft eds. (New York, 1936), his middle name is spelled "Jeffrey." Tom Hood, who was his friend and wrote his obituary in *Fun* (Apr. 30, 1870, p. 76), spells his name "Jeffray." *British Authors* also says "from 1856 onward he wrote regularly for *Fun* . . ." but *Fun* was not founded until 1861.

10. There are 42,375 words in the 79 ballads under consideration. This count was made with an electric word counter which greatly reduces the time required for such a chore and almost completely eliminates error.

11. *The Athenaeum,* April 10, 1869, p. 502, col. 1.

12. Deems Taylor, preface to *Plays and Poems of W. S. Gilbert* (London, 1932).

13. The forty-four ballads collected by Gilbert in *The "Bab" Ballads* (1869) and the thirty-five in *More Bab Ballads* (1872) are the basis of this study. No account is taken of the so-called "lost" ballads.

Robert A. Hall, Jr.

*T*he *S*atire *of* The Yeomen of the Guard

(1958)

It has long been recognized that *The Yeomen of the Guard* does not fit into the general pattern of the Savoy operas. Most critics formulate the difference between the *Yeomen* and the other Gilbert and Sullivan operettas by saying that in it, Gilbert eschewed his customary satirical vein of humour and Gilbertian "topsy-turvydom." [1] Yet discussions of the *Yeomen* in general sentimentalize it and thereby obscure its true significance. To regard the *Yeomen,* as some do, as a "tender little romance which mingles laughter and tears," [2] or as "the romantic, somewhat relenting exception" to Gilbert's satire,[3] will not suffice to explain its peculiar effect on the spectator. To an audience expecting Gilbert's rollicking cheerfulness, it offers a mood hovering between wry jest and serious drama; and instead of a final solution of all difficulties, it presents an ending in which an apparently "happy" outcome is marred by the discomfiture, not only of Jack Point, but also of Sergeant Meryll and his daughter Phoebe. The sensitive spectator leaves a performance of the *Yeomen,* not cheered, but saddened—not merely because of Jack Point's falling "insensible" (whether in a faint or dead) at the end, but because of the actions of the characters and the mood of the play as a whole.

This peculiar effect of the *Yeomen* has not as yet been satisfactorily explained. It has, of course, been observed that some of the situations in the *Yeomen* parallel those of Fitzball's libretto for Wallace's *Maritana*—not only the last-minute wedding of condemned man and heavily-veiled bride,[4] but also the use of the deliberately delayed reprieve. Some of the characters and situations derive clearly from Gilbert's earlier operettas, notably the *Mikado:* Goldberg [5] has called our attention to the presence of the wandering minstrel, the public executioner, and the hasty marriage for a brief time that turns into a lifetime. Dame Carruthers is another of Gilbert's typical predatory middle-aged females, and perhaps the most sadistic of the lot (cf. "When our gallant Norman foes"). Yet it is not in these details, but in the nature of the characters in relation to the plot as a whole, and in the relation of the *Yeomen* to the preceding Savoy operas as a group, that we must seek its significance.

The key to an understanding of Gilbert's "normal" characters—i.e. those who live in Gilbertian topsy-turvy-dom—has been furnished by Clarence Day, Jr., in a penetrating analysis.[6] He points out that Gilbertian characters derive their special characteristics from the unusual and incongruous emotional fortitude which they manifest in wildly improbable situations:

> Now the Anglo-Saxon race . . . really come out strongest when they take up their stand on frontiers. It's when they work at building civilizations in rough, untamed regions, and at teaching law and order to cut-throats, that the world most admires them. Their bourgeois and inartistic desire to make things smooth and even, that has given us so many dull cities and stiff, stupid homes, is a trait of great value when exercised on a frontier.
>
> To go back to Gilbert, the people in his operas are frontiersmen: not geographically, but emotionally. The orderly emotional surroundings that most of us know are exchanged in these operas for scenes of the most frightful turbulence. And mark the result. Just as the Anglo-Saxon pioneer lays primness aside, and becomes a big, vigorous man when he goes to the Rockies, so the frontiersmen of emotion in Gilbert lay aloofness one side, and obtain an astonishing kind of emotional strength.

Apply this conception to the characters of the *Yeomen,* however, and what do we find? A group of people, all of whom are quite ordinary, and all but two of whom are un-heroic, un-generous, and the very opposite of the Gilbertian "frontiersmen of emotion." It is as if Gilbert had decided for once to show how a group of people, similar to his stock characters but without their emotional strength and resilience, would react in a melodramatic situation of the type he was fond of parodying. The result is a sorry mess: the rescue of Fairfax does come off, but boomerangs on its planners; the "happy ending" is only for the rather superficial and callous "hero" Fairfax and "heroine" Elsie; the only two really generous personages, Phoebe and Sergeant Meryll, are rewarded for their generosity by having to promise to marry the repulsive Shadbolt and Dame Carruthers respectively; and the weak, selfish, irresolute Jack Point realises too late where his true happiness lay and loses it miserably.

To see the *Yeomen* in this light—which I believe to be the true one—we must revise the currently prevalent view of a number of personages of the play, a view which unduly sentimentalises and distorts them, Jack Point most of all. The appeal of this character, particularly in "I have a song to sing, O!" and in his final collapse, has led most critics to idealise him: he has been referred to as "the prince of jesters," the play's "chief source of wit and philosophy," [7] "a merryman of infinite wit," [8] who is no ordinary strolling player but has a taste for pretty wit and nimble repartee.[9] Various critics have seen in Point a reflection of Gilbert's own personality,[10] his "essential self" and an "idealised Gilbert," [11] and have considered the *Yeomen* to be Gilbert's "spiritual testament." [12] These estimates of Point are based primarily on the philosophy of professional humour expressed in the songs "I've jest and joke and quip and crank" (Act I) and "Oh! a private buffoon is a light-hearted loon" (Act II). But the philosophy of these two songs is at variance with Point's actual behaviour; basing our analysis purely on the internal evidence of the dialogue, we must come to a quite different estimate of his character. From his first appearance in the play, he is in a sorry state, not merely because he has been "down on his luck," [13] but because he is in fact a failure, professionally and personally. He was not skillful enough to judge the Archbishop of Canterbury's mood properly, so that he got himself discharged ignominiously for a jest out of season, and the samples of his jokes which he gives in his conversation with the Lieutenant and elsewhere are stale and "corny." At his best, he relies on a series of already-excogitated "gags" ("my best conundrum wasted!" he exclaims when the Lieutenant fails to take his cue); at his worst, he pilfers his jests from a joke-book. They are, as Granville-Barker observed,[14] very like the feeble humour of the Victorian burlesque à la Planché which Gilbert's wit replaced.

Physically, Point is anything but heroic, as evidenced in his dealing with the angry crowd at his first entrance; in his personal relations he is indecisive and selfish. He is willing enough to run the risk of losing Elsie for the sake of a hundred crowns, as long as he thinks the gain certain, especially since he has not at all made up his mind whether he really wants to marry her or not ("for though I'm a fool, there's a limit to my folly," he tells the Lieutenant). When he has definitely lost her, however, he is suddenly torn by self-pity, which grows throughout the second act until he falls insensible at Elsie's feet at the end of the play, through a sorrow which he has brought on himself by his earlier indifference to her and his eagerness to make a hundred crowns quickly and effortlessly.

Elsie is a rather empty-headed, selfish lass,[15] who takes her luck where she finds it, and is quite callous towards Jack Point.[16] Fairfax, likewise, is a superficial character, rather unfeeling, and the kind of man who would "test his wife's principles" by making love to her incognito and who would bait her at the end of the play before revealing his identity.[17] It is worthy of notice that neither Elsie nor Fairfax give any thanks to Phoebe and Sergeant Meryll, to whom they owe Fairfax's escape and survival—a lack of gratitude quite in keeping with their personalities.

Both Wilfred Shadbolt and Dame Carruthers are obviously unpleasant characters (Shadbolt none the less so because of his humourous aspects).[18] They fit well into the general pattern of the Gilbertian anti-hero (e.g. Ko-Ko, Dick Deadeye) and anti-heroine, (e.g. Katisha, Lady Jane, or Ruth the piratical nursemaid) respectively; and Sullivan gave Dame Carruthers an excellent musical characterisation in "When our gallant Norman foes" and "Rapture, rapture!" They are both essential to the plot, however, as the repulsive persons whose silence Phoebe and her father must purchase by consenting to marry them. From this point of view, the scene between Dame Carruthers and Sergeant Meryll, culminating in the "Rapture, rapture!" duet, does not deserve the condemnation it has received from some critics;[19] nor should this scene be omitted in performance, since it fits perfectly with what has gone before and is necessary to complete the disagreeable outcome of Phoebe's and Sergeant Meryll's efforts (*v. infra*).

The only two likable characters in the *Yeomen* are, in fact, Phoebe and her father.[20] They are the ones who are unselfish and, because of their love for Fairfax, engineer his rescue, which promptly recoils on them in such a way that not only does Phoebe lose him, but she and her father have to yield to Shadbolt's and Dame Carruthers' unwelcome suits.[21] If there is any tragedy in the *Yeomen,* it lies, not in Jack Point's misfortunes, but in the undeservedly unhappy outcome for Phoebe and Sergeant Meryll.

In effect, Gilbert is saying to us in the *Yeomen*: "Up to now you have been witnessing, in the previous Savoy operas, the quite impossible and hence amusing antics of the unusual characters of my stock tomfoolery; now see what happens to ordinary human beings when they are put into a similar—nay, a much less impossible—situation. They are callous, selfish, ungrateful, if not actively repulsive: those who are so naïve as to be generous and self-sacrificing not only lose the benefit of their efforts, but have to marry the most unpleasant persons, who in my topsy-turvydom are normally reserved for each other." Satire there is in the *Yeomen,* and in plenty; but it is the bitterest of all satire, that of a man mocking his own work. The *Yeomen* is, in other words, Gilbert's satire on Gilbertian tomfoolery,[22] and as such does indeed occupy a special place in the series of the Savoy operas, but in a different sense from the interpretation that has customarily been given to it. It confirms, in a direct artistic manifestation, what we are told concerning Gilbert's attitude towards his "topsy-turvydom": "Gilbert had an extremely high opinion of his contribution to what he believed to be the higher drama, and while Sullivan turned to comic opera with relief, Gilbert turned to it with regret." [23]

Gilbert gave the *Yeomen* the somewhat colourless subtitle "The Merryman and his Maid." Possible alternative subtitles might have been "Unpoetic Justice," or, with reference to *Fidelio* and its kind, "The Rescue that Boomeranged."

Notes

1. Cf., for instance, W. A. Darlington, *The World of Gilbert and Sullivan* (London and New York, 1951), p. 126; G. W. Gabriel, Introduction to *H.M.S. Pinafore and Other Plays* (New York, Modern Library, n.d.), p. iv; A. H. Godwin, *Gilbert and Sullivan: A Critical Appreciation* (London—Toronto—New York, 1926),

pp. 25-6, 47, 252; H. Pearson, *Gilbert and Sullivan: A Biography* (London and New York, 1935), p. 181; H. Saxe-Wyndham, article "Sullivan" in Grove's *Dictionary of Music and Musicians,* 5th ed., vol. VIII, p. 177; etc.

2. Godwin, *op. cit.,* p. 47.
3. Gabriel, *loc. cit.*
4. As pointed out by A. Williamson, *Gilbert and Sullivan* (London, 1953; 2nd edition, 1955), pp. 201-3.
5. I. Goldberg, *The Story of Gilbert and Sullivan, or The "Compleat" Savoyard* (New York, 1928), p. 364.
6. C. Day, Jr., Introduction to *The Mikado and Other Plays* (New York, Modern Library, n.d.), pp. ix-x.
7. Williamson, *op. cit.,* p. 207.
8. Godwin, *op. cit.,* p. 26.
9. *Ibid.,* p. 282.
10. Goldberg, *op. cit.,* p. 364; Godwin, *op. cit.,* pp. 62-4.
11. Pearson, *op. cit.,* p. 181.
12. Goldberg, *op. cit.,* p. 359.
13. N. O. M. C[ameron], *The Gramophone,* vi (1929), 450.
14. Cf. H. Granville-Barker, "Exit Planché—Enter Gilbert" in *The Eighteen-Sixties* (Cambridge, Eng., 1932), pp. 102-48; pp. 147-8: "He [the Lieutenant, after interviewing Point] departs, looking very much as a man may look after reading a round dozen of those mid-Victorian burlesques. After him exit Jack Point, crestfallen. And exit after him . . . [the mid-nineteenth-century authors of burlesques, Planché etc.]"
15. As pointed out by Godwin, *op. cit.,* pp. 153-4.
16. Williamson reports (*op. cit.,* p. 215, fn. 1) that for the 1897 revival, Gilbert changed "who laughed aloud" in Elsie's stanza of "I have a song to sing, O!" in the finale, to "who dropped a tear"; if Gilbert did so, he was falsifying Elsie's character for the sake of a sentimental ending.
17. Cf. Godwin, *op. cit.,* pp. 208-9; Williamson, *op. cit.,* p. 204.
18. Cf. Godwin, *op. cit.,* pp. 138-40; Williamson, *op. cit.,* pp. 217-8.
19. E.g. Williamson, *op. cit.,* pp. 204-5; E. Blom, in fn. 1 to p. 177 of H. Saxe-Wyndham's article "Sullivan" in Grove VIII.
20. Cf. Darlington, *op. cit.,* p. 128; Godwin, *op. cit.,* p. 140; Williamson, *op. cit.,* pp. 215-6.
21. We can hardly agree with Godwin's opinion (*op. cit.,* p. 140) that "we need offer him [Sgt. Meryll] no commiseration, in that Dame Carruthers should make him a splendid mate for this sturdy old yeoman"—an observation which misses one of the major points of the play.

22. It is also, in the history of opera as a whole, a parody of the classical "rescue opera" of the type of Beethoven's *Fidelio* and Cherubini's *Les Deux Journées* (cf. D. Grout, *A Short History of Opera* (New York, 1947), pp. 259, 302 ff., 308 ff.); but this aspect of the *Yeomen* seems less important than its significance within the series of Savoy operas.

23. Pearson, *op. cit.,* p. 98.

Herbert Weisinger

The Twisted Cue

(1963)

It is disheartening to realize that after almost a century of continuous performance the libretti of W. S. Gilbert are still not taken seriously. The reason for this failure is not hard to find: the wit of the words and the charm of the music to which they are set divert the reader from the more profound and significant meanings which lie hidden in the texts. Other instances of similar distraction caused by the attractiveness of surface texture over inner depth will clarify this point; the lush lure of Spenser's imagery which stunts his readers' growth in mental health; the glow of poetry in the final plays of Shakespeare which obscures their celebration of the resurrection and renewal in Christian ritual; the simple grace of Herrick's "Corinna's going a-Maying" which quiets the clash between the pagan and Christian world views going on within it; the polished ease of Gray's "Ode on a Distant Prospect of Eton College" which makes the reader miss the substantive object first geometrized and then turned into a rate of motion in such phrases as "chase the rolling circle's speed" instead of "roll the hoop"; the overpowering style of Conrad's *Lord Jim* which glosses over its Manichean heresy; and the elemental simplicity of Hemingway's *The Old Man and the Sea* in which such a seemingly natural act as the old man's passing of the spear of the fish to the boy actually represents in a kind of double phallic symbol the mutability of virility and the immortality of continuity, that is, the replacement of the old and dying god by the young and virile god who himself will be replaced, and so on in an endless cycle of death and renewal. It is along the line of this strategy of criticism that I propose to examine the libretti of W. S. Gilbert in an effort, first, to disclose in them the presence of the paradigms of ritual, and, second, and more significantly, to portray them as exemplars of Christian belief. In so doing, I hope at the same time to reveal their hitherto undetected source.

If we abstract from the plots of the libretti of the leading operettas their quintessential action (taken in the Aristotelian sense of the term), we find their basic pattern of action to consist of some such arrangement as this. The protagonist is a young man of unknown or apparently low birth who falls in love with, and is in turn loved by, a young lady of high or even royal station. To gain the young lady's love and hand in marriage, he undergoes a series of trials and tests; in particular, his way to consummation is blocked by an older woman who uses every device at her command (devices often diabolic in their conception and execution) to prevent the achievement of his goal; we shall return to the significance of this older woman later on. At the moment of his deepest despair, when he is on the verge of loss of love or banishment or even death, his true identity is disclosed, often by the same older woman who has hitherto tried to prevent his marriage, and he is revealed to have been as highly born as his lady and assuredly worthy of her in every respect. The play ends with their marriage and its attendant celebrations.

This basic plot structure is clearly seen in the vicissitudes of Ralph Rackstraw in *H.M.S. Pinafore,* in Frederic in *The Pirates of Penzance,* in Strephon in *Iolanthe,* in Sir Ruthven Murgatroyd in *Ruddigore,* in Nanki-Poo in *The Mikado,* in Colonel Fairfax in *The Yeomen of the Guard,* and in Luiz in *The Gondoliers.* The most representative illustration is to be found in *The Mikado.* Disguised as a wandering minstrel, Nanki-Poo seeks the love of his lady Yum-Yum who is, however, betrothed to her guardian, Ko-Ko, the Lord High Executioner; at the same time, Nanki-Poo is under the order of the Mikado to marry Katisha, an elderly lady of the Court, and it is to flee this sentence that he has assumed the guise of a Second Trombone and has come to the town of Titipu to join with his true love. When the Mikado decrees that an execution is to take place in Titipu, the town having been quite derelict in its duty in this respect, a victim must be found, and, in despair over the frustration of his love, Nanki-Poo volunteers to be executed. As a reward for his civic enterprise, he is permitted to marry Yum-Yum for a period of a month, and the marriage is in fact about to be celebrated when Katisha bursts in to stop it; at the same time, she almost discloses his true identity. The approach of the Mikado is now announced, and, on his arrival, he is informed that an execution has been duly performed. Though he says that he would have been truly interested in so expeditious an execution, the main purpose for his visit to Titipu is to find his son, reported to be there. When he discovers that it is the Heir Apparent himself who has been the leading figure in the execution, he angrily orders those responsible for the fiasco executed as well. But Nanki-Poo is alive and married to Yum-Yum, and he assumes his rightful station; his other problem is solved when it is discovered that Katisha has married Ko-Ko. All difficulties having been surmounted, the play ends with the rites of the marriage celebration. I should add that the reversal of fortune of the protagonist is perhaps more sharply handled in *H.M.S. Pinafore* and in *The Gondoliers;* in *The Pirates of Penzance, Ruddigore,* and *The Yeomen of the Guard,* the reversal takes the form of freeing the protagonist from a false position or an unfair obligation; Gilbert has masterfully diversified his plots to bring out the great variety of treatment to which the basic action can be fruitfully submitted. The two basic requirements of the drama, reversal of the situation and recognition, are thus fully met.

In *The Hero with a Thousand Faces,* Joseph Campbell has given a most succinct description of the structure of action of the mythological hero's alternations of fortune in the form of a symbolic journey as follows:

> The mythological hero, setting forth from his common-day hut or castle, is lured, carried away, or else voluntarily proceeds, to the threshold of adventure. There he encounters a shadow presence that guards the passage. The hero may defeat or conciliate this power and go alive into the kingdom of the dark (brother-battle, dragon-battle: offering, charm), or be slain by the opponent and descend in death (dismemberment, crucifixion). Beyond the threshold, then, the hero journeys through a world of unfamiliar yet strangely intimate forces, some of which severely threaten him (tests), some of which give magical aid

(helpers). When he arrives at the nadir of the mythological round, he undergoes a supreme ordeal and gains his reward. The triumph may be represented as the hero's sexual union with the goddess-mother of the world (sacred marriage), his recognition by his father-creator (father atonement), his own divinization (apotheosis), or again—if the powers have remained unfriendly to him—his theft of the boon he came to gain (bride-theft, fire-theft); intrinsically, it is an expansion of consciousness and therewith of being (illumination, transfiguration, freedom). The final work is that of the return. If the powers have blessed the hero, he now sets forth under their protection (emissary); if not, he flees and is pursued (transformation flight, obstacle flight). At the return threshold the transcendental powers must remain behind; the hero re-emerges from the kingdom of dread (return, resurrection), the boon that he brings restores the world (elixir).

This ideal version of the monomyth is substantiated in many ways by Lord Raglan's study of the myth of the hero, in which, from an analysis of the stories of Oedipus, Theseus, Romulus, Heracles, Perseus, Jason, Bellerophon, Pelops, Asclepios, Dionysos, Apollo, Zeus, Joseph, Moses, Elijah, Watu Gunung, Nyikang, Siegfried, Llew Llawgyffes, Arthur, and Robin Hood, he arrives at a pattern made up of the following incidents, all or most of which occur in the life of the hero:

1. The hero's mother is a royal virgin;
2. His father is a king, and
3. Often a near relative of his mother, but
4. The circumstances of his conception are unusual, and

5. He is also reputed to be the son of a God.
6. At birth an attempt is made, usually by his father or his maternal grandfather, to kill him, but
7. He is spirited away, and
8. Reared by foster-parents in a far country.
9. We are told nothing of his childhood, but
10. On reaching manhood he returns or goes to his future kingdom.
11. After a victory over the king and/or a giant, dragon or wild beast,
12. He marries a princess, often the daughter of his predecessor, and
13. Becomes king.
14. For a time he reigns uneventfully, and
15. Prescribes laws, but
16. Later he loses favour with the Gods and/or his subjects and
17. Is driven from the throne and city, after which
18. He meets with a mysterious death,
19. Often at the top of a hill.
20. His children, if any, do not succeed him.
21. His body is not buried, but nevertheless
22. He has one or more holy sepulchres.

Lord Raglan rightfully suggests that the considerable number of coincidences points to a ritual pattern as the origin of the myth of the hero and he notes that the three principal incidents in the life of the hero, his birth, his accession to the throne, and his death, correspond to the three principal *rites de passage,* at birth, at initiation, and at death. A somewhat similar pattern is depicted by A. M. Hocart in *Kingship* on the basis of his investigation of the Fijian, Brahamanic Indian, modern Cambodian, ancient Egyptian, Hebrew, Roman, Byzantine, Abyssinian, and European coronation ceremonies. This pattern is corroborated in turn by Tor Irstam's study of the coronation rites in the central belt of Africa, by G. Widengren's analysis of the Canaanite enthronement ritual, by R. Patai's study of the rites in the installation ceremonies of the Hebrew Kings, and by S. H. Hooke's description of the ideal myth and ritual pattern of the ancient Near East. And indeed, in the Annex II to V. V (ii) (a) titled, "Christus Patiens," in the sixth volume of *A Study of History*, Toynbee goes so far as to show no less than seventy-eight points of similarity between the life of Christ and the lives of a number of pagan heroes. The picture is thus completely filled out in all of its confirming details: the protagonist of the drama descends from and owes his power to move us to his incarnation as the dying-reborn god-hero-king of ancient myth and religion; he is our surrogate through whose sufferings and triumphs we are vicariously purged and redeemed.

We must not, however, expect the structure of religious ritual to be reproduced literally and exactly in the structure of drama which, in the course of its descent from and development of religious ritual, has omitted, telescoped, expanded, and thus changed the elements of religious ritual into a more compact and meaningful (from the point of view of formal aesthetic requirements) shape. We may therefore assert with some confidence that the basic action structure of the libretti of W. S. Gilbert is in the long run ultimately derived from the pattern of action of religious ritual and it is the immanent power and thrust of this pattern, infused and diffused through them, which gives them both their architecture and their capacity to move audiences, even when both artist and audience may be quite unaware of its presence in them. Nevertheless, we must raise these two questions: from what source did W. S. Gilbert most directly derive this pattern, and, was it from this source that the specific Christian coloring of the libretti comes?

I would suggest that Gilbert's source is Spenser's *The Faerie Queene*. Now, it is true that nowhere does Gilbert specifically allude to Spenser either in his libretti or in his letters. At the same time, it is equally true that Gilbert was extraordinarily attracted to the concept of the Fairy Land. The locale of two of the operettas, three of the verse plays, and many of the Bab Ballads is wholly and explicitly Fairy Land. Moreover, Gilbert, like Spenser before him, uses the Fairy Land as a symbol of the golden age, both as a criterion of judgment of contemporary manners and aspirations and as an ideal to be attained. To be sure, this is circumstantial evidence, but when Gilbert's libretti are read in the light of *The Faerie Queene,* when we place side by side the narratives of the adventures of, let us say, the Redcrosse Knight, with a typical Gilbert protagonist, let us say, Luiz in *The Gondoliers,* then the pattern of action will be seen to be startlingly and surely not coincidentally alike. In both cases, the pattern of action takes the form of the adventures of a young man of seemingly humble birth who sallies forth to do battle for the love of his lady; he encounters (physically and spiritually) enemies both without and within him (again physically and spiritually); he is apparently defeated by his own defects of character but learns through his actions and their reactions on and in him the lessons of Christian humility, obedience, and love; he overcomes his final great adversary; and, in the end, has earned the right to be proclaimed, and to be treated as, a true Christian knight. Thus the mythological journey of the hero has been allegorized into the pattern of Christian triumph over temptation and of resurrection over fall. G. Wilson Knight has written of Shakespeare: "Though his drama is no passive reflection of Christian dogma it certainly does very often, in matters both infernal and paradisal, demonstrate, not indeed the truth of the dogma, but the truth of *that* the truth of which the dogma exists to establish." The same may be said of Spenser, and, therefore, of Gilbert as well.

Revealing as this similarity is, it may be objected that it is rather too general, too capable of universal and therefore non-discriminating application. There is, however, one other point of comparison which is to my mind clear-cut and convincing. I have already referred to the mysterious older woman who plays such a key role in Gilbert's libretti. This figure takes the form of Little Buttercup in *H.M.S. Pinafore,* Ruth in *The Pirates of Penzance,* Iolanthe in the opera of the same name, Lady Blanche in *Princess Ida,* Katisha in *The Mikado,* Dame Hannah in *Ruddigore,* and Inez in *The Gondoliers.* This figure plays a double role in the action: on the one hand, she is often an obstruction in the path of success of the protagonist; on the other hand, she is just as often the revealer of truth whose story finally clears the way for him. She is thus in her dual role the reincarnation of the Great-Terrible Mother of ancient religion and myth; she is Lilith-Eve, Isis-Osiris, Asherath-Anath-Ashtaroth, Athene-Aphrodite, Mary-Mary, vampire-wife, temptress-sister, the Great Goddess, in short in her two-fold character of witch-mother, seductress-protectress. The anthropological, archaeological, mythological, and psychological evidence for the power and persistence of the idea of the Great Mother in the ancient world has been fully set forth by Bachofen in *Das Mutterrecht,* Bruno Bettelheim in *Symbolic Wounds,* Robert Briffault in *The Mothers,* Frazer throughout *The Golden Bough* and especially in *Adonis Attis Osiris,* Freud in *Totem and Taboo* and *Moses and Monotheism,* Arnold van Gennep in *The Rites of Passage,* S. Giedion in *The*

Eternal Present: The Beginnings of Art, Jung in virtually every one of his papers and books, Gertrude R. Levy in *The Gate of Horn,* Margaret Murray in *The God of the Witches,* Erich Neumann in *The Origins and History of the Consciousness* and in the fuller *The Great Mother,* and by Otto Rank in *The Myth of the Birth of the Hero.* Mircea Eliade who has treated the archetype of the Great Mother with learning and discernment in several of his books well sums up its double character in *Myths, Dreams and Mysteries:* "To men of the traditional cultures . . . all life was a hierophany, a manifestation of the sacred. Creation—at every cosmic level—presupposed the intervention of a holy power. Accordingly, the divinities of life and of fertility represented sources of holiness and of power and of this their androgyny was confirmatory. But *androgyny extends even to divinities who are pre-eminently masculine, or feminine.* This means that androgyny has become a general formula signifying *autonomy, strength, wholeness;* to say of a divinity that it is androgyny is as much as to say that it is the ultimate being, the ultimate reality." The penetration of the archetype into myth and thence into literature has been documented by Joseph Campbell in *The Hero with a Thousand Faces,* Mario Praz in *The Romantic Agony,* Lord Raglan in *Jocasta's Crime,* but above all by Robert Graves who attests to the potency of the goddess in his own person and poetry, that poet, who with crookedly broken nose, furrowed cheeks, and coarse grey hair, ". . . still stands ready, with a boy's presumption,/To court the queen in her high silk pavilion."

But nowhere in modern literature, to my knowledge at least, has the theme of the duplex female been more elaborated than in *The Faerie Queene.* It is true that the white devils and insatiable countesses of Jacobean drama still excite the reader with horror; the Romantic period proliferated, as Praz tells us, the Matilda of Lewis, the Velleda of Chateaubriand, the Salammbô of Flaubert, the Carmen of Mérimée, the Cecily of Sue, the Conchita of Pierre Louys, the Cleopatra of Gautier, in addition to the Mater Lachrymarum of De Quincey and the "La Belle Dame sans merci" of Keats; and later in the century there are in England Swinburne, Pater, and Wilde; in Italy D'Annunzio; and in France Baudelaire, Huysmans, and Laforgue. But in none of these are the changes of the theme rung with such variety, subtlety, and range of symbolic significance as in *The Faerie Queene*. For every Una, there is a Duessa; just as Nature destroys, so she creates; and if the challenge to Zeus and the reign of law is made by woman in her guise as Change, so she is put down by woman in her other guise as Nature:

> Then forth issewed (great goddesse) great Dame
>   Nature,
> With goodly port and gracious majesty, . . .
> Yet certes by her face and physnomy,
> Whether she man or woman inly were,
> That could not any creature well descry: . . .
>
> This great grandmother of all creatures bred,
> Great Nature, ever young yet full of eld,
> Still mooving, yet unmoved from her sted,
> Unseene of any, yet of all beheld, . . .

No student of Spenser has more penetratingly perceived the ambivalent (and thus simultaneously the androgynous) role of woman in *The Faerie Queene* than has A. C. Hamilton when he writes in *The Structure of Allegory in "The Faerie Queene"*:

The simultaneous awareness of the power of virtue and the wretchedness of life drives the poem into metaphor. Consequently its central visions are always twofold: Una is veiled, woman's beauty is combined with the serpent's tail in Error and Duessa, the glorious Lucifera as the fallen Faery Queen, Florimell and the false Florimell, Amoret bound, Venus with the snake wound around her feet, Isis and the crocodile. By exploring these visions the poem moves towards an image of man seen perfected in Arthur and also the image of Nature. As Arthur appears in the various knights, Nature appears in her various forms, from that original vision of the Faery Queen and the primary vision of Una to Belphoebe, Amoret, Florimell, Britomart, Colin's damsel surrounded by the graces and maidens, until Nature herself appears in the Mutability Cantos. We see this unfallen Nature herself in opposition to fallen Nature, her counterpart in the twofold vision. Since this nature is both without and within man, we see unfallen man in the images of virtue at one with nature opposed to fallen man in the images of vice. Once we see that opposition on all levels, Nature is redeemed, and therefore man. It is in this sense that Spenser delivers in his poem a golden world.

I believe that this tradition of the two-fold image of woman yielding up in the end the two-fold vision of Nature and therefore of man's redemption through suffering operates with sufficient force to account for its presence in Gilbert's libretti, and I am therefore sure that it is not at all necessary to attribute it to personal, psycho-analytical reasons as does Hesketh Pearson when he observes of Gilbert: "The other aspect of his work that appears to be related to impressions of the period of his youth is the mockery he makes in his operas of ageing females. Though this has some connection with his strong attraction for pretty women, held in check by an equally strong moral sense, the origin is possibly to be found in his total lack of sympathy with his mother, amounting in time to active dislike, his feeling revenging itself on all women whose age and insensitiveness called her to mind." Whatever the reason, this archetypal ambivalence, whose descent from myth through Spenser to Gilbert we have just traced, does play a most crucial part in the libretti. Thus, when we place Fidessa's letter to the King of Eden, intended to prevent the betrothal of the Redcrosse Knight to Una:

> "To thee, most mighty king of Eden fayre,
> Her greeting sends in these sad lines addresst . . .
> And bids thee be advized for the best,
> Ere thou thy daughter linck in holy band
> Of wedlocke to that new unknowen guest:
> For he already plighted his right hand
> Unto another love, and to another land.
>
> To me, sad mayd, or rather widow sad,
> He was affyaunced long time before,
> And sacred pledges he both gave, and had,
> False errant knight, infamous, and foreswore!"

side by side with Katisha's plaint:

> Your revels cease! Assist me, all of you!
> I claim my perjured lover, Nanki-Poo!
> Oh, fool! to shun delights that never cloy!
> Come back, oh, shallow fool! Come back to joy!
> > The hour of gladness
> > Is dead and gone;

> In silent sadness
>   I live alone!
> The hope I cherished
>   All lifeless lies,
> And all has perished
>   Save love, which never dies!
> Oh, faithless one, this insult you shall rue!
> In vain for mercy on your knees you'll sue.
> I'll tear the mask from your disguising.
>
> My wrongs with vengeance shall be crowned!
> My wrongs with vengeance shall be crowned!

when we place these situations side by side, then, the links in the chain have been closed and the knot between myth, Christianity, Spenser, and Gilbert has been tied.

Gilbert, like Spenser, delivers a golden world, yet again, as in Spenser, we cannot escape hearing in him a note of melancholy, an overtone of despair. The very fact that Spenser left his grand structure uncompleted is a melancholy thing in itself; considering that there are already signs of loss of strength and imagination in Books V and VI, we cannot help wondering what the remaining sixteen books would have held for us. Similarly, after *The Gondoliers* and the break with Sullivan, Gilbert turned out libretti of the order of *The Mountebanks* and *His Excellency,* and even the renewed collaboration with Sullivan could produce nothing better than *Utopia, Limited* and *The Grand Duke.* Even in the most golden operettas, the Sophoclean note is struck:

> Is life a boon?
>   If so, it must befall,
>   That Death, whene'er he call,

Must call too soon. . . .
Is life a thorn?
   Then count it not a whit!
   Man is well done with it;
Soon as he's born
   He should all means essay
   To put the plague away; . . .

Nor is it even certain that art itself can triumph over time:

Is it, and can it be,
Nature hath this decree,
   Nothing poetic in the world shall dwell?
Or that in all her works
Something poetic lurks,
   Even in colocynth and calomel?
                I cannot tell.

"I cannot tell"—this, perhaps, is the final answer of the poet. No wonder, then, that art and criticism and life itself, all alike, are played:

On a cloth untrue,
With a twisted cue,
And elliptical billiard balls!

John Bush Jones

In Search of
Archibald Grosvenor:
A New Look at
Gilbert's Patience

(1965)

Ever since an anonymous first-night critic attempted
to equate Archibald Grosvenor with Algernon Swinburne
eighty-four years ago,[1] scholars, critics, and assorted devotees of Gilbert and Sullivan have tried their hand at
identifying the prototypes of the two rival poets in *Patience*. Most of the attention has been given to Reginald
Bunthorne, and, amidst some rather wild and haphazard
guesses, a few sound theories have been put forth. Most
of the earlier writers on the subject favored an equation
of Grosvenor with Swinburne and Bunthorne with Oscar
Wilde.[2] It was not until a decade ago that Leslie Baily
and Audrey Williamson (independently, it appears) offered

more satisfactory suggestions, suggestions which need little additional support in order to establish a fairly positive identification for the prototype of Bunthorne.[3] However, neither Mr. Baily nor Miss Williamson hazards a guess at the identity of a model for Grosvenor, the latter finally despairing of the fact that Grosvenor's poems "can hardly be conceived as the parody of any known writer of the day." [4] It is my present purpose to add a few new bits of evidence in support of Miss Williamson's identification of Bunthorne and to suggest possible prototypes for Grosvenor which I believe to be not only plausible, but accurate, not only consistent with the satiric intent of *Patience,* but also instrumental in adding a new dimension to that satire.

The conclusion to be drawn from Miss Williamson's cogent arguments is that Reginald Bunthorne is a composite of the appearance, mannerisms, physical attributes, and artistic tastes and abilities of several of the Pre-Raphaelite and "Aesthetic" figures of Gilbert's day. Though the character embodies a few characteristics of Whistler, Burne-Jones, and Rossetti, and rather more of Oscar Wilde, the primary component both of Bunthorne's poems and personality is Algernon Swinburne. While carefully comparing evidence from *Patience* with the careers of these men, Miss Williamson stops short of examining the poetry itself. She only remarks in passing that "Bunthorne's literary style, as exemplified in his recited poetry and conversation, is without doubt the parody of a particular literary style, not (like the language of the girls) just a general reflection of the aesthetic jargon." [5] A look at the poetry, I believe, will add even further weight to Swinburne's dominant position in the character of Bunthorne.

If Gilbert was seeking a living model for his poetic

parodies which the theatre-going public would have recognized, he would not have had too many resources open to him. Oscar Wilde's first collection of poems appeared in June of 1881, three months after the opening of *Patience*. Rossetti's output was confined to the single volume, *Poems,* of 1870 and its subsequent editions. Swinburne, on the other hand, had published seven substantial volumes of poetry before 1881, most of which went through several editions.[6] It might also be added that Swinburne was better known to the general public than Rossetti, thanks to his vitriolic counterattack on Buchanan's "Fleshly School" and his other defenses of the Pre-Raphaelites.

In addition to the argument for notoriety and familiarity through sheer bulk of publication, there is evidence in Bunthorne's poems themselves that points directly to Swinburne. Metrically, none of Rossetti's poems published before the writing of *Patience* bear even a distant resemblance to "Oh Hollow! Hollow! Hollow!," whereas the structure of the first six lines (of eight-line stanzas) of at least two of Swinburne's poems, "To Victor Hugo," and "Blessed Among Women," are reproduced exactly in Bunthorne's lyric:

> Yet though all this be thus,
> Be those men praised of us
> Who have loved and wrought and sorrowed and
>   not sinned
> For fame or fear of gold,
> Nor waxed for winter cold,
> Nor changed for changes of the worldly wind; [7]

> When from the poet's plinth
> The amorous colocynth
> Yearns for the aloe, faint with rapturous thrills,

How can he hymn her throes
Knowing as well he knows,
That they are only uncompounded pills? [8]

It is partly the meter, but, more important, the "verbal tricks" and inverted repetition of ideas in such a poem as Swinburne's *"Satia Te Sanguine"* that are echoed in Bunthorne's "Heart Foam":

I wish you were dead, my dear;
I would give you, had I to give,
Some death too bitter to fear;
It is better to die than live.[9]

Oh, to be wafted away
From this black Aceldama of sorrow,
Where the dust of an earthy to-day
Is the earth of a dusty tomorrow!   (p. 38)

Swinburne's heavy use of alliteration is mimicked in such lines as,

What time the poet hath hymned
The writhing maid, lithe-limbed
Quivering on amaranthine asphodel,   (p. 33)

in a way similar to his own anonymous self-parody of 1880, "Nephelidia."

From the depth of the dreamy decline of the dawn
through a notable nimbus of nebulous
noonshine.[10]

These literary parallels concur in every respect with Miss Williamson's arguments to make Swinburne the most likely candidate for the primary, though not sole, source of the person and poetry of Reginald Bunthorne.

The character and literary efforts of Archibald Grosvenor also suggest a composite prototype. Miss Williamson's attempt to write off Grosvenor's good looks, insipid manner, and child-like poetry as leftovers from Gilbert's earlier draft in which the rivals were curates rather than poets, is a disappointing anti-climax to her careful analysis of Bunthorne. Granted, Grosvenor is less clearly drawn and not as fully developed as the "Fleshly Poet," but there are plenty of hints to suggest that Gilbert had some of his contemporaries in mind while creating this "Idyllic Poet." This term, "Idyllic Poet," occurs in the *Dramatis Personae* of *Patience,* but, unlike Bunthorne's appelation "Fleshly," it does not immediately suggest a generic identification with a particular school or group of poets. "Idyllic" suggests, rather, a type of poetic composition—more or less simple, romantic narrative verse often depicting peace, happiness, and contentment. Tennyson's *Idylls of the King* comes first to mind, but the Poet Laureate may be summarily dismissed as the object of Gilbert's satire since none of Grosvenor's characteristics jibe with the popular impression of Tennyson. Besides, in spoofing Tennyson's *The Princess* in 1870, Gilbert carefully called his play "A Respectful Per-version"; there is nothing respectful about the treatment of contemporary poets in Grosvenor.

A second, far more plausible, conjecture is William Morris. Virtually all of Morris' major poems published before 1881 are narratives and may, without stretching the term too far, be classified as idylls. In addition to this hint in the *Dramatis Personae,* there are several characteristics of Grosvenor's manner and career that point to Morris as at least one of the models. Before discussing these, however, I would like to offer one further—though slightly tangential—implication of the term "idyllic" as applied to Grosvenor. Ever watchful for a pun, even in such a mature work as *Patience*, Gilbert may have labelled Grosvenor "idyllic" in reference to Morris' well-known phrase, "An idle singer of an empty day." This seemingly far-fetched suggestion draws further strength from the similarity of the sentiment expressed in Grosvenor's "*They* [his poems] will not cure thee of thy love" (p. 53) and Morris'

> I cannot ease the burden of your fears,
> Or make quick-coming death a little thing,
> Or bring again the pleasure of past years,
> Nor for my words shall ye forget your tears[11]

Grosvenor's other similarities to Morris begin with his general physical appearance. In contrast to the diminutive George Grossmith's portrayal of Bunthorne in the original production of *Patience* (Swinburne was a small, odd-looking individual), the handsome and stocky Rutland Barrington was cast as Grosvenor. William Morris was known generally as a strikingly handsome man "rather below the middle height, deep-chested and powerfully made, with a head of singular beauty." [12] At one point in the second act of *Patience*, Bunthorne declares that he will make Grosvenor "cut his curly hair" (p. 60). A glance at photographs of Morris in any of the many biographies—not to mention the outlandishly exaggerated hair in contemporary caricatures—reveals wildly curly locks to be a predominant physical feature of Morris.

Taking handsomeness as an attribute drawn from

reality, Gilbert warps the picture by a flight into the realm of caricature. By extension of Grosvenor's good looks, he furnishes Grosvenor with an overbearing conceit: "It is pleasant to be able to gaze at leisure upon those features which all others may gaze upon at their good will! . . . Ah, I am a very Narcissus!" (p. 65).

Before 1881 Morris had begun his lectures on art and crafts, and several of these speeches had appeared in pamphlet form: *The Lesser Arts* (1877), *The Art of the People* (1879), and *The Beauty of Life* (1880). These writings already reveal in Morris what he was later to call his passionate "desire to produce beautiful things," [13] and a part of his idea of beauty is that the beautiful is basically the simple. Grosvenor describes himself both as "a trustee for Beauty" and "the Apostle of Simplicity" (p. 42) both possible reflections of Morris' published artistic mission.

Even Morris' socialistic views, juxtaposed with his personal wealth and landholdings in a typically Gilbertian fashion, do not escape a wry notice:

> I may say at once, I'm a man of propertee—
>   Hey willow waly O!
>   Money, I despise it,
>   Many people prize it.   (p. 41)

Though Morris did not found the Socialist League until 1884, he was already treasurer of the National Liberal League and had proclaimed his socialistic views in the lectures mentioned earlier and in the *Manifesto to the Working Men of England* in 1877. It may be assumed fairly safely that these views were known widely enough to allow for a sly dig in a theatrical performance. I also feel that Morris' socialism as a referent helps to make clear the rather befuddling contrast between Grosvenor's apparent wealth and hatred of money.

Reference to Morris alone, however, cannot account for the full portrait of Grosvenor, nor does it seem likely that Gilbert even had Morris uppermost in his mind. Morris was not the only narrative poet to achieve popularity in the decades preceding *Patience,* and the appellation "idyllic" more rightly applies to Coventry Patmore than to the "idle singer of an empty day." Patmore's poems were more familiar to many Englishmen than those of Morris, especially *The Angel in the House* and *The Victories of Love,* those horrendously long poetic tracts on the bliss of domestic and marital love. In the first few editions of the former poem, the several sections were designated "Idyl I," "Idyl II," and so forth, although in the later editions they were labelled cantos. That these poems, which Frederic Harrison referred to as "goody-goody dribble," [14] were still familiar enough for public satire in the 1880's is evidenced by Swinburne's parody "The Person in the House," appearing in his anonymous *Heptalogia* the year before the production of *Patience.* The popularity of Patmore is further attested to by the fact that between the first edition of 1854 and 1896, the year of the poet's death, an estimated quarter million copies of *The Angel in the House* were sold, not counting the popular edition of 1887.[15] Patmore's popularity and peculiar brand of poetry, then, would have made him an easy target for theatrical satire, and his narrative verse and incessant theme of marital joy strongly suggest him as a model for the "idyllic" Grosvenor.

If Grosvenor embodies Morris' physical attributes and a few of his ideas on art and society, even more does he display the personality traits of Patmore as they were popularly thought of from the public's reading of *The Angel in the House*. Patmore was generally thought to be of an "insipid amiability," [16] to be "a mild, soft, and rather sentimental personality." [17] This description jibes with Grosvenor's behavior as well as with Bunthorne's comments on it: "I know what it is; it's his confounded mildness . . . . But I will show the world I can be as mild as he. If they want insipidity, they shall have it" (p. 59). It matters not at all that Patmore's true nature was "haughty, imperious, combative, sardonic, susceptible, and capable of deep tenderness." [18] For the purpose of public satire, the popular notion of the poet's personality is a fitter subject than his real character.

Patmore was also generally thought to be sanctimonious as well as insipid.[19] Grosvenor's "holier-than-thou" attitude, if taken as a reflection of Patmore's supposed religiosity, helps to explain a point about *Patience* that has long troubled critics. The line "Your style is much too sanctified—your cut is too canonical" (p. 59) has hitherto been interpreted as a remnant of the earlier "rival curates" version of the play. However, the description applies equally well to the self-righteous and almost clerically mild and moral poet as it would have to the clergyman of the original draft. Taken as an aspect of the popular notion of Patmore's character, then, "canonical" may be viewed as an integral part of the literary satire of *Patience* rather than as an anomalous leftover from Gilbert's original plan for the play.

The poems of Grosvenor comprise the final piece of evidence suggesting that this character is a composite of familiar aspects of the person and poetry of William Morris and Coventry Patmore, with the emphasis on the latter. Both of Grosvenor's "decalets," as well as most of his song "A magnet hung in a hardware shop," are written in somewhat irregular octosyllabic couplets. This metrical arrangement and rime scheme was a favorite of both narrative poets on whom Grosvenor appears to be based. Several of Morris' shorter pieces ("A Good Knight in Prison," "The Haystack in the Floods," and "The God of the Poor") and substantial portions of "The Blue Closet," *Love is Enough,* and *The Life and Death of Jason* follow this scheme, while Patmore's lengthy *The Victories of Love* is in octosyllabic couplets throughout. Some of Morris' simple narrative technique and the "story-telling" quality of his verse have their counterparts in Grosvenor's poems:

> There was a lord that hight Maltete,
> Among great lords he was right great,
> On poor folk trod he like the dirt,
> None but God might do him hurt.[20]

> Gentle Jane was good as gold,
> She always did as she was told;
> She never spoke when her mouth was full,
> Or caught bluebottles their legs to pull.   (p. 53)

However, in homely diction and mundane subject matter, Grosvenor's poems more closely approximate the domestic verse of Patmore:

> I hope you're well, I write to say
> Frederick has got, besides his pay,
> A good appointment in the Docks;
> Also thank you for the frocks
> And shoes for Baby.[21]

He punched his poor little sisters' heads,
And cayenne-peppered their four-post beds,
He plastered their hair with cobbler's wax,
And dropped hot halfpennies down their backs.

(p. 54)

Finally, Patmore's constant reiteration of the rewards of virtue and the bliss of marriage is echoed in Grosvenor's

And when she grew up she was given in marriage
To a first-class earl who keeps his carriage. (p. 53)

The Patmore-like morality of these lines about a very good girl Grosvenor declares is not "calculated to bring the blush of shame to the cheek of modesty" (p. 53).

The evidence for an irrefutably positive identification of a prototype for Archibald Grosvenor is, to be sure, fragmentary. But, until a document is discovered wherein Gilbert has expressly declared his intentions and sources, the text of *Patience* itself must serve as the only source of information. From the evidence available at this time, I feel more than justified in offering the foregoing suggestion of a composite of Morris and Patmore, primarily Patmore, as the foundation of the "Idyllic Poet" Grosvenor.

Furthermore, I find that this interpretation is not only consistent with the satire embodied in *Patience,* but also serves to reveal an aspect of that satire not yet considered by critics. It is true that an audience or reader can appreciate the opera without knowing that Grosvenor is modelled on Morris and Patmore; this knowledge is not necessary to understand the humor of the fluctuating poetic tastes of the "rapturous maidens." However, in

viewing Grosvenor in this new light, it becomes apparent
that Gilbert is having his fun with the Philistines as much
as with the so-called aesthetes. Morris was somewhat on
the fringe of the Pre-Raphaelites, the bulk of his poetry
displaying few of the elements of the esoteric lyric flights
of those men. Patmore, by anybody's definition, was a
"popular" poet; the mundane, almost anti-poetic, nature
of his subject matter and the mode of his presentation of
the idyll of married love were directed at a public taste
far different from, perhaps below, that of the people who
really understood or blindly followed the Pre-Raphaelite
and aesthetic poets. Gilbert, in having the girls vacillate
in their affections between the "aesthetic" Bunthorne and
the "commonplace" and almost Philistinian Grosvenor, is
ridiculing the "popular" as well as the cultivated poetic
tastes of his day. The satire takes an even sharper turn
when Bunthorne convinces Grosvenor to become

> An every-day young man:
> A commonplace type
> With a stick and a pipe
> And a half-bred black-and-tan.   (p. 68)

When Grosvenor appears at the end in his business suit
and bowler, he is the living picture of the middle-class,
un-aesthetic, Philistine taste that his poetry had expressed
all along. His aesthetic pretensions are broken down completely, his true "anti-culture" nature is revealed, and—
by extension—Gilbert has taken his final swipe at the
Philistines with as much vigor as he had earlier bludg-
eoned the aesthetes.

The common accusation that Gilbert is militantly
pro-Philistine in *Patience* no longer seems justified.

Rather, the identification of the insipid Grosvenor with the commonplaces of Patmore's poetry makes the rivalry between him and the "highly spiced" Bunthorne more clearly defined and the satire, now double edged, more pointed.

Notes

1. "An Aesthetic Opera" (anon. rev.) London *Times,* April 25, 1881, p. 10.
2. This point of view is most fully presented by S. J. Adair Fitz-Gerald in *The Story of the Savoy Opera* (London, 1924), pp. 80-82, and by Isaac Goldberg in *The Story of Gilbert and Sullivan,* rev. ed. (New York, 1935), pp. 252-261 *passim.*
3. See Baily's *The Gilbert and Sullivan Book* (London, 1953), pp. 175-180, and Miss Williamson's *Gilbert & Sullivan Opera* (New York, 1953), pp. 80-85.
4. Williamson, p. 85.
5. *Ibid.,* pp. 83-84.
6. *Atalanta in Calydon:* 1865 (First ed.), 1865 (2nd ed.), 1866, 1868, 1875; *Poems and Ballads:* 1866 (First ed.), 1866-67 (2nd ed.) , 1868, 1871, 1873; *Songs Before Sunrise:* 1871, 1874, 1877, 1880; *Songs of Two Nations:* 1875; *Poems and Ballads, Second Series:* 1878 (First ed.), 1878 (2nd ed.), 1880; *Songs of the Springtides:* 1880 (First ed.), 1880 (2nd ed.); *Studies in Song:* 1880.
7. "To Victor Hugo," in *The Works of Algernon Charles Swinburne* (Philadelphia, n.d.), p. 65—hereafter cited as "Swinburne."
8. William Schwenck Gilbert, *Patience,* in *Selected Operas, First Series* (London: Macmillan, 1956), p. 33. This edition of Gilbert's comic operas, no better or worse than any other readily available edition, does not number the lines. Future references to *Patience* are incorporated in the text by page reference to this edition.
9. Swinburne, p. 43.
10. Swinburne, p. 654.
11. *The Earthly Paradise,* "An Apology," ll. 2-5.
12. J. W. Mackail in *DNB* s.v. "William Morris."
13. Quoted in *Victorian Poets and Poetics* ed. Walter E. Houghton and G. Robert Stange (Boston, 1959), pp. 583-584.
14. Quoted in J. C. Reid, *The Mind and Art of Coventry Patmore* (London, 1957) , p. 3.

15. Reid, p. 3.
16. Richard Garnett in *DNB* s.v. "Coventry Patmore."
17. Basil Champneys, *Memoirs and Correspondence of Coventry Patmore* (London, 1900), I, 394.
18. *DNB,* loc. cit.
19. *Ibid.*
20. "The God of the Poor," in *The Collected Works of William Morris,* ed. May Morris (London, 1910), IX, 157.
21. "From Jane to Mrs. Graham," *The Victories of Love,* in *The Poems of Coventry Patmore,* ed. Frederick Page (London, 1949). p. 260.

David A. Randall

The Gondoliers
and Princess Ida

(1965)

There has never been a satisfactory bibliography of
Gilbert and Sullivan. The late Townley Searle published
one in 1931, but even then it was unreliable and it is now
hopelessly out-of-date. Though he deserves high praise
for pioneering, he had not the slightest interest in the
accurate transcription of his knowledge and almost no
power to set forth a complicated situation with clarity.
The late Carroll A. Wilson was well along with what
promised to be the definitive work, but he never did get
around to finishing it. He was defeated, not by the complexities of the task itself, as a writer in *The Times Literary Supplement* recently implied, but by death. When
his library was sold, his widow retained his beloved Gilbert and Sullivan collection, hoping to finish the work
herself, which never happened. The Lilly Library re-

cently acquired the Wilson collection, with the exception of Reginald Allen's, now at the Pierpont Morgan Library, the most extensive known. But somehow in the decade and a half following Wilson's death, his manuscript bibliography disappeared. Fortunately, however, many of the volumes still have his rough notes laid in. These will be of inestimable value to anyone who can gather the temerity to tackle the formidable task of a full-dress Gilbert and Sullivan bibliography.

The collection is particularly rich in American editions, some of which contain material that has never appeared elsewhere. Reginald Allen's "Prologue" to his *The First Night Gilbert and Sullivan* (New York, 1958), explains how this came about.

As our concern in this edition is to present the texts as actually performed on the first nights, we are fortunately relieved of the complex considerations educed by prepublication librettos. Gilbert all too frequently made important changes at the last moment, rewrote or excised complete lyrics within a day or two of first-night curtain-time. His nimble publishers could evidently keep up with him on twenty-four hours' notice. But for our purposes these changes of creative fancy, however fascinating, are like authors' manuscript drafts and never of first-night textual significance. What! Never? Well, hardly ever!—as you will see. There was one exception, *The Pirates of Penzance,* which alone of all the operas had its first public run in America and had no published libretto for many months thereafter. So its first-night text was, of necessity, a prepublication text and differed considerably from the first published version.

The first American librettos of other Gilbert and
Sullivan operas after *The Pirates of Penzance*
(whether pirated or authorized) were textually at
least as early as the London first-night librettos, and
in some instances were based on even earlier Gilbert
drafts. This is readily understood when one recog-
nizes that a transatlantic crossing for the manuscript
took ten or twelve days, the American printer required time for setting and his or Carte's lawyer
time for copyright registry, and the American company at least a couple of weeks for rehearsal, if the
first New World performance was to follow closely
the London première. So it is not improbable that
the manuscript for the first American libretto was a
month earlier than Chappell & Company's final
proofs—and in a month's time during rehearsals Gilbert could do an amazing amount of rewriting.
Thus, the earliest American printing of *Patience,
Princess Ida, The Gondoliers, Utopia (Limited),* and
The Grand Duke discloses material that never appeared in published British librettos, showing clearly
their origin in Gilbert's prepublication manuscript
proofs.

This is particularly true of *The Gondoliers,* where a
song, part of a song, and considerable dialogue appear in
the first American edition but not in the English. The
following material is taken largely from Wilson's notes
laid in his various copies, with additional information
supplied by Reginald Allen.

The Gondoliers

December 7, 1889-June 20, 1891
(Savoy Theatre)

Collation: 48 pp. (1) (2) Title page; verso, Dramatis Personae; (3)-47, Text, with imprint under a rule at foot of p. 47 reading: Henderson & Spalding, Printers, 3 & 5 Marylebone Lane, London, W.; (48), blank. Size 8⅜ x 5⅜ inches.

Blue-gray wrappers. Front wrapper corresponds to title page. Outside the box, at the top: An Edition of GILBERT'S EIGHT COMIC OPERAS, price, cloth, 2/6; at the bottom, copyright notice; at the left, in caps, reading up, Vocal Score, 5/-Net.; at the right, in caps, reading down, Pianoforte Solo, 3/-Net. Inner front wrapper advertises *Mikado*. Inner back wrapper advertises *Ruddigore,* outer the *Yeomen.*

FIRST EDITION, with p. 48 blank. The speech on p. 6:—"Are you peeping? Can you see me?"—is given to the non-existent character "Fer" and p. 16, line 16 has the error: "of that is no possible doubt." But the most important change occurs on pages 12-13. One will recall the entry, early in the first act, of the Duke and Duchess of Plaza-Toro and their much-snubbed "suite," Luiz. The Duke sings "In enterprise of martial kind," with its battery of adjectival quadrisyllabics, the Duke and Duchess retire, and Luiz and Casilda "rush to each others' arms" and sing what the first edition calls a "Recit," followed by a ballad by Luiz, "Thy wintry scorn I dearly prize."

In the second edition, they sing a "Recit and Duettino," the ballad is dropped and is replaced by the familiar two-part song with its sighing ending, "Ah, well-beloved." "Fer," p. 6, is changed to the still incorrect "Ter," and the error on page 16 is corrected.

Later editions have the speech on page 6 correctly attributed to "Tessa."

The first American libretto of *The Gondoliers* is a gray wrappered 12mo, n.d., with imprint of The John Church Co., Cincinnati, of 48 pages, p. (2) being blank, and the text ending at p. 48. The top of the front cover denominates it the "only authorized and correct edition." It was duly copyrighted. A pirated printing was put out by Richard A. Saalfield, New York, in pink wrappers, using Church's text. (Saalfield also pirated the early American "Yeoman" libretto from the authorized Wm. Pond issue.) The next Church edition carried on page 2 an announcement of the date and place of the first English performance and gives the English cast, and the text ends on p. 46. It may be inferred that the first libretto was printed sufficiently in advance of the English opening that either its date, or some of the characters, had not been decided upon. The title, not determined until December 2, could of course have been cabled.

Upon examining the text, it appears that one song, part of a song, and a considerable amount of dialogue appear only in the first American libretto. This follows the English first edition text but with a major addition appearing nowhere else, at the very end of Act 2. Here we have definite evidence that the elision was made at the last minute. Sullivan's diary reads:

> December 2d . . . Gilbert came down after rehearsal at Savoy at 11:15. Finally settled title "The Gondoliers" or "The King of Barataria." Good title

I think. Also settled to cut out dangerous dialogues
at the end of the piece.

What were these "dangerous dialogues?" The American edition tells us.

Early in the first act Marco and Giuseppe, the "Gondoliers," had married Gianetta and Tessa, respectively.
Very quickly the gondoliers learn that one of them is the
son of the King of Barataria, secretly smuggled out of
the country for reasons of state when just over six months
old. Unfortunately, typical Gilbertian baby-mixing by
their parent, or purported parent, had followed, so that—

> That highly respectable gondolier
> Could never declare with a mind sincere
> Which of the two was his offspring dear,
> And which the Royal stripling!

So far, their wives are not unduly disturbed. It is not
until later in the second act that the four principals learn
that, just before the smuggling process, the King-baby
had been married by proxy to Casilda, in love with Luiz,
so that one pair of principals is not married at all. (Of
course eventually Luiz turns out to be the real King-
baby, by reason of a previous Pinafore-like substitution,
thus validating both marriages, but that is not revealed
until the climax.) The four principals are left alone with
Casilda, and discuss the superfluity of spouses. Casilda
says to Gianetta and Tessa (1st English edition, p. 45):

> My good girls, I don't blame you. Only before
> we go any further we must really arrive at some

satisfactory arrangement, or we shall get hopelessly complicated.

—and there follows the quintette beginning "Here is a fix unprecedented."

In the American first libretto, however,—and this pretty clearly was the form of the opera up to five days before it opened—we have another quintette, and much more conversation. It continues (p. 45), from Casilda's speech:

MAR.   It's a difficult position. It's nobody's fault— let us treat it good-humoredly and make the best of it.
CAS.   Oh yes; let's make the best of it by all means.
TESS & GIU.   Certainly, let's make the best of it.
MAR.   Very well. It seems that we two have married you three. Now I have a proposition to make which I think will meet the difficulty.

QUINTETTE.

MARCO, GIUSEPPE, CASILDA, TESSA, GIANETTA.
MAR.   Till time shall choose
                    To solve the hitch
                    Which wife is whose—
                    Whose wife is which,
        Our three young brides must please agree
        To act as one and not as three.

CAS., TESS., GIA. Your three young brides hereby agree
                    To act as one, and not as three.
                    Then you must be, till that is done,
                    Two gentlemen rolled into one.

MAR. & GIU.   Then we will be, till that is done,
Two gentlemen rolled into one.

ALL.   Till time shall choose
To solve the hitch
Which wife is whose—
Whose wife is which,
The three young brides hereby agree
To act as one and not as three;
And both their lords, till that is done,
Two gentlemen rolled into one!

GIA., TESS. & CAS. (*speaking together*).   I think that is a very satisfactory arrangement.

MAR. & GIU. (*speaking together*).   Ingenious, isn't it, Jenny?

GIA., TESS. & CAS. (*surprised*).   Jenny?

MAR. & GIU.   I must call you something, you know.

GIA., TESS. & CAS.   Well, if you call me Jenny, I shall call you Thomas.

MAR. & GIU.   Oh hang it all—Tommaso!

GIA., TESS. & CAS.   No—Thomas.

MAR. & GIU.   But it's so British!

GIA., TESS. & CAS.   Never mind that. The question is, will you always be true to me?

MAR. & GIU.   My dear Jenny, can you doubt it?

GIA., TESS. & CAS.   Certainly. How can I trust a husband who married one-third of me when I was a baby and waited twenty years before he married the remainder?

MAR. & GIU.   It does sound dilatory. Regard it as an instalment on account.

GIA., TESS. & CAS.   And now I come to think of it, you've only married two-thirds of me, after all.

MAR. & GIU.   I've married as much as I might.

GIA., TESS. & CAS.   But I've married the whole of you!

MAR. & GIU.   Pardon me—one-third of you is still single.

GIA., TESS. & CAS.   My dear Thomas, what is the use of one-third of me being single when I don't know which third it is?

The American libretto then follows with "Here is a fix unprecedented," as a second quintette by the same five, and thereafter accords with the English first, except that Marco's "Solo," at the end of Act I, has four lines which appear nowhere else:

> And the birds all twitter
>   Through the winter weather,
> Like a spinnet and a zither
>   That are played together.

The Act 2 Quintette and the "dangerous dialogues" have their first reprinting in *The Gilbert and Sullivan Journal* in its inaugural issue, No. 1, February 1925.

Recollecting that the title was determined on the same night when this long passage was eliminated, and that the American libretto of course has a title, it is a bit hard to understand how it survived in printed American form, but there it is.

The second American libretto, announcing itself as the "newly revised and only authorized and correct edition" with the same "The John Church Co." imprint, omits all the above passages, and to that extent accords with the English first. It contains, however, some rewriting for American ears. Much of this is understandable, and does no offense to the spirit of the text, e.g., the turning into American legal language of such English

Ducal phrases as "floated at a premium," "registered under the Limited Liability Act," "join the Board after allotment." Less defensible is the turning of the Barataria servant's hall into the "kitchen"; and quite indefensible is the alteration of the rusk which Giuseppe offers the Grand Inquisitor, to a "Boston cracker." One wonders how far, if at all, Gilbert approved these changes; the edition in which they appear is the authorized American copyright form.

Later American librettos have the imprint of "The John Church Company." All of these contain the misprint "Yoemen" on the title page.

Princess Ida

January 5, 1884-October 9, 1884
(Savoy Theatre)

Collation: 48 pp. (1) (2), Title page; verso, Dramatis Personae; (3)-48, Text p. 48 containing the imprint, under a rule, "Henderson, Rait, & Spalding, Printers, 3 & 5 Marylebone Lane, London, W."

Blue-gray wrappers, the outer front wrapper with copyright notice. Inner front wrapper advertises *Pirates of Penzance,* inner back wrapper advertises *Patience,* outer back wrapper advertises *Iolanthe,* "now being performed at the Savoy," etc.

The FIRST EDITION, FIRST ISSUE, as described above, is in a prologue and two acts. The minor part of Ada is played by "Miss Twynam," and not by "Miss Lillian Carr."

A later binding is identical with the above except

that the line about *Iolanthe* "now being performed at the Savoy" is removed.

The Second Edition on both title page and cover has "In Three Acts" instead of "In Two Acts" and "Act I" replaces "Prologue" on page (3). Ada is now played by Miss Lillian Carr. There are no textual changes, even the misprints persist (e.g., "Sacharisa, p. 16, l. 1).

The first American libretto is a wrappered 12mo, copyright in 1884 by J. M. Stoddart, Philadelphia, of 50 pages, the text ending on p. 49. Some copies have the imprint of Oliver Ditson, of Boston, on the front cover. These are, however, the same sheets. *Princess Ida* opened in America simultaneously at the Fifth Avenue Theatre, New York, and the Boston Museum, Boston, on Monday evening, 11 Feb. 1884, both productions being authorized. The Dramatis Personae, on the verso of the title page, does not give the names of the players or the date of the first American performances. Later American editions transfer the Dramatis Personae to the inner front wrapper and begin the text on the verso of the title page.

As related in the standard biography of Sullivan:

> Sullivan was late with the music. . . . Rehearsals and the composition now became so concentrated that he scarcely slept. He rehearsed the piece with Gilbert late into the night, and then returned to Queen's Mansions to compose till daylight. . . . On New Year's Day he completed the music which four days later was to be performed.

The American libretto can reasonably be assumed to be contemporaneous, as the copyright law would demand, with the English libretto for the production at the

Savoy on 5 January, and in fact the Library of Congress copyright deposit copy is stamped 7 Jan. 1884.

The American libretto indicates that the lateness above referred to was not all Sullivan's fault. Two *entire songs,* and two verses of other songs, differ in both matter and meter from the English libretto. The only possible assumption seems to be that these differing songs and verses were parts of the opera when the libretto left England for the American copyright printing, and that in the interval came Gilbert's alterations to the form now printed.

Of course a large part of the dialogue comes word for word from Gilbert's earlier "whimsical allegory," *The Princess,* London, n.d. (8 Jan. 1870), but in the earlier play Gilbert fitted his songs to existing airs, whereas here, as in all the Gilbert and Sullivan operas (with one minor exception in *Utopia Limited*), Gilbert wrote his songs and choruses as he would, and Sullivan fitted music to them.

The following lyrics are found only in the first American libretto.

1. Chorus of courtiers (p. 7), the first four lines according with the English first:

From the distant panorama
Come the sons of royal Gama.
    Who, to-day, should cross the water
    With his fascinating daughter—
    Should she not refuse.
They are heralds evidently,
And are sacred consequently,
Let us hail the sons of Gama,
Who from yonder panorama
    Come to bring us news.

2. Chorus given to ALL (p. 21):

> In this college
> Useful knowledge
> Everywhere one finds;
> And already,
> Growing steady,
> We've improved our minds.

3. Quintette of Psyche and Melissa with Hilarion, Cyril and Florian (p. 27):

PSY.

> If we discharged our duty clear,
> We should denounce your presence
>   here,
>   What we should do
>   We plainly view
> *In speculum veluti.*

HIL.

> If that's the case, don't wait a bit,
> But trick it, cheat it, swindle it;
>   'Twere pity great
>   To hesitate,
> Distinctly "do" your duty!

ALL.

> Oh duty, when you check our ease,
> Uncertain, coy, and hard to please,
> When you are "done," as you are
>   now,
> An unimportant person thou.

MEL.

> But if we "did" our duty thus,
> The consequence might fall on us;
>   'Twould give you pain
>   To see us slain
> In all our youth and beauty!

CYR.   If "doing" it distress you so,
            Dismiss it, sack it, let it go;
                Don't pause a whit,
                Dispense with it;
            In fact, "discharge" your duty!

ALL.   Oh duty, when you check our ease,
            Uncertain, coy, and hard to please,
            When you're discharged as you are
                now,
            An unimportant person thou!

4. Last verse of Gama's "nothing whatever to grumble at" song replaced by "I offered gold in sums untold" (p. 43):

            Upon the stage
            Plays, ripe with age,
        And not too much protracted,
            With faultless taste
            Were always placed
        And excellently acted;
            Now when he sees
            Good comedies
        It irritates King Gama,
            With no excuse
            For rank abuse
        Who can enjoy the Drama?

5. Chorus, and song by Arac, replaced by "This helmet, I suppose," etc. (p. 45):

CHO.   With hearts resolved and courage
                grave,

The warriors now begin.
May fortune's shield protect the brave,
And may the best men win!

SOLO—ARAC.
Whene'er we go
To fight the foe
We never throw a chance away,
And at last
We always cast
Each useless circumstance away.
A helmet bright
Is far from light
(Life-guardsmen know how true it is.)
(*Taking off helmet.*)
A bright cuirass
We also class
With useless superfluities. (*Taking off
cuirass.*)
All this array
Is in the way
It is, upon my word it is—
For who can fight
When locked up tight
In lobster-like absurdities?

(*By this time they have removed all their armour and
wear nothing but a close fitting shape suit.*)

Though brasses
And tasses
And showy cuirasses
Are all very useful to dazzle the lasses.
He classes with asses
Who cumbers with masses

Of metal
His fettle,
Tra la la la la!

THE THREE.   Yes, yes, yes,
Tra la la la la!

ALL.   Yes, yes, yes,
Tra la la la la!

6. Added second verse of the following soldiers' chorus *in re* the "doughty sons of Hungary" (p. 46):

But if our hearts assert their sway,
(And hearts are all fantastical)
We shall be more disposed to say
These words enthusiastical:
Hilarion!
Hilarion!
Oh prosper, Prince Hilarion!
In mode complete
May you defeat
Each meddlesome Hungarian!

John Bush Jones

The Printing of The Grand Duke: Notes Toward a Gilbert Bibliography

(1967)

The state of descriptive bibliography for W. S. Gilbert, as David A. Randall has recently reminded us, is a sorry one.[1] Both he and Reginald Allen have discredited much of Townley Searle's *Topsy-Turvy Adventure* (the only book-length Gilbert bibliography) for unreliability, inaccuracy, and the failure to allow the reader to "identify the true first issues."[2] Much of the inadequacy of Searle's book may be attributed not only to insufficient information, but also to the flagrant mishandling of bibliographical language. Note: "Only the first two of the Gilbert and Sullivan, none of the German Reed, Lacy, French, or Phillips items is dated, and most of them

have later editions and variant states (issues or editions)."
And again, "The reason why actual first editions are
rarely seen is that they were soon superseded by a second
issue." [3] In the first quotation Searle, in addition to jug-
gling with bibliographical vocabulary, has lumped together
the names of authors, theatrical managers, and publishers in a heap which only the most devoted Gilbert en-
thusiast could hope to unscramble. The carelessness ex-
hibited by Searle in his random use of precise technical
terms is also evident in the form of his descriptions. He
makes no real attempt at a quasi-facsimile title page; he
gives the size and total number of pages, but no pagina-
tion or collational formula; he pays some attention to advertisements (relying too heavily on them for the priority
of what he calls issues, even when they are not conjugate
with any gatherings of the text); and he takes a fleeting
look at the binding (often making the same error in
judgment as he does with the advertisements). Above all,
Searle provides a "full" description of only the "first
edition" (in his vocabulary) with no systematic account of
the variants distinguishing the impressions, issues, or
states. What he has in actuality provided, although I
question whether he was fully cognizant of the fact, is a
loose description of the first state of the first issue (when
applicable) of the first impression *of the first edition*.

So much for a capsule review of a book long since
dead. It is now my intention, first, to present a tentative
model for a complete description of the first edition, first
impression of a Chappell & Company Gilbert libretto
(exclusive of "Typography" and "Notes"), and, second,
to discuss the printing of *The Grand Duke* with the aim
of firmly fixing the bibliographical nature of those copies
which reveal significant departures from the first state
of the first impression. It will be seen that where I differ

most from earlier attempts at a Gilbert bibliography is in my criteria for what may be properly distinguished as editions.

My findings were greatly aided by the use of the Hinman Collator at Northwestern University, by G. Thomas Tanselle's suggestions with regard to the organization and presentation of materials, and, especially, by David A. Randall's courtesy in giving me access to the Gilbert collection in the Lilly Library.

THE GRAND DUKE, Chappell & Co., 1896
First Edition (English) [4]
First Impression:

THE GRAND DUKE; [fancy] | OR, | THE STATU-TORY DUEL. | A Comic Opera in Two Acts. [script] | [short double rule (1 $13/16$)] | WRITTEN BY [space] COM-POSED BY | W. S. GILBERT. [space] ARTHUR SULLI-VAN. | [short rule ($1 1/32$)] | PRICE ONE SHILLING. | [short rule ($1 1/32$)] | CHAPPELL & CO., 50, NEW BOND STREET, W. | AGENTS: | NEW YORK: T. B. HARMS & CO. | [short rule ($1 15/16$)] | [paragraph indentation] *All Rights reserved under the International Copyright Act. Public Perform-* | *ance forbidden, and Right of Representation reserved. Single detached numbers* | *may be sung at Concerts, not more than two in all from the various Operas by* | *Mr. W. S. Gilbert and Sir Arthur Sullivan at any one Concert, but these must* | *be given without Stage Costume or Action. In no case must such performances* | *be announced as a "Selection" from the Opera. Applications for the right of* | *performing the above Opera must be made to* "MR. R. D'OYLY CARTE, *Savoy Theatre, London."* | [short rule ($5/16$)] | COPYRIGHT, MDCCCXCVI., BY R. D'OYLY CARTE. [sans serif]

Collation: (8¹¹⁄₃₂ x 5¹³⁄₃₂): *unsigned, 1 ³⁰*, 30 leaves, pp. *1-3* 4-59 *60*, stapled between pp. 30 and 31. Page numbers centered at top of type page.

Contents: p. *1*, title; p. *2*, head title, 'THE GRAND DUKE; | OR, | THE STATUTORY DUEL. | **Produced at the Savoy Theatre, London, under the management of** | **Mr. R. D'Oyly Carte, on Saturday, 7th March, 1896.** | [short rule (1³⁄₁₆)]' list of the cast and staff of the production headed '𝔇𝔯𝔞𝔪𝔞𝔱𝔦𝔰 𝔓𝔢𝔯𝔰𝔬𝔫𝔞𝔢.'; p. *3*, head title 'THE GRAND DUKE; | OR, | THE STATUTORY DUEL. | [short decorative rule (1¹⁄₁₆)]' with text headed 'ACT I.'; p. *34*, text ending with 'ACT DROP.'; p. *35*, text headed 'ACT II.'; p. *59*, text ending with 'THE END. | [short rule (2)]' imprint 'HENDERSON & SPALDING, Printers, 1, 3 and 5, Marylebone Lane, W.'; p. *60*, advertisement headed 'CHAPPELL & CO.'S | 𝔑𝔢𝔴 & 𝔓𝔬𝔭𝔲𝔩𝔞𝔯 𝔖𝔬𝔫𝔤𝔰 & 𝔅𝔞𝔩𝔩𝔞𝔡𝔰. | (SEASON [*sans serif*] 1896.) | [decorative rule]' [41 titles arranged by composers beginning with '**ARTHUR SUL-LIVAN . . . . . . "Bid me at least Good-bye"** ' and ending with ' "[ditto mark] **"A Spring Song"** . . . . Sung by MADAME AMY SHERWIN'] followed by short rule (1¹³⁄₃₂) and 'PRICE TWO SHILLINGS NET, EACH. | [decorative rule] | CHAPPELL & CO. . 50, New Bond St., London, W.'

Paper: White wove unwatermarked, all edges cut.

Binding: light bluish-gray paper; printed in dark grayish-blue ink. *Front cover,* within single rules extending beyond their points of intersection: THE GRAND DUKE; | OR, | *THE STATUTORY DUEL.* | 𝔄 ℭ𝔬𝔪𝔦𝔠 𝔒𝔭𝔢𝔯𝔞 𝔦𝔫 𝔗𝔴𝔬 𝔄𝔠𝔱𝔰 | WRITTEN BY | W. S. GILBERT. | COMPOSED BY | ARTHUR SULLIVAN. | [short decorative rule (½)] |

CHAPPELL & CO., 50 New Bond Street, London, W. |
Agents: | New York: T. B. HARMS & CO. | [short rule
($2\frac{1}{32}$)] | [8 line copyright notice, same as on title page] |
[below bottom rule] COPYRIGHT MDCCCXCVI., BY
R. D'OYLY CARTE. [*sans serif*] *Verso of front cover,*
advertisement headed 'Popular Comic Operas [fancy] |
WRITTEN BY [*sans serif*] | W. S. GILBERT. [*sans serif*]
| COMPOSED BY [*sans serif*] | ARTHUR SULLIVAN.
[*sans serif*] | AND PUBLISHED BY [*sans serif*] *CHAP-
PELL & CO., 50, New Bond St., London, W.' Back cover,*
advertisement for vocal score, piano solo, and separate
sheet music of *The Grand Duke,* noted as being 'IN THE
PRESS.' *Recto of back cover,* advertisement for musical
scores headed 'UTOPIA | LIMITED | OR, | THE
FLOWERS OF PROGRESS. | An Original Comic Opera
| WRITTEN BY [space] COMPOSED BY | W. S. GIL-
BERT. [space] ARTHUR SULLIVAN.'
Leaves and covers are fastened by two metal staples through
the center of the single gathering and the binding.

The Grand Duke opened at the Savoy Theatre on
Saturday, 7 Mar. 1896, and—as was the case for all the
operas save *The Pirates of Penzance*—the printed libretto
was available for the first-night audience. This last of the
Gilbert and Sullivan collaborations was not a success,
having had a run of only 123 performances. Consequently, the printing history of this Chappell libretto is
the shortest in the series; public demand has never been
great enough to warrant a reprinting of this opera as an
individual libretto subsequent to its initial publication,
although it has appeared in several collected volumes of
Gilbert's works. Yet it is precisely because *The Grand
Duke* failed both in the theatre and in the bookstores
that the bibliographer has a small controlled body of

material to serve as a model for further investigation of the Gilbert canon.

The texts of *The Grand Duke* once again reveal Gilbert's usual practice of continuing to revise his productions—and, consequently, his published libretti—even after the start of public performances. The libretto of thirty leaves described above is followed shortly (probably within a matter of weeks, although precise dating is almost impossible) by one of twenty-eight leaves. The major revisions are largely in the form of cuts in the lyrics and dialogue, most conspicuously the omission of three entire songs for the Baroness, the Prince of Monte Carlo, and Duke Rudolph (all in Act Two), the shortening of the Duke and Baroness's duet in Act One, and numerous excisions in long dialogue scenes.

It has been customary up to now to refer to this revised version of *the text* as the "second edition," not in the case of *The Grand Duke* alone, but with reference to all the Gilbert libretti which exhibit an analogous pattern of authorial revision.[5] The designation of the shorter version as a new edition has been based solely on the evidence of major substantive changes in the text rather than on the proper criterion of the physical production of the book. If this practice were carried to its *reductio ad absurdum,* it could be argued that any copy of a Gilbert libretto revealing a single substantive variant would constitute a separate edition.

Of course, if it could be shown that the twenty-eight-leaf version was printed from a complete and total resetting of the type (the primary bibliographical qualification for an edition), then indeed those copies containing the authorial revisions noted above would comprise a second edition. Such, however, is not the case. Comparison on the Hinman Machine of the *unrevised* portions of the thirty- and twenty-eight-leaf copies reveals that the horizontal alignment of pairs of type-lines is the same, and that all instances of type batter are identical. It is especially the recurrence of type batter which discloses that, in cases where the excision of a lyric would have left a gap on the page before the ensuing dialogue, the type for this dialogue has been lifted bodily from its position for the printing of the thirty-leaf version to fill the blank space on the page in the shorter version. In effect, all the standing type was used for the unrevised portions of the revised libretto, the bibliographical result being that the twenty-eight-leaf copies may not be correctly designated the "second edition," but rather (perhaps to the chagrin of collectors) the first edition, *second impression.*[6] Or, perhaps for further descriptive clarity, the twenty-eight-leaf version might be identified as "second impression (with revisions)" or "second impression (first revised impression)."

The matter of "issue" is not relevant to the printing of *The Grand Duke,* for the creation of the twenty-eight-leaf version of the libretto involved the setting-up, primarily from the standing type, of an entirely new set of sheets from the thirty-leaf version, this being a criterion of impression rather than issue. No evidence has been found to suggest changes made in some of the sheets in order to allow for reissue of the unsold sheets, a part of Bowers' stipulation for an issue. Nor does there appear any attempt on the part of the publisher to give public notice, by way of advertisement or an addition to the title page, of a reissue of the libretto. Hence, we may move from a discussion of the two impressions of *The Grand Duke* to an identification of the states.

The first impression of this libretto exists in three states, the first two differing only in the failure of a single piece of type to print, and the third a result of corrections made from postpublication proofreading working toward ideal copy, along with further instances of "dropped type." [7] Three copies of the uncorrected first impression are in the Lilly Library. In one of these, the stage direction on page 53, line 39, ends *"stakes.)"*; the other two copies read *"stakes."*. This is clearly a case of dropped type rather than emendation, for the reading without the parenthesis occurs again in the otherwise corrected third state (see below). Virtually all stage directions in Gilbert libretti are enclosed in parentheses, and it seems unlikely that the printer would have printed an early run of copies without the end parenthesis, inserted it for a continuation of the run, and then omitted it again. Its omission in the third state, next to be discussed, is clearly an oversight of the proofreader.

The remaining copy of the first impression in the Lilly Library contains a series of corrections made in an attempt to achieve ideal copy; this corrected libretto comprises the third state. The variants may be summarized as follows, the numbers referring to page and line:

	First State	Third State
2.12	TANNHAUSER	TANNHÄUSER
2.28	CHAMBERLAIN	CHAMBERLAINS
17.1	QUINTETTE	QUINTET [8]
38.15	byegone	bygone
40.46	(*Shuddering*	∧ ~ [dropped type]
53.39	*stakes.*)	~. ∧ [dropped type]
55.24	ELSA	LISA
59.21	*falls.*)	~. ∧ [dropped type]
60.28	Courtship"	~ " Sung by Miss ELLA RUSSELL
	[line ends]	

The rarity of this third state has been noted by Carroll A. Wilson (calling it a second issue), and indeed there is only one copy in the Lilly collection and very few in Reginald Allen's extensive collection at the Morgan Library. This scarcity may best be explained by the possibility that soon after the presses began to run off the corrected third state of the first impression, Gilbert had made his cuts and revisions, and the shorter, revised second impression was set up and printed. This second impression thereby quickly supplanted the few copies of the first impression, third state which reached the market.

The above data clearly suggest a positive priority of states within the first impression: the uncorrected version *with* the parenthesis on page 53 first, the uncorrected version *without* that parenthesis second, and the corrected version third. Hence, it is with certainty that we may label chronologically the first, second, and third states of the first impression.

The second impression is made up of two states,[9] the variants in the second again being products of continued proof correction, and one instance of what appears to be type batter. The complete list which follows is presented as an easy means for identification of the second impression's two states.

		First State	*Second State*
15.11		stated $_\wedge$	~.
21.40		Oh $_\wedge$	~,
22.22		Still $_\wedge$	~,
28.21		lose $_\wedge$	~,
28.26		ones $_\wedge$	~!
29.14		shoeses $_\wedge$	~!
30.29		monarch	Monarch

37.32	live!	~,
39.10	see ∧	~,
39.32	seeking ∧	~,
40.19	thrilled ∧	~,
42.21	Tol the riddle ∧	~,
43.36	violet!	~. [type batter?]
49.13	elevated ∧	~.
49.15	rich ∧	~,
52.35	me	you
52.35-	∧Baroness	⎰ ~
37	∧Julia	⎱ ~
	∧Lisa	~
53.15	banns ∧	~!
54.26	*falls.*	~.)
56.26	[no line of type]	EDWIN . . . DAVIES

As is the case for the first impression, the priority of states in the second impression may be firmly established. The punctuation marks in the right-hand column of the list are invariably added to settings of type which had been used in printing all copies of the libretto down from the first state of the first impression. Hence, the copies containing these corrections comprise the second, and, to my knowledge, the final state of the second impression of *The Grand Duke*. With this run of the presses, the printing of the first (and only individual) English edition of the last Gilbert and Sullivan libretto came to an end.

The foregoing enumeration of states is, however, not meant to be exhaustive. The possibility does remain that there are states yet to be discovered and identified; the general scarcity of *Grand Duke* libretti has resulted in a limited number of copies available for immediate inspection. My endeavor has not, however, been to present a complete catalogue of the variant forms of a particular libretto, but rather to establish rigorous bibliographical criteria, and to demonstrate something of the method employed for separating and describing, accurately and without confusion, the editions, impressions, and states of the W. S. Gilbert libretti published by Chappell. It is my hope that, by an extension of these principles, a solid base can be established for making some bibliographical sense out of the complexities of the entire Gilbert canon.

Notes

1. David A. Randall, "The Gondoliers," *PBSA*, 59 (1965), 193.
2. Reginald Allen, ed., *The First Night Gilbert and Sullivan* (New York, 1958), p. xviii.
3. Townley Searle, *Sir William Schwenck Gilbert: A Topsy-Turvy Adventure* (London, 1931), pp. 8, 100.
4. The first American edition of this and many other of the libretti presents quite another bibliographical story. These texts appear to be derived largely from Gilbert's prepublication copies used in rehearsals and from the License copies deposited with the Lord Chamberlain. They warrant a bibliographical investigation and discussion all to themselves.
5. Even expert bibliographers and Gilbert enthusiasts such as Carroll A. Wilson, Reginald Allen, and David A. Randall have fallen into the "second edition" error. However, this may be readily excused because of the unavailability of, or failure to use, the Hinman Collator to investigate the nature of the type, reliance being placed instead upon major substantive variants easily discovered by sight collation.
6. Furthermore, the ease with which sections of the type were moved from one setting to another suggests that the libretto was printed from type, not plates.
7. I use the term "dropped type" here to designate a piece of type which fails to print altogether, either because it has dropped too low to print or because it has fallen out altogether. This is in contradistinction to "type batter," referring to a piece of type which, while printing, reveals a peculiar flaw indicating damage to the type.

8. This change in spelling is clearly for conformation with the printing-house style. In his manuscripts, Gilbert consistently uses the spelling "quintette," "quartette," etc.

9. Carroll A. Wilson's manuscript notes in the Lilly Library note the existence of three states (he calls them "issues"). Exhaustive collation on the Hinman Machine has, however, brought to light only the two noted here. Perhaps Wilson was including binding states in his definition, but these comprise a positive bibliographical nightmare in conjunction with the Gilbert libretti. Even some fairly late states and impressions have been discovered with the early bindings advertising the vocal scores still in the press.

Jane W. Stedman

The Genesis of Patience

(1968)

In the W. S. Gilbert Papers deposited in the British Museum there are twenty-one almost illegible pages which constitute the earliest draft yet known of *Patience; or, Bunthorne's Bride*.[1] This fragment, about two-thirds of Act I, follows Gilbert's usual method of composition; that is, he has written the lyrics but not the dialogue, connections being supplied by short "epitomes" of action or reaction.[2] At this stage, the rival poets of the final version are still the competitive clergymen whom Gilbert borrowed from his own Bab Ballad, "The Rival Curates."

From almost the first, the plot line of *Patience* was fundamentally that of the finished work, produced at the Opera Comique, London, on April 23, 1881,[3] but the identity of its leading characters seesawed between the Grosvenor Gallery and the Anglican church for some six

months. Gilbert's original intention seems to have been
to make aesthetes of Bunthorne and Grosvenor (long
before these names had been settled upon),[4] but he drew
the outlines of his plot from three earlier works, each
dealing with clergymen.

"The Rival Curates" (a Bab Ballad, published in
Fun, October 19, 1867) describes the chagrin of the
Reverend Clayton Hooper, famed for mildness, upon
whom a competitor, the even more insipid Reverend
Hopley Porter, unexpectedly bursts. Hooper sends his
sexton and beadle ("On Sundays they were good—/On
weekdays they were minions") to annihilate Porter unless
he consents to become more secular. Porter, overjoyed,
exclaims, "For years I've longed for some/Excuse for this
revulsion: / Now that excuse has come / I do it on compulsion!!!" He curls his hair, smokes, and ogles, while
Hooper once again enjoys his reputation of "the mildest
curate going." [5] Here is the structure of the aesthetic
rivalry between the fleshly and idyllic poets of *Patience*
as well as its resolution: Grosvenor's becoming commonplace upon compulsion. In the ballad, however, there are
no Rapturous Maidens (unless we count the old maids in
whose albums Hopley Porter sticks seaweed). The feminine chorus of adulation rises in another Bab, "The
Ladies of the Lea" (*Fun,* October 30, 1869), and in Dr.
Daly's song, "Time was, when Love and I were well
acquainted" (*The Sorcerer,* 1877).[6]

To the village of Jessie, Jane, and Margaret, "the
Ladies of the Lea," comes a new curate, James De Vyse,
"young and fair, and comfortably off, / With the gentlest
indication of a sweet consumptive cough." He also has
"pretty little legs, and little hands, and little feet," which
so charm the ladies that they resolve to atone for their
neglect of his elderly predecessor. "Mortify[ing] the body

with fatiguing exercise," they embroider braces, knit gloves, and work slippers for James. But so long have the ladies been out of practice that their offerings are all the wrong size. Nevertheless, the curate puts them on, believing it a duty "to conciliate parishioners—at all events at first." The sight of James, ungainly in their gifts, so disappoints the ladies that "they all became Dissenters, and he never saw them more." This is the final bourgeois *volte face* of the later Rapturous Maidens, but without as yet a counter-character for them to turn to.

In *The Sorcerer,* Dr. Daly, vicar of Ploverleigh, continues the comic motifs of "The Ladies of the Lea," but less grotesquely. He recalls that in his youth, he, too, was an adored pale young curate:

> A saintly youth, with worldly thought untainted—
> None better-loved than I in all the land!
> Time was, when maidens of the noblest station,
> Foresaking even military men,
> Would gaze upon me, rapt in adoration—
> Ah me, I was a fair young curate then! [7]

These verses foreshadow the relationship of the male and female choruses of *Patience,* and the "military men" proved to be as effective contrasts to the "long-haired aesthetics" as to consumptive curates.

These three works gave Gilbert a dramatic structure and established certain character outlines. At some time during the very earliest, perhaps the merely speculative, stages of planning the new opera, Gilbert's original idea of "a rivalry between two aesthetic fanatics, worshipped by a chorus of female aesthetics," had become "a couple of clergymen worshipped by a chorus of female devotees." As he reminded Sullivan in a much later letter (November 1, 1880), he had abandoned his first intention "because I foresaw great difficulty in getting the chorus to dress & make up aesthetically." [8] In the same letter he admitted that, although he now had completed two-thirds of the libretto, he mistrusted "the clerical element" and felt hampered "by the restrictions which the nature of the subject places on my freedom of action." He wanted to return to a satire of aestheticism. "I can get much more fun out of the subject as I propose to alter it, & the general scheme of the piece will remain as at present. The Hussars will become aesthetic young men (abandoning their profession for the purpose)—in this latter capacity they will all carry lilies in their hands, wear long hair, & stand in stained glass attitudes." During the curate phase of the plot, the soldiers were to have taken religious orders.

Gilbert's decision to alter the profession of his characters seems to have been taken instantaneously. In an introductory note to the 1902 edition of *Patience*,[9] he describes himself as feeling "crippled at every turn by the necessity of protecting myself from a charge of irreverence." Lying awake (no doubt with a dismal headache) one night, searching for "a group of personages" to fit the plot "as already devised," the idea of making the rivals into "yearning aesthetics" flashed upon him. "Elated . . . , I ran down at once to my library, and in an hour or so I had entirely rearranged the piece upon a secure and satisfactory basis." [10]

At this point he presumably sent Sullivan the letter quoted above. The composer readily agreed, for on November 7, 1880, Gilbert wrote to Clement Scott, the critic, that he had begun his libretto all over again after finishing two-thirds of it.[11] Two weeks later he was somewhat startled to discover that James Albery's new play *Where's the Cat?* was making capital out of the eccentricities of contemporary aesthetes. Gilbert immediately and somewhat disingenuously wrote to Albery (November 21, 1880) [12] that, "by an odd coincidence, I have completed the greater part of the libretto of a two act opera (designed six months ago) [13] in which this preposterous school [of "lily-bearing poets"] plays a very prominent part." Gilbert marked his letter "private" and asked Albery not to make its contents known "unless necessity arises." He confided the secret only to prevent Albery from later supposing that the new opera "was in some way suggested by a successful character in your work." [14]

Gilbert's letters to Sullivan, Scott, and Albery imply that the reversal from curates to poets came after he had worked out a detailed scenario and had written a considerable number of the lyrics, but not the dialogue, which he habitually left to the last. This estimate would fit his repeated statement that the new piece was two-thirds done, would not contradict his assertion that it had been "designed" six months earlier, and would correspond to his usual sequence of composition. It would also support W. A. Darlington's perceptive observation that many of the lyrics of *Patience* seem to be held over from "The Rival Curates" stage, while the satire of aestheticism comes largely through the dialogue.[15]

This is indeed the case in the British Museum fragment printed below. It includes several lyrics which have achieved their final well-known form or something very near it. Although the manuscript ends shortly before the point at which a Grosvenor character would appear, the epitomes of action it does contain develop the now-familiar plot of *Patience*.

Gilbert begins with a stage direction, underlined as are most of his manuscript stage directions.[16]

Act 1.   1

*Scene. Exterior of country Vicarage. Ladies dis-
covered seated on lawn in despairing attitudes,
headed by Angela Ella & Saphir. They are waiting to
congratulate Rev.ᵈ Lawn Tennison on his birthday, &
to give him slippers, comforters, braces &ᶜ which they
are working upon* [17]

Chorus

Twenty love-sick maidens we,
    Sitting by a running rill [18]
Twenty years hence we shall be
    Twenty lovesick maidens still!
        Ah, Miserie! [19]

All our love is all for one
    Yet that love he prizes [20] not
He is coy and cares for none
    Sad & sorry is our lot!
        Ah Miserie!

Solo, Angela, accompanying herself on mandolin.[21]

Love feeds on hope, they say, or love must [22] die.
            Ah Miserie!
Yet my love lives although no hope have I.
            Ah Miserie!
Alas, poor heart, go hide thyself away
            Ah Miserie.[23]
To weeping concords tune thy roundelay
            Ah Miserie.
All   Oh Miserie—Ah Miserie.[24]

———

Saphir [25]   2

Go, breaking heart,
   Go dream of love requited—
Go, foolish heart,
   Go dream of lovers plighted
Go, madcap heart,
   Go dream of never waking,
And, in thy dream,
   Forget that thou art breaking!
All   Ah Miserie! [26]

Chorus

Twenty lovesick maidens we
   Sitting by a running rill [27]
Twenty years hence we shall be—
   Twenty lovesick maidens still!
             Ah Miserie!

3

Dialogue showing their love for Revd L. Tennison
His exceeding mildness
His lamblike innocence—
His unfortunate insensibility to their admiration
former admiration for Twenty-first hussars—But their
recent [28] discovery [word crossed out] hussars are
vanities.
Approach of Patience who alone of all the village
maidens is insensible to the charms of Revd L. T.
In point of fact Patience has never loved—does not
know what it is.
Her entrance to recitative.
She is pained to see the girls so unhappy—
She is aware that it is owing to their love for Rev.
L. Tennison
Still that conveys no idea to her mind, as she cannot
realize what love is.

Recit 4

Angela.   See—hither comes the village school-
        mistress [29]
        Poor Patience—who alone of womankind
        Remains insensate to his calm attractions!
Saphir   Unhappy girl—her heart has ne'er known
        love—
Ella   Benighted creature!
Angela   Miserable maid!
        Patience appears on rock L [30]
Patience   Your pardon ladies—I intrude upon you
        —(*going*)
Angela   Come hither, Patience—tell us—is it true
        That you have never loved?
Patience (*coming down*)   Most true indeed!
Sopranos   Most marvellous!
Contraltos   And most deplorable!

Song Patience .
I cannot tell what this love may be
That cometh to all and [31] not to me—
It cannot be kind, as they'd imply,
Or why do these gentle [32] ladies sigh?
It cannot be joy & rapture deep
Or why do these gentle ladies weep?
It cannot be blissful as 'tis said,
Or why are their eyes so wondrous red?
    Though everywhere true love I see
    A coming to all but not to me
    I cannot tell what this love may be!
        For I am blithe & I am gay
        While they sit sighing all night all day[33]
        Think of the gulf twixt them & me—
    F. /// / / & Miserie! [34]

———

[5]

Chorus

She is blithe & she is gay
While we sit sobbing all night—all day— 35
Think of the gulf twixt them & me—
Patience   Fal la la la—
Chorus   And Miserie!

Patience

If love is a thorn they show no wit
Who foolishly hug & foster it—
If love is a weed, how simple they
Who gather & gather it, day by day.36
If love is a nettle that makes you smart
Why do you keep it next your heart 37
And if it be none of these, say I,
Why do [word crossed out] you sit & sob & sigh? 38
   Though everywhere true love I see
   A-coming to all but not to me
   I cannot tell what this love may be—
     For I am blithe & I am gay
     While they sit sighing all night—all day— 39
     Think of the gulf 'twixt them & me—
     Fal lalala—& Miserie! 40
Chorus   For she is blithe &c

After dialogue showing that they are there to give
birthday presents to [illegible] Tennison ladies express
surprise that 41

―――――

Dialogue showing that ladies are waiting to congratulate Rev. Tennison on his birthday.
Patience had no idea it was his birthday

Astonishment of ladies that anyone could be unaware of it.

She has brought no present.

Ladies offer her some of their superfluity, as they have several.

She declines—she doesn't [word crossed out] want to give him present.

Yes, she likes him—he is a good man

But she wishes he wouldn't squeeze her hand. &ᶜ.

Girls look significantly at each other.

Enter Lawn Tennison from the house. He is preceded by the Sexton & the Beadle (whose duties are to keep the girls off) & followed by two grim and portentous middleaged females dressed in heavy black—who stand about in gloomy Manfred-like attitudes, as injured people who owe Society a grudge. They are called Sister Jane & Sister Ann.

————————

7

Chorus of Ladies.

Sir, on your birthday
  We have brought you posies
May your guileless way
  Lie among the roses.
Pray you, if you please,
  Listen to our carol,
And accept of these
  Items of apparel (*giving slippers, braces &ᶜ*)
Worthier rewards
  All for you are fated
To the House of Lords
  When you are translated.

*(He accepts the various gifts unwillingly, & with the
air of a man who is bored with admiration.) The
ladies run down & sing confidentially to audience:*

Chorus
Though to him we make a simultaneous advance
I do not think the others have the shadow of
    a chance.
For he will give his love to *me*, if he has
    any sense—
This, of course, I mention in the
    strictest confidence.

They retire up.
Lawn *(taking Patience aside)*
    Is there any known invention
      Scheme or method, plot or plan,
    To dispense with this attention *(indicating gifts)*
    Which is quite a yearly pension?
      You alone the flame could fan
      Of this hapless clergyman
    Never mind [?] my condescension—.

        ———————

8

Patience *(taking Sisters Ann & Jane aside)*
        Though no doube he's rather pleasing.
        Never understand I can
        Why my fingers he is seizing [42]
        Patting, flattring [?], teasing, squeezing!
        Ere my hand in marriage ban
        I'd give any clergyman,
        I declare I'd rather eat it.
        Though I hope you won't repeat it—
Two Sisters. No, no no, we'll not repeat it.

Sisters *(taking Beadle & Sexton aside)*
    We are maidens consequential
    $\left\{\begin{array}{l}\text{She is}\\\text{I am}\end{array}\right\}$ Jane & $\left\{\begin{array}{l}\text{I am}\\\text{she is}\end{array}\right\}$ Ann
    With affection reverential
    We discourage all potential
        Rivals who may form a plan
        To entrap our clergyman.
    Which we think is most essential—
    This of course is confidential.
Beadle & Sexton Certainly its confidential.
Beadle & Sexton, taking Angela aside.
    $\left\{\begin{array}{l}\text{Im the}\\\text{Hes the}\end{array}\right\}$ sexton $\left\{\begin{array}{l}\text{he's the}\\\text{Im the}\end{array}\right\}$ Beadle
        Both are under Cupids ban
    Women never coax or wheedle
    Or [43] the Sexton or the Beadle
        If they only think they can
        Captivate the clergyman.
            But you'll understand we'd rather
            That this statement went no farther
Angela—   Your remarks shall go no farther.
            [Illegible] we make a similtaneous
            advance.[44]

9

The two sisters whose attentions to Tennison have
been quietly repelled by him, during the preceding
scene are left sitting gloomily on the stage brooding
over the slights that they are continually receiving
from men.
They deplore the popular taste for frivolity

Also the general indifference to their solemn charms.
They work themselves up into a fury of indignation.
Is nothing in Nature interesting, but that which is
fragile & insignificant?

———————

10

Sister Jane
Song. [*two words crossed out*] 45
Is there no grandeur in the growling gale?
Is there no beauty in the bellowing blast? 46
Is there no pathos in the whirlwind's wail?
Is Mount Vesuvius played out at last?
Have thunderbolts lost their appalling zest
Does not the heart leap to the bombshell's boom?
Are battle yells devoid of interest
Or the gaunt 47 sepulchre's absorbing gloom?
Or the [word crossed out] 48 Earthquakes
magnificent avidity?
Is all insipid—saving insipidity?
Has Red Rebellion lost its dread delight
And ironclads their grim & ghastly grace?
Is there no charm in dormant dynamite
Are tigers tame & cobras commonplace?
Has mustard lost its zest—is pepper dead
Has curry ceased to tickle human gums
Is there no market now for cayenne red?
Have pickles given place to sugar plums?
Why what unwritten law of Nature teaches
That nothing's fit to eat but cream & peaches?

———————

11

They hear a sound of martial music
They look off—Hurrah—a regiment of Hussars is
approaching.

It is the Twenty first, who formerly exercised such
fascination in the village.[49]
Now we shall see whether, when he is cut out by
Hussars, the Revd L. Tennison will not gladly revert
to them (Sisters Jane & Ann) *Exeunt Jane & Ann.*
Entrance of Hussars.

----

[12]

Chorus of Hussars [50]

The twenty first hussars [51]
  Are linked in friendly tether
Upon the field of Mars [52]
  They fight the foe together
There every mothers son
  Prepared to fight & fall is
The enemy of one
  The enemy of all is!

United as a clan
  We have arranged between us
To introduce this plan
  Within the courts of Venus
With one emotion stirred
  Beneath our belts of leather,
The Colonel gives the word
  And all propose together.

----

[13]

Patter-song. Temple.[53] Colonel of Hussars.
If you want a receipt for that popular mystery
  Known to the world as a British Hussar,[54]
Take all the remarkable people in history

Choose the best points from each eminent star [55]
    Take of these elements all that is fusible
    Melt 'em all down in a pipkin or crucible
    Set 'em to simmer & take off the scum,
    And a British Hussar is the residuum!
Chor.   Yes, yes, yes, yes
    A British Hussar is the residuum.

The pluck of Lord Nelson on board of the
    Victory—
    Genius of Bismarck devising a plan
The humour of Fielding—which sounds contra-
    dictory—
    Wit of Macaulay who wrote of Queen Anne.[56]
The Science of Jullien, the eminent musico— [57]
    Coolness of Paget about to trepan
The pathos of Paddy as rendered by Boucicault—
    Style of the Bishop of Sodor & Man—
    The dash of a D'Orsay, divested of quackery
Narrative powers of Dickens & Thackeray
Victor Emmanuel, peak-haunting Peveril
Thomas Aquinas & Doctor Sacheverel
    Tupper & Tennyson—Daniel Defoe,
    Anthony Trollope & M^r. Guizot— [58]
    Take of these elements &c.

14
If you want a receipt for this soldierly [59] [word
    crossed out] paragon
    Get at the wealth of the Czar (if you can)
The family pride of a Spaniard from Arragon—
    Swagger of Roderick heading his clan
A smack of Lord Waterford, reckless & rollicky.
    Force of Mephisto pronouncing a ban—

The keen penetration of Paddington Pollaky
   Grace of an Odalisque on a Divan—
[A flavour of Hamlet—the Stranger, a touch of
     him—] [60]
The genius strategic of Caesar or Hannibal
Skill of Sir Garnet in thrashing a cannibal
Flavour of Hamlet—the Stranger, a touch of him—
Little of Manfred (but not very much of him)
   Beadle of Burlington—Richardson's show,
   M^r. Micawber & Madame Tussaud.
     Take of these elements all that is fusible
     Melt 'em all down in a pipkin or crucible
       Set 'em to simmer & take off the scum,
       And a British Hussar is the residuum.
Chor: Yes, yes, yes, yes
     Take of these elements [61]

———————

15

They congratulate themselves on their probable success with the young ladies of the village.
They recal [*sic*] their conquests, last time they were quartered here.
Their flirtations with Angela
      "   with Ella
      "   with Saphir.
They hear that they are all still unmarried.
No doubt they have kept single for their sakes.
They see a procession [62] approaching.
Can it be? Yes—it is the clergyman, followed by all their young ladies
Confound these clergymen—they always cut one out!

———————

[16]

Song, Colonel [63]

When I first put this uniform on
I said as I looked in the glass
    Its one to a million
    That any civilian
This [64] figure & form will surpass.
    Gold lace has a charm for the fair
    And I've plenty of that, and to spare.
While a lover's professions
When uttered in Hessians
    Are eloquent everywhere.
        [This] like Elkingtons window I shone—
        When I first put this uniform on. [65]

Chorus.   By a simple coincidence few
        Could ever have counted upon,
        The same thing occurred to me, too
        When I first put this uniform on.

I thought,[66] when I first put it on,
    Its [67] plain to the veriest dunce
    That every beauty
    Will feel it her duty
To yield to its glamour at once
    But though I am freely gold-laced [68]
    In a uniform handsome & chaste
[word crossed out] [69] The glitter ecstatic
of cope & dalmatic [70]
        Is [71] very much more to their taste
        Which I never counted upon
        When I first put this uniform on! [72]

---

[17]

Chor of Officers up Revd L.T. enters followed by
girls & led by Clerk & [illegible] [73]
Now is not this ridiculous & is not this preposterous

And is it not to suicidal act enough to urge a man [74]
Instead of rushing eagerly to cherish us & foster us
They all prefer this excellent but very prosy clergyman.[75]
    Instead of slyly peering at us
    Casting looks endearing at us
      Flushing at us—
      Blushing at us— [76]
    Flirting with a fan—
They're actually jeering at us, sneering at us, fleering at us [77]
Pretty sort of treatment for a military man!

Chorus of Maidens
In a melancholy train [78]
    Two & two we walk all day.
Pity those who love in vain [79]
    None so sorrowful as they,
    Who can only sigh and say
    Woe is me: alack-a-day!

First lady [80]
Gentle vicar: [81] hear our prayer—
    Twenty lovesick maidens we,
Young and pretty,[82] dark & fair,
    [4 lines illegible] [83]

———

18

Mr. L. Tennison Though my book I seem to scan
    Like a studious [illegible]
    Like a serious clergyman [84]
    Who despises female clay

I hear plainly all they say
Twenty lovesick maidens
they!

Beadle & Sexton—(*to Officers*) He hears plainly all
they say
Twenty lovesick
maidens they [85]

Officers to each other— He hears plainly all
they say—
Twenty lovesick
maidens they!

Second lady (?Sister Ann) [86]
Though so excellently wise
For a moment mortal be.
Deign to raise thy gentle [87] eyes
From thy dry theology— [88]
Twenty lovesick maidens see—
Each is kneeling on her knee! (*all
kneel*)

Chorus of maidens Twenty lovesick maidens
see
Each is kneeling on her
knee!

Officers, Beadle & Sexton Twenty lovesick maidens
see
Each is kneeling on her
knee! [89]

Vicar aside Though, as I remarked
before
Anyone convinced
would be
That a work of musty
lore [90]
Is monopolizing me
Round the corner I can
see

Each is down upon her
knee [91]

----

[19]

Beadle & Sexton to Officers—Round the corner he
can see
Each is kneeling on
her knee—
Officers to each other   Round the corner he
can see
Each is kneeling on
her knee!
Ensemble [92]

Officers, Beadle & Sexton	Ladies	Rev. L.T.
Now is not this ridiculous &c	Though so excellently wise	Though as I remarked before—

Exeunt Officers, Beadle & Sexton

----

[20]

The ladies remain.
He is still absorbed in his folio [word crossed out]
black-letter, rubricated
They wonder what theological lore is monopolizing
him.
They gaze at him in ecstasy [93]
He is so learned—so wise—yet [94] so simple—so mild
They implore him to communicate some of the lore
to them
He consents—lifts up his voice & reads—

Gentle Jane [95]

LT   Little May was as good as gold
She always did as she was told
She never spoke when her mouth was full
Or caught blue bottles their legs to pull!
Or spilt plum jam on her nice new frock
Or put white mice in the eight day clock
Or vivisected her last new doll
Or fostered a passion for Alcohol.
    And when she grew up she was given in marriage
To a first class Earl who keeps his carriage.

All—Oh may we all endeavour to gain
        The happy reward of Gentle Jane! [96]

LT   Teasing Tom was a very bad boy [97]
A great big squirt was his favorite toy—
He put live shrimps in his fathers boots
And sewed up the sleeves of his Sunday suits
He punched his poor little sisters' heads
And cayenne peppered their [word crossed out] four-
    post beds
He plastered their hair with cobblers' wax
And dropped hot halfpennies down their backs!
    The consequence was he was lost to*tally*
And married a girl in the *corps de ballet!*

All: Oh may we all take warning from
        The wicked career of Teasing Tom!

In this manuscript the order of entrances and musical
numbers differs from that of the final version. Lawn
Tennison comes on stage before the soldiers appear;
Bunthorne, not till some time later. The Colonel's patter
song in the fragment precedes "Now is not this ridic-

ulous" but follows it in *Patience*.* Bunthorne recites his poems between these two numbers; Tennison reads his verses aloud only after the Hussars leave. When Tennison became the highly spiced Bunthorne, these cautionary verses were inappropriate and were transferred as "original" works to Grosvenor in Act II. The idyllic Archibald thus preserves the mildness of his clerical antecedents and continues the identification of aesthetes and nursery rhymes made in some of du Maurier's cartoons.[98] Gilbert has given up the amusing discrepancy between the inane content of the rhymes and the black-letter, rubricated tome in which they are printed, while his economy in retaining these tractlike verses deprived Grosvenor of any very recognizable literary parody.[99] Bunthorne, however, was suitably furnished with the new, Swinburnian "Oh Hollow! Hollow! Hollow!" and "Heart-Foam."

The chief differences in *dramatis personae* of the fragment and the corresponding portion of *Patience* are the presence of Bluebeardishly named Sister Ann and the absence of the Duke of Dunstable. Ann is an undeveloped character, decidedly inferior in interest to her sister, who became Lady Jane in *Patience*. Perhaps Ann was to be funny simply as an echo or duplicate of Jane, numerical extension being one of Gilbert's customary comic devices; certainly two female Manfreds would have lent themselves to more absurd stage pictures than could one. It seems likely that the sisters were ultimately to have married the sexton and the beadle.[100]

The addition of the Duke gave Jane a new partner, however, and Sullivan a tenor. This character may be implicit in the fragment, but he has not been differenti-

---

* This is an error; in the opera as in the MS. this song immediately follows the choral entrance of the soldiers. The reversed order does, however, apply to the colonel's other song, "When I first put this uniform on."—Ed.

ated from his fellow Hussars. Yet in the corresponding portion of the finished libretto, he has appeared (before Bunthorne has), and his wealth, as well as his detestation of deference, has been established. Nevertheless, on the evidence of the license copy of *Patience,* it seems that Gilbert must have devised the Duke before his mistrust of "the clerical element" began.

The license copy of *Patience* consists of galley proof and represents the penultimate version of the libretto as submitted to the Lord Chamberlain for approval.[101] Gilbert habitually made heavy deletions during his last rehearsals and even after opening night;[102] he often altered dialogue and occasionally wrote new verses. A song for the Duke,[103] present in the license copy but deleted from the text of *Patience* as performed, indicates quite clearly that the Duke was part of the Lawn Tennison plot.

SONG.—DUKE

Though men of rank may useless seem,
   They do good in their generation,
They make the wealthy upstart teem
   With Christian love and self-negation;
The bitterest tongue that ever lashed
   Man's folly drops with milk and honey,
While Scandal hides her head, abashed,
   Brought face to face with Rank and Money!

ALL   Yes, Scandal hides her head, abashed,
      Brought face to face with Rank and Money

Society forgets her laws,
   And Prudery her affectation,
While Mrs. Grundy pleads our cause,
   And talks "wild oats" and toleration;
Archbishops wink at what they'd think
   A downright crime in common shoddy,

Although Arch*bish*op's shouldn't wink
At anything or anybody!

ALL   A good Archbishop wouldn't wink
At anything or anybody!

These verses are appropriate to Gilbert's general satire of hypocrisy, but their connection with the action is tenuous, and their references to Christian love and temporal-minded archbishops do not suit the context of rival poets.

The license copy's version of the "marionette" trio in which the Duke takes part is another holdover.

It's clear that medieval art alone retains its zest,
To charm and please its devotees we've done
    our little best
We're not quite sure if all we do has the Early
    English ring;
But, as far as we can judge, it's something like
    this sort of thing:
    You hold yourself like this [*attitude*],
    You hold yourself like that [*attitude*],
By hook and crook you try to look both angular
    and flat [*attitude*].
    To cultivate the trim
    Rigidity of limb,
You ought to get a Marionette, and form your
    style on him [*attitude*].

Here the references to medieval art and Early English belong as much to a caricatured Oxford Movement as to a parodied Aesthetic one. Unmistakable allusions to High Art and Aesthetic tastes come only in a later insertion of ten lines between lines 7 and 8 above, turning the trio into a two-verse number. In his letter to Sullivan, Gilbert made it clear that he intended to substitute soldiers imitating artistic deportment for soldiers taking religious orders. In the trio we see this change in the process of being made.[104]

Lady Jane is also in transition in the license copy. The fragment describes her as "grim and portentous middleaged . . . dressed in heavy black . . . stand[ing] about in gloomy Manfred-like attitudes." These traits are repeated in a license-copy stage direction: "JANE, *a gaunt*,[105] *formidable, portentous, black-haired, heavy-browed aesthete, sits gloomily apart,* (R.) *with her back to audience, wrapt in grief.*" In the dialogue of the license copy and of *Patience*, itself, however, she is massive, not morbid; brusque, not broody. Her only Byronism is the black Japanese costume which the actress who played her wore on stage as a Rapturous Maiden. Jane's first-act solo in the fragment, "Is there no grandeur in the growling gale," with its foreshadowing of Katisha, has disappeared in the license copy. There, as in the final libretto, her solo is "Silvered is the raven hair," which opens Act II on a note of comic nostalgia reminiscent of Dr. Daly's "Ah me, I was a fair young curate then!" That this Jane should be chosen by the Duke is laughable but not grotesque.[106]

The general outcome of Gilbert's hesitation between High Church and High Art was an increased breadth of satiric effect, concentrating on principles more than persons and universalizing parody into a criticism of affectation as a motivating principle in human nature. (The Dragoons are as devoted to effective costumes as the poets are.) *The Times'* reviewer even took the librettist to task for lacking topicality: "All the more disappointing if one considers how amusing a clever parody of certain tricks and mannerisms of modern poetry might have been made." But the Reverend Charles Dodgson, who a year before had publicly denounced Gilbert for laughing at pale young curates, breathed a sigh of relief. "The play of *Patience* is I think a little weak as a whole," he told his diary, "but it has funny bits, and the music is very pretty. It is entirely unobjectionable, which one is glad to be able to say of one of Gilbert's plays." [107]

Fortunately, he had never heard of a vicar named Lawn Tennison.

Notes

1. These sheets are pressed copies of a missing original. Gilbert evidently made them at some later time when practicing with a copying machine. They obviously represent only a very small part of the mass of scenario, drafts of lyrics, etc., through which *Patience* must have passed. Permission to make use of unpublished material in the British Museum has been given by the owner of the subsisting copyright in the works of Sir William Schwenck Gilbert.

2. Gilbert described this process, in varying detail, to Edith Browne, Percy Fitzgerald, and William Archer. Scenarios in the Gilbert Papers also attest to his habits of composition.

3. Transferred to the newly built Savoy on October 10, 1881.

4. Even up to opening night, Grosvenor's first name was Algernon, not Archibald.

5. Gilbert admitted that this ballad was his source for *Patience,* and the relationship was recognized by reviewers of the first production, as well as by writers on the subject ever since.

6. Many more Bab Ballads contain hints for *Patience,* such as "The Scornful Colonel" (*Fun,* September 25, 1869), who drills his men in sneering: "Prepare to 'Bah'! By sections, 'Phew.' " He anticipates Colonel Calverley's order: "By sections of threes—Rapture!" Isaac Goldberg lists some antecedents in *The Story of Gilbert and Sullivan* (New York, 1928), pp. 253-55.

    It is not my intention to discuss Gilbert's self-borrowings at length here; for the background of *Patience,* see my doctoral dissertation, "William S. Gilbert: His Comic Techniques and Their Development" (University of Chicago, 1955).

7. *The Savoy Operas* (London, 1962), I, 31. In the second verse of his song, Dr. Daly repeats the motif of De Vyse's "sweet consump-

tive cough": "Did I look pale? then half a parish trembled; / And when I coughed all thought the end was near!" He was, he says, loved beyond all other men: "Fled gilded dukes and belted earls before me— / Ah me, I was a pale young curate then!" (*ibid.*, I, 32).

Punch ("Comic Clerics," XCIV [March 17, 1888], 129), reporting that "the Comic Cleric is ubiquitous," rather fancied that the type had been originated by Gilbert with Dr. Daly. Certainly it was a character for which Gilbert always had a penchant. As late as 1888 in the unsuccessful *Brantighame Hall,* he gave a clergyman a speech that was pure Savoy Opera. "Rev. Noel Ross" explains that he had come to Australia because he could not cope with female parishioners at home: "With half the women of my parish setting their caps at me, I wasn't safe. They never left me. Presents showered down upon me. It literally rained carriage-rugs, altar-cloths, birthday books, paper-knives, letter weights, pocket diaries, knitted waistcoats, and presentation inkstands. . . . My photographs bought up as fast as they could be printed! Half-a-dozen ladies of exalted rank were carried out in convulsions whenever I preached!" These amusing lines were markedly inappropriate to the "realistic" melodrama that *Brantinghame Hall* was intended to be.

8. Press copy in the Gilbert Papers. This letter is also reprinted by Sidney Dark and Rowland Grey in *W. S. Gilbert: His Life and Letters* (London, 1923), p. 83, and by others.

   The letter continues: "but if we can get du Maurier to design the costumes, I don't know that the difficulty will be insuperable." George du Maurier, whose elegantly satiric anti-aesthetic cartoons were a weekly feature of *Punch,* did not, after all, do costumes for *Patience.* The "Aesthetic Dresses," as the program described them, were designed by Gilbert himself.

9. Published in New York.

10. In this note, Gilbert acknowledges his debt to "The Rival Curates" but gives no indication of having originally considered poets. Goldberg considers that the note contradicts Gilbert's earlier letter to Sullivan. It is possible that Gilbert, twenty years later, had forgotten the original sequence, but it seems unlikely that in 1880 he would have written "as you remember" to Sullivan if he had not at least mentioned the possibility of aesthetes to the composer.

11. Quoted by Reginald Allen. *The First Night Gilbert and Sullivan* (New York, 1958), p. 139.

12. Copy in Gilbert Papers. This letter is also reprinted by Hesketh

Pearson in *Gilbert: His Life and Strife* (London, 1957), p. 111. Gilbert had just read the reviews of Albery's play, produced at the Criterion on November 20, 1880. It contained perhaps the first stage caricature of Oscar Wilde. The *Athenaeum* (November 27, 1880) described *Where's the Cat?* as "hopelessly nonsensical."

13. This phrase, inserted as an afterthought, seems carefully ambiguous, for it had been only three weeks since Gilbert had written Sullivan that he wanted to eliminate the clerical characters. But if we take it to mean that the shape of the libretto had long been determined or that six months ago it had been in its first, aesthetic, stage, the statement is accurate enough for a dramatist who sees himself threatened by possible accusations of plagiarism.

14. Gilbert was very touchy about originality in an era when dramatists borrowed freely. The program of *Patience* carried another disclaimer: a statement that the libretto had been comleted "in November last," i.e., before F. C. Burnand's very popular anti-aesthetic farce, *The Colonel,* had been performed. The *Daily Telegraph,* reviewing *Patience,* thought this note unnecessary: "Although Mr. Gilbert sometimes chooses to economize his ideas by using them again and again, no one suspects him of lacking originality so far as to be obliged to borrow from other people."

   Albery's play must have seemed a threat to Gilbert or he would not have given away the closely guarded secret of what the new opera was to be about.

15. W. A. Darlington, *The World of Gilbert and Sullivan* (London, 1952), pp. 78-83. On these grounds, Darlington also accounted for the country setting rather than South Kensington, for the emphasis on love, and for the raffle.

16. The manuscript is untitled. Titles of the Savoy Operas were secrets guarded almost as closely as their subjects, and, as a letter from Gilbert to Clement Scott (March 20, 1881) shows, *Patience* was without a title until the last moment (Reginald Allen, *W. S. Gilbert: An Anniversary Survey* [Charlottesville, Va., 1963], p. 53).

   In giving the text of the British Museum fragment, I have followed Gilbert's punctuation, such as it is. He frequently depended on position of lines on the page as an indication of end punctuation, which he supplied later, and he often used a very short dash and a sketchy ampersand. In this fragment, as elsewhere in his manuscripts, he carefully indicated appropriate, often intricate, indentation in stanzas; he usually underlined stage directions, which would be italicized in type; and he wrote most of the epitomes of action in the form of lists of single sentences or phrases rather than in paragraphs.

Gilbert himself numbered most of the pages, as I have, at the upper right-hand corner. A page number in square brackets indicates that I have supplied it. I have shown page endings in the manuscript by a centered line. I have indicated Gilbert's own crossings-out and the word crossed out if it is decipherable. In the few instances where a word not crossed out cannot be read, I have indicated an illegibility in the text.

When a lyric has been retained in the final version of *Patience*, I have shown that fact in a footnote, together with any changes in wording or order of lines. I have not taken notice of repetitions which appear in the final version as a result of the musical setting.

All variants shown in footnotes represent the final text as printed in the 1962 Oxford edition of *The Savoy Operas*.

17. The "which" clause seems to have been added later: it is crowded into the space beneath the end of the line.

18. "Love-sick all against our will." This chorus and the two solos which follow it were retained with very few changes.

19. This line is replaced by: "Twenty-love-sick maidens we, / And we die for love of thee."

20. "heedeth"

21. Angela's solo comes between the two verses for chorus in the final version, and there is no stage direction.

22. "will"

23. Omitted.

24. Omitted.

25. Sung by Ella.

26. Ella repeats her last line after "Ah Miserie."

27. "Love-sick all against our will."

28. The phrases beginning "former admiration" have been interlined and are evidently additions.

29. Patience is finally a dairy maid. A schoolmistress could hardly have received Bunthorne's verses with sufficient naiveté.

30. The following recitative and song appear with very minor changes in the final version. There Angela's lines read: "Nay pretty child, come hither. Is it true / That you have never loved?"

31. "but"

32. Omitted.

33. "sighing night and day"

34. " 'Fal la la la!' and 'Miserie!' "

35. "Yes, she is blithe, and she is gay / While we sit sighing night and day."

36. "Who gather it, day by day!"

37. "Then why do you wear it next your heart?"

38. "Ah, why do you sit and sob and sigh?"
39. "While they sit sighing night and day."
40. " 'Fal la la la!'—and 'Miserie!' "
41. Gilbert crossed out these prose lines in the original.
42. A word has been crossed out and "seizing" written in above it.
43. Obviously here in the sense of "either."
44. The illegible half-line is presumably the same as in the earlier chorus.
45. The first word may be "Lady."
46. This song, deleted before *Patience* reached the stage, is the basis for Katisha's "There is beauty in the bellow of the blast, / There is grandeur in the growling of the gale" in Act II of *The Mikado*. In this duet with Ko-Ko there are also references to volcanoes, thunderbolts, gales, and tigers. Such allusions are more comic when they are spoken to or by the timid tailor of the later opera. Katisha's solo verse addressed to Yum-Yum in the finale of Act I, "Pink cheek, that rulest / where wisdom serves!" serves much the same function as Sister Jane's solo.
47. Gilbert had originally written "grim" but crossed it out and inserted "gaunt" above it, presumably because he had used "grim" again in line two of the second stanza.
48. The first syllable is "flood."
49. These hussars have become the Thirty-fifth Dragoon Guards by the final version.
50. The first verse of this chorus was retained, with changes noted below; the second verse was dropped.
51. "The soldiers of our Queen"
52. "Upon the battle scene"
53. The name has been crossed out, but Richard Temple did play the Colonel. The patter song, with changes noted below, is preserved in the final version of *Patience*. When Gilbert reprinted it in *Songs of a Savoyard* (1890) he changed the "humour of Fielding" * to "The grace of MOZART, that unparalleled musico—": and in the second stanza "Sir Garnet" became "LORD WOLSELEY." Neither change, however, has been made in performance.
54. "Known to the world as a Heavy Dragoon." "Heavy Dragoon" has replaced "British Hussar" *passim*.
55. "Rattle them off to a popular tune"

* Actually, the line about Fielding is retained in *Songs of a Savoyard*. What Gilbert did replace with the Mozart allusion is "The science of JULLIEN, the eminent musico."—Ed.

56. In the final version this line and the sixth line are transposed; the same is true for the fourth and sixth lines of the second verse.

57. "The" seems to have been added at the beginning of this line, since it conspicuously breaks the indentation pattern of the other lines.

58. This line ends "Guizot! Ah!—" in Miss Bridget D'Oyly Carte's MS emendation of the Oxford text. An "Ah!" is also added in verse 2 after "Madame Tussaud!"

59. "soldier-like"

60. This line has been crossed out by Gilbert.

61. At this point the manuscript is too faint to decipher; the chorus must have continued its reprise, however.

62. Gilbert originally wrote "ladies," crossed it out, and inserted "a procession" above it.

63. This song was retained with the changes noted below.

64. "My"

65. These two lines, which are omitted from the final version, have been squeezed in between the surrounding lines; the initial "This" was crossed out, evidently as soon as written. Elkington & Co. was a well-known firm of silversmiths in Regent Street.

66. "I said"

67. "It is"

68. "They will see that I'm freely gold-laced"

69. The word crossed out may be "But."

70. "But the peripatetics / Of long-haired aesthetics"

71. "Are"

72. The chorus repeats its earlier quatrain with line 3 changed to "I didn't anticipate that" in the final version.

73. It is possible that the illegible word is "sexton." Certainly the beadle and sexton are on stage a little later in this number. This ensemble-*cum*-solos was retained in the final version with appropriate changes to suit it to a poet.

74. "A thorough-paced absurdity—explain it if you can."

75. "They all prefer this melancholy literary man."

76. These two lines were transposed in the final version.

77. "They're actually sneering at us, fleering at us, jeering at us!"

78. "In a doleful train. . . ." In the final version, this chorus precedes the men's chorus.

79. "For we love in vain!"

80. Angela in final version.

81. "Mystic poet"

82. "wealthy"

83. The sheets of this number are almost unreadable. The last word

of the second line seems to be "ecstasy." In the final version, there is only one line: "All of county family," which is followed by a couplet: "And we die for love of thee— / Twenty love-sick maidens we!" In the fragment, the last line seems to be some variant of "we die for love of thee."

84. "In a rapt ecstatic way, / Like a literary man"
85. The Sexton & Beadle dropped out here and later.
86. The parenthesis, including the question mark, is Gilbert's. It is much darker than the writing on the rest of the page and seems to have been written in after the rest. In the final version, the second lady's solo is sung by Saphir.
87. "purple"
88. "From thy heart-drawn poesy."
89. These two lines are omitted in the final version.
90. "That some transcendental lore"
91. "Each is kneeling on her knee!"
92. This ensemble was finally sung by officers and ladies only, the ladies singing "In a doleful train. . . ."
93. "At him" has been repeated at the end of this sentence and then crossed out.
94. A superfluous "yet" has been crossed out after the (—).
95. The title appears to have been added later. Both "Gentle Jane" and "Teasing Tom" were retained in the final version but transferred to Grosvenor in Act II. There the first "poem" begins, "Gentle Jane was as good as gold."
96. This line originally read, "The bright example of gentle Countess May." "Bright example" and "Countess May" have been crossed out heavily with the same sort of stroke; "gentle" has been crossed out more lightly in a different stroke. "Unhappy reward" and "gentle Jane!" have been written in above the line and the "un" of "unhappy" crossed out. This couplet does not appear in the final version, nor does the "All" couplet for "Teasing Tom."
97. A word has been blotted out at the beginning of this line. Judging from the indentation pattern, it was not part of the verse.
98. Particularly in "Nincompoopiana," *Punch*, LXXVII (December 20, 1879), 282. Here male aesthetes lounge about in attitudes of rapture, two of them bearing a faint resemblance to Wilde. Du Maurier's accompanying text explains that "surfeited with excess of 'cultchah,' Prigsby and his Friends are now going in for extreme simplicity."

Prigsby. "I considah the words of 'little Bopeep' Freshah, Love-liah, and more Subtile than anything Shelley evah wrote!
[*Recites them.*
Muffington. "Quite so. And Schubert nevah composed anything quite so precious as the Tune!"
[*Tries to hum it.*
Chorus. "How Supreme!"
Bunthorne also announces that "High diddle diddle" / will rank as an idyll, / If I pronounce it chaste!"

99. John B. Jones, in his article "In Search of Archibald Grosvenor: A New Look at Gilbert's *Patience*" (*Victorian Poetry*, III [Winter, 1965], 45-53) discusses Grosvenor's possible relationship to contemporary poets.

100. The sexton and the beadle are not needed as "minions" in the final version, Bunthorne himself threatening Grosvenor at the instigation of Lady Jane. Darlington (cited in n. 15 above) points out that their duet, "So go to him," contains such "rival curates" lines as "Your style is much too sanctified—your cut is too canonical" and therefore must be one of the lyrics retained from an earlier draft (p. 82).

101. The Lord Chamberlain's collection of plays submitted for licensing is now in the British Museum. In addition, in the Gilbert Papers there is a prompt copy of *Patience* with MS notes, some indicating deletions.

102. Discarded lyrics or dialogue was sometimes retained in the first American edition of Gilbert's libretti. See Allen, *The First Night Gilbert and Sullivan* (cited in n. 11 above) pp. xvii-xviii. The first-night libretto of *Patience* is substantially that of the Oxford edition; the license copy's extensive variants do not appear in the American libretto except for a second verse to the duet for Patience and Angela in Act I. It is reasonable to suppose, therefore, that the rest were cut before *Patience* reached the stage. I have included in this article only the license-copy lyrics and dialogue that are relevant to the change in characters.

103. This solo follows his explanation that he joined the regiment for the pleasure of being snubbed.

104. Another transitional passage, later deleted, was Grosvenor's announcement that "I am here to preach, in my own person, the principles of perfection. I am as it were, a Banquet of Beauty upon which all who will may feast. It is most unpleasant to be a Banquet, but I must not shirk my responsibilities." This sounds like a mixture of *agape* and opening remarks by Oscar Wilde.

105. Alice Barnett, the gigantic first Lady Jane, was decidedly not gaunt, suggesting that Gilbert did not originally conceive the role with her in mind, as he did Colonel Calverley for Temple. A gaunt Lady Jane could scarcely sing, "Still more corpulent grow I."
106. The speech in which the Duke chooses Jane is in prose in *Patience,* but it is a musical number in the license copy, beginning with a recitative for the Colonel which introduces a solo by the Duke, repeating the theme of his earlier, deleted verses. It concludes:

> I have resolved—for men of high degree
>> Should show the way in self-denying actions—
> To give it to that maid who seems to be
>> Most wanting in material attractions!
>>> Jane!

107. *The Diaries of Lewis Carroll,* ed. R. L. Green (New York, 1954), II, 403. In spite of Dodgson's modified rapture, *Patience* seems to have been the standard by which he judged later Gilbert and Sullivan productions. He found *Iolanthe* "very inferior to to *Patience*" (11, 469).
Patience" (II, 412) and *The Yeomen of the Guard* "not equal

Selected Bibliography

This bibliography is restricted to book-length works on W. S. Gilbert and the Savoy Operas. Books devoted primarily to a study of Sir Arthur Sullivan are excluded from the list. Readers should bear in mind that several of the works listed here, like some of the essays in the present volume, are presented chiefly for the historical interest of their contents. Gilbert's works, like those of any writer who has been more attractive to dilettantes than to serious scholars until very recently, have been the subject of much fanciful interpretation and his life, surrounded as it is by numerous apocryphal stories, has been recounted and revaluated, to use Dick Deadeye's phrase, "in many various ways."

BIBLIOGRAPHY

Allen, Reginald. *W. S. Gilbert: An Anniversary Survey and Exhibition Checklist.* Charlottesville, Virginia, 1963.

Searle, Townley. *Sir William Schwenck Gilbert: A Topsy-Turvy Adventure.* London, 1931.

REFERENCE

Dunn, George E. *A Gilbert and Sullivan Dictionary.* London, 1936.
Halton, F. J. *The Gilbert and Sullivan Operas: A Concordance.* New York, 1935.
Moore, Frank Ledlie. *Crowell's Handbook of Gilbert and Sullivan.* New York, 1962.
Rollins, Cyril, and Witts, R. John. *The D'Oyly Carte Opera Company In Gilbert and Sullivan Operas: A Record of Productions.* London, 1962.

BIOGRAPHY AND HISTORY

Allen, Reginald (ed.). Prologue, introductions, and postscripts to *The First Night Gilbert and Sullivan.* New York, 1958.
Baily, Leslie. *The Gilbert & Sullivan Book.* London, 1952. Revised edition, 1956. Reprinted, 1966.
Browne, Edith A. *W. S. Gilbert.* London and New York, 1907.
Cellier, Francois, and Bridgeman, Cunningham. *Gilbert, Sullivan, and D'Oyly Carte.* London, 1914.
Dark, Sidney, and Grey, Rowland. *W. S. Gilbert: His Life and Letters.* London, 1923.
Fitz-Gerald, S. J. Adair. *The Story of the Savoy Opera: A Record of Events and Productions.* London, 1924.
Goldberg, Isaac. *The Story of Gilbert and Sullivan.* New York 1928. Revised edition, 1935.
Pearson, Hesketh. *Gilbert & Sullivan.* New York and London, 1935.
———. *Gilbert: His Life and Strife.* London, 1957.

Rees, Terence. *Thespis: A Gilbert & Sullivan Enigma.* London, 1964.

Stedman, Jane W. (ed.). Introduction to *Gilbert before Sullivan: Six Comic Plays by W. S. Gilbert.* Chicago, 1967.

Walbrook, H. M. *Gilbert & Sullivan Opera: A History and a Comment.* London, 1922.

CRITICAL STUDIES

Darlington, W. A. *The World of Gilbert and Sullivan.* New York, 1950.

Fitzgerald, Percy. *The Savoy Opera and the Savoyards.* London, 1894.

Godwin, A. H. *Gilbert & Sullivan: A Critical Appreciation of the Savoy Operas.* London, 1926.

Goldberg, Isaac. *Sir Wm. S. Gilbert: A Study in Modern Satire.* Boston, 1913.

Williamson, Audrey. *Gilbert & Sullivan Opera.* London, 1953.

JUVENILE BOOKS

Purdy, Claire Lee. *Gilbert and Sullivan: Masters of Mirth and Melody.* New York, 1946.

Wymer, Norman. *Gilbert and Sullivan.* New York, 1963.